THE PRETTIEST GIRL ON STAGE IS A MAN

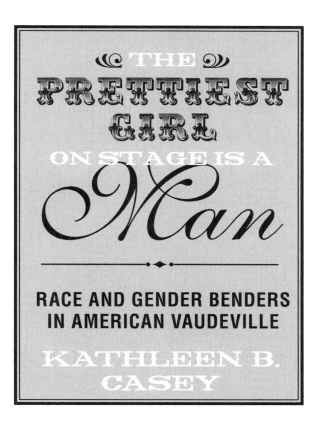

THE PRETTIEST GIRL

ON STAGE IS A *Man*

RACE AND GENDER BENDERS IN AMERICAN VAUDEVILLE

KATHLEEN B. CASEY

The University of Tennessee Press
Knoxville

"Sex, Savagery, and the Woman Who Made Vaudeville Famous" originally appeared
in *Frontiers: A Journal of Women's Studies*, vol. 36, no. 1., pp. 87–112.
Copyright © 2015 by The University of Nebraska Press. Reprinted by permission.

"'The Jewish Girl with a Colored Voice': Sophie Tucker and the Sounds of Race and Gender
in Modern America" originally appeared in *Journal of American Culture*, vol. 38, no. 1, pp. 16–26.
Copyright © 2015 by John Wiley and Sons. Reprinted by permission.

The paper in this book meets the requirements of American National Standards Institute /
National Information Standards Organization specification Z39.48-1992 (Permanence of Paper).
It contains 30 percent post-consumer waste and is certified by the Forest Stewardship Council.

Library of Congress Cataloging-in-Publication Data

Casey, Kathleen B.
The prettiest girl on stage is a man : race and gender benders in American vaudeville / Kathleen B. Casey.
pages cm
Includes bibliographical references and index.
ISBN 978-1-62190-165-5 (hardcover)
1. Vaudeville—United States.
2. Female impersonators—United States.
3. Blackface entertainers—United States.
4. Entertainers—United States.
5. Gender expression—United States.
6. Racism—United States.
I. Title.

PN1968.U5C37 2015
792.70973—dc23

2014038345

"One Hundred Years from Now,"
performed by Eva Tanguay, 1915

In the year two thousand and fifteen, we'll all be turned around
And the female of the species will on every hand be found
We'll have a woman mayor and a woman president
The men will do the housework and the women pay the rent (maybe)
We'll all be then 'up in the air' and all own aeroplanes
And when we call, we'll simply rap at top floor window panes
The poor men will be rich at last for Andrew Carnegie
Will give us each a million—you just live that long and see.
A hundred years from now, there'll be some change
We won't have Roosevelt then, I will seem so strange
We'll have no Barnes around us to raise a row
But Tanguay will be 'running' still
A hundred years from now

—Eva Tanguay Papers,
Benson Ford Research Center, The Henry Ford

CONTENTS

ILLUSTRATIONS

ACKNOWLEDGMENTS

Writing a book is, to put it simply, an arduous process, and it does not happen without help from many people and places. Therefore, it is a pleasure to express my gratitude in writing to the individuals and institutions that supported this project over the last several years. First, this work would not have been possible without financial support from various institutions. While working on this manuscript as a dissertation during graduate school, the University of Rochester's Department of History, College Writing Center, and Susan B. Anthony Institute for Gender and Women's Studies provided me with funding that allowed me to work on this project continually. More recently, Virginia Wesleyan College supported this work by awarding me a Summer Faculty Development Grant during a critical final stage.

This work would never have materialized without the assistance of the dedicated staff of many institutions. The interlibrary loan and circulation departments at the University of Rochester and Virginia Wesleyan College libraries, and the archival staff at the Schomburg Center for Research in Black Culture, the New York Public Library for Performing Arts, the Houghton Theatre Library at Harvard University, the International Center of Photography in New York City, the Institute for Jazz Studies at Rutgers University, and the Benson Ford Research Center at the Henry Ford Museum have been especially helpful. In particular, the assistance of Linda Skolarus at the Henry Ford Museum, Micah Hoggatt at Harvard University's Houghton Theatre Collection, Barbara Stratyner at the New York Public Library, Dan Morgenstern at Rutgers Institute for Jazz Studies, and Mary Yearwood and Edwina Ashie-Nikoi of the Schomburg Center for Research in Black Culture have helped me acquire documents from archives across the country and made my research trips efficient and pleasurable. Jim Orr of the Henry Ford Museum, Thomas Lisanti of the New York Public Library, and Claartje van Dijk of the International Center of Photography assisted me in acquiring high quality copies of many of the photographs and illustrations that help tell the story of this book. In addition, the Strauss Peyton Studio gave permission for their photographs to appear in the book. I am also thankful that Lillyn Brown's former student, actor Robert Kya-Hill, gave permission to quote his descriptions of her performances as he remembered them late in her life. I am also grateful to *Frontiers: A Journal of Women's Studies* for their permission to reprint excerpts of a previously published article on Eva Tanguay and to the *Journal of American Culture* for granting permission to reprint sections of a recent article on Sophie Tucker.

I owe many thanks to individuals whose interest, enthusiasm, and faith pushed this work along. Of course, I owe a great debt to Victoria Wolcott, my graduate school advisor, whose productive insights on each chapter, persistent encouragement, and sage professional advice helped push this book along. Her own careful scholarship on race in America also provided me with an excellent model for my own. I am also thankful for my departmental colleagues at Virginia Wesleyan College, especially Dan Margolies, who encouraged me to forge ahead with this project and Rich Bond, who provided me with feedback on the introduction. While at the University of Wisconsin at Milwaukee, I was and continue to be thankful for the friendship and feedback of my former colleague, Robert Emmett.

While in graduate school, I benefited from the kinship of fellow students, especially Michelle Finn, who first introduced me to Lillyn Brown and offered helpful feedback on Chapters Two and Three. I would also like to thank Jeremy Saucier and Jamie Saucier, who read and commented on excerpts of Chapter One. I am grateful to Aviva Dove-Viebahn, for her friendship, optimism, and willingness to read anything I asked her to. Over several years, I have also benefited from participating in multiple lively, interdisciplinary writing groups in various places. Paula Booke, Krystal Frazier, Laura Hill, Aubrey Westfall, Kellie Holzer, Jennifer Slivka, and Taryn Myers are just a few readers who provided feedback, support, and friendship which nourished this project immensely. In Virginia, two friends in particular, Leslie Caughell and Daniel Howland, read much of this work with a careful and patient eye. They have sustained and enriched this work and my life in many ways. I am also indebted to Linda Mizejewski, for her thoughtful and constructive feedback on an earlier draft of this manuscript. The incisive criticisms of a second anonymous reader also helped me to produce a more polished final draft of the book. Thomas Wells and Emily Huckabay at the University of Tennessee Press have also been instrumental in making the road to publication a smooth one.

The support of my family also helped make this work possible. I am grateful to my parents, Ann and Dennis Casey, for never discouraging me from making less than practical professional choices even when I know they did not always understand why—or even what—I was doing. My oldest sister, Eileen Casey, also commented on early drafts of Chapters One and Two, despite the demands of her own career.

Finally, I dedicate this book to Lynn Gordon, who passed away in 2012 after fighting cancer for more than a decade. Whether sick or healthy, throughout graduate school and beyond, Lynn provided me with a model of intellectual and personal generosity that humbles me still. She and her wonderful husband, Harold Wechsler, repeatedly gave me a place to stay in New York City, while I buried my head in theater scrapbooks at the New York Public Library. She offered me home-cooked meals, invited me to spend holidays with her family, and when temperatures reached beyond 90 degrees, offered me an air-conditioned room in which to write in the sweltering summers of graduate school. She seemed to have bottomless faith in my ability to think historically, and it made all the difference to me. Without her indefatigable energy and efforts, this project would not exist.

INTRODUCTION

In 1914, Caroline Caffin challenged readers of *Vaudeville: The Book* to "watch the audience trooping into a New York Vaudeville house. There is no more democratic crowd to be seen anywhere." Caffin believed that vaudeville offered "something for everyone and, though the fastidious may be a little shocked (the fastidious rather like to be shocked sometimes), they must not be offended, while the seeker for thrills must on no account be bored."[1] Vaudeville was one of the most popular forms of American entertainment from the 1890s through the 1920s. It reflected the motley crowds of Americans who regularly sought its shocks and thrills in the form of laughter, drama, escape, and satire. Spectators came from vastly divergent economic, social, and ethnic backgrounds to a shared urban space, where performers used humor to invite viewers to turn a self-conscious eye upon themselves, the Other, and their fracturing culture.

Audiences paid as little as ten cents or as much as two dollars to occupy the 1,000 to 2,000 seats available in each big-time vaudeville theater.[2] Though white performers far outnumbered black acts, they took turns occupying the stages of the largest vaudeville houses across the country.[3] At most of these houses, however, theaters remained highly racialized spaces, where black audiences were relegated to the cheapest seats in the balcony and fair-skinned patrons, both native-born and more recent European immigrants, sat front and center in the orchestra pit. Often segregated by physical space, these racially, socially, and economically diverse audiences witnessed the same sensational performances. Though managers discouraged rowdiness, audiences clapped their hands, stomped their feet, cheered, stood, and hissed to express their delight or disapproval.[4] Vaudeville was cheap, interactive, and because it featured six to ten different acts per night, it had something to offer everyone. *The New York Times Magazine* suggested it was "very nearly the people's art."[5]

In the 1880s, the first generation of vaudevillians picked up on performative traditions established by nineteenth-century American minstrel performers. At the height of their popularity, between 1840 and 1850, minstrel shows competed with concert saloons and dime museums. These shows catered primarily to working-class men who could smoke, swear, and drink alcohol inside the theaters. Minstrel players claimed their performances were based upon careful observation of the behavior of "plantation Negroes." According to Eric Lott, every aspect of the minstrel show "was supposedly taken from the observance of authentic slave life" and was presented as an accurate representation of black culture.[6] Though minstrel shows had virtually disappeared by the turn of the century, many successful vaudevillians got their training as members of minstrel troupes, touring small towns in the 1880s and 1890s. By 1900, however, vaudeville replaced minstrel shows as one of the most popular pastimes in a culture that increasingly commercialized the mass consumption of leisure.

Led by innovators like Tony Pastor, pioneering vaudeville theater owners seized upon opportunities to reach new audiences and expand profits.[7] Pastor, followed by B.F. Keith, strove to distinguish vaudeville theaters from more disreputable places like variety and burlesque houses that still allowed prostitutes and alcohol to pass through their doors. In the twentieth century, vaudeville houses attempted to attract middle class women by hosting "Ladies' Nights," giving "away prizes of groceries, coal, dress patterns, dishes" and advertising "clean shows that were first-rate entertainment."[8] Such houses also established "dirt brigades" to censor acts, forcing performers to abandon vulgar or obscene content. These efforts helped vaudeville gain a reputation as high-class entertainment. Women who came in pairs or with dates, and mothers with husbands and children became a core part of the new audiences. At the height of vaudeville's popularity in 1910, women constituted at least one-third of the evening vaudeville clientele and the majority of patrons at matinee performances.[9]

The demographic changes visible in the audiences mirrored those taking place on stage. By one scholar's count, in 1870 there were just 780 working actresses in America; by 1920, there were close to 20,000 and actresses outnumbered actors twenty-five to one.[10] Actresses' salaries also skyrocketed during this period. Outside of prostitution (to which some conservative critics still thought it comparable), stage-work provided single women the prospect of financial independence, wealth, and fame. Bonafide female celebrities emerged; their names gained household fluency, their faces became internationally recognized, and their salaries allowed them to purchase multiple homes equipped with personal servants.

Vaudeville performances placed particular emphasis on physical humor, masquerade, and metamorphosis. Women, in particular, wore flashy costumes, danced, and told jokes that insisted on their newly heightened visibility. Bodily display was also a central component of novelty acts performed by magicians, acrobats, and strongmen who sometimes strode the stage in revealing clothing. In a performance genre that emphasized intimate interaction between the audience and the performer, the most successful vaudevillians relied on their bodies and their voices to carry off highly physical performances.

Masquerade was also the central conceit of vaudeville's most popular and highly paid novelty performers, gender impersonators. These performers were men and women who donned the clothes and affected the voice, comportment, and demeanor associated with a different gender.[11] Popular in the nineteenth century on the male-dominated minstrel stage, theatrical cross-dressing developed new meaning in vaudeville when men began to perform as women alongside women. This effectively nullified old rationales for gender impersonation, making it clear that audiences were interested in cross-dressers for the sake of cross-dressing itself. Sometimes these acts surprised audiences when performers removed their wigs at the end of the act, revealing their "real" gender. On other occasions, the audience was aware of the trick from the beginning. Despite their long history, the popularity of gender impersonations peaked between 1900 and 1920.[12]

Just as gender impersonation survived several changes of venue, twentieth-century vaudevillians borrowed from their minstrel predecessors by using blackface and dialect in their performances as well. Around 1900, many bills featured at least one blackface performer. Although blackface acts were primarily performed by men, a few women also worked under the burnt cork mask, including Sophie Tucker, Josephine Gassman, Lulu and Mabel Nichols, and a group called The Minstrel Misses.[13] Though the use of blackface began to wane in the 1920s, performers continued to mimic ethnic dialects and joke about racial stereotypes throughout the twentieth century. Not coincidentally, the popularity of gender and racial impersonations peaked in the midst of tremendous gender, sexual, and racial upheaval. According to Ann Douglas, turn-of-the-century American moderns were obsessed with revealing the "arts of exactitude, of distinguishing one thing from all else that may resemble it."[14] The illusions presented by gender and racial impersonators offered them exciting new challenges.

While each evening's show typically featured only one female or male performer whose entire act was structured around gender or ethnic impersonation, many vaudevillians offered audiences race and gender bending acts. For example, Jewish comedienne Fanny Brice sang, "I'm an Indian" in Yiddish, and the Gordon Sisters performed as boxers who styled themselves as "Amazonian athletes."[15] Other performers relied on costumes and song lyrics to more subtly suggest an ambiguous racial and gender identity that did not conform to existing categories. But all of these performances drew attention to the ways in which gender and race were flexible cultural projects, actively revised, contested, and rebuilt through each other.

The enduring presence and undeniable success of performers who offered audiences race and gender bending performances raise several important questions: What explains the endurance of the race and gender bender in the twentieth century and how did these performances work in tandem? How did representations of race rely upon, reinforce, and challenge understandings of gender and vice versa? Why did so many working and middle-class urbanites spend time and money to watch these performances? How did critics respond to performers who transformed themselves from black to white, to Jewish, to Indian, from male to female, and savage to civilized? How did critics' responses change over time? This book attempts to answer these questions.

———

Vaudevillians took to the stage at the same time social changes were dramatically altering the American landscape around them. By the late nineteenth century, the industrial order of America had been dramatically restructured. Instead of working with their hands on a farm or as artisans in their own shop, more Americans became factory and clerical workers earning wages doled out by middle-managers. Many waged workers crowded into factories, which offered alienating, backbreaking labor, unsafe working conditions, and low wages. While women entered the work force in greater numbers, men lost the power to control the pace, production, and outcome of their work.[16] Together, these changes caused many American men to feel uneasy about their relative loss of independence in a rapidly changing world.

By poking fun at these changes and using the stage to transport audiences to a different time and place, vaudevillians offered Americans the opportunity to laugh, cry, and—ultimately—cope with the increasing mechanization and regimentation of life. While some performers sang nostalgically about a pre-industrial rural past on stage, modern cities continued to expand. Millions of Americans flocked to cities, newly illuminated by electricity and easily navigable by streetcar. Other advances in technology unleashed sweeping changes that altered the pace at which Americans communicated and moved through daily life. By 1920, more than half of Americans lived in urban areas, where movies, automobiles, skyscrapers, and airplanes dotted the roads and skies.[17] In the American home, wristwatches, telephones, light bulbs, radios, and refrigerators changed the rhythm and hue of domestic life.[18]

Throughout this era, gender norms also underwent rapid revision and vaudeville performances dramatized these changes as well. In the late nineteenth century, the middle-class, white New Woman became the dominant female icon, replacing the True Woman of the Victorian era. One of the most important characteristics of the New Woman was her desire to attend college, which she did in greater numbers than previous generations.[19] Many such women became nurses, clerical workers, teachers, and social workers and a select few managed to break into male-dominated fields of medicine and law. New Women were also more likely to join activist and politically-oriented clubs, and to advocate for the rights of consumers and universal suffrage. They often worked and played outside the home, and were more likely to remain single than any previous generation of American women. If she did marry, the New Woman often did so later in life and had fewer children, a fact that worried not a few pundits. Though much of the controversy surrounding New Women was exaggerated, real changes were, in fact, taking place. Indeed, between 1800 and 1900, the birth rate dropped 40 percent to 3.56 children per woman, and it continued to decline as women exercised more control over their fertility.[20] Due to legislative reforms, rates of divorce also rose in the early twentieth century.[21] By singing about suffrage and joking about women ruling the world, vaudevillians caricatured, celebrated, and satirized the New Woman on stage.

The New Woman's emergence coincided with the increasingly public face of sex in American life. Beginning in the 1880s, a new generation of experts sought to grapple with challenges of modern life by studying gendered and sexual behavior. In particular, sexologists like Richard von Krafft-Ebing and Havelock Ellis became interested in deviance and paid particular attention to "inverts" they believed were inappropriately gendered.[22] By the early twentieth century, sexologists were explaining gender non-conformity by asserting that effeminate men had inverted their gender and become females on the inside, while remaining anatomically male.[23] They had similar worries about assertive New Women who believed in suffrage, wore pants, or failed to reproduce. While doctors believed many inverts were homosexual, there was little consensus on the causes or correlation of the two phenomena.[24]

Sexologists also wrote about the drag balls of New York City where, between 1890 and World War II, upper-class urbanites came to watch participants upend existing gender, racial, and class hierarchies by cross-dressing and dancing with same-sex partners. In Harlem and Greenwich

Village, drag balls made a spectacle of gay life and even hosted competitions and awarded prizes to the best male and female impersonators.[25] Though such activities were censured on the streets, ball organizers obtained police permits, allowing attendees to cross-dress and race-cross without fear of harassment or arrest.[26] In the same period in which gender impersonators dominated the vaudeville stage in large and mid-sized cities, then, the drag balls of New York City offered elite spectators an opportunity to become cultural and sexual tourists.

Throughout this era, gender and sexuality were primarily read visually, so things as seemingly insignificant as hairstyle, complexion, and clothing became sources of obsessive scrutiny. As Marjorie Garber has argued, "clothing—and the changeability of fashion—is an index of destabilization."[27] With a quick costume change, a wig, and a little makeup, modern men became women and whites became Others. Performers who illustrated this knowledge by changing multiple times per performance—sometimes even *on* stage—often had a disruptive effect on gender and racial norms. Just as eugenicists and phrenologists pointed to hair texture, skull size, and lip shape as visual markers of a fixed racial identity, sexologists watched changing fashion trends and pointed to clothing and hair as signs of sexual inversion. They began to insist that women who wore their hair short or "who dress in the fashion of men" were most likely lesbians.[28] Though the stage was a safer space to experiment with norms than the street, what audiences and theater managers tolerated on stage was still tethered to what was permissible off stage.[29] As gender norms contracted during the Great Depression and experts focused increasingly on homosexuality, gender impersonators who cross-dressed on stage, then, came under increasing pressure to distinguish themselves from gay men and women.

The proliferation of new technologies, the field of sexology, the invert, and the New Woman all appeared at the same historical moment that Americans began to police racial boundaries with new zeal. Throughout most of the nineteenth century, Nordic immigrants came to America from northern and western Europe, including Denmark, Norway, and Sweden. In the early twentieth century, however, the source of this exodus shifted to southern and eastern Europe. This brought Italian, Russian, Polish, and Jewish immigrants through Ellis Island to compete with working-class blacks and whites for industrial jobs and over-crowded urban housing. Combined with the declining birth rates of white New Women, the increased immigration of non-Nordics alarmed eugenicists, politicians, pundits, and legislators that old-stock Americans were committing race suicide.

In the twentieth century, new laws attempting to preserve resources and maintain racial boundaries placed strict limits on immigration. In 1924, the Johnson-Reed Act established nationality quotas, limiting the number of non-Nordic immigrants allowed entrance to the United States. This new immigration policy sought to preserve racial homogeneity and was extremely effective in stemming immigration from those perceived as undesirable, and not coincidentally, less-than-white.[30] While new immigration laws excluded virtually all Asian immigrants, they also disproportionately limited the number of immigrants from countries such as Italy, Russia, Hungary, Greece, and Poland. Vaudevillians tapped into these anxieties by lampooning unassimilated Irish, Jewish, and Italian immigrants on stage.

While immigrants were still pouring in through New York City, in 1896, the landmark U.S. Supreme Court case, *Plessy v. Ferguson*, helped usher in the nadir of race relations between black and white Americans. The Louisiana case stipulated that racial segregation was legal throughout the United States, so long as accommodations were "separate but equal."[31] Following this ruling, Jim Crow quickly spread, not just in the South, but throughout the nation. The legal codification of physical boundaries separating the races, however, did not preclude the continued escalation of racial tensions, and in many cases, deadly violence. In 1919, for instance, when a fourteen-year-old African American boy floated on a raft across an invisible color line at a beach in Chicago, he was stoned by white bathers and then drowned. When police refused to arrest his assaulters, a riot erupted lasting seven days, leaving nearly forty people dead.[32] Known as the "red summer" of 1919, riots also broke out in several other cities across the country, resulting in untold bloodshed and hundreds of deaths. Part of these new tensions stemmed from a major demographic shift known as the Great Migration. With the onset of World War I, half a million black Southerners relocated to cities like Detroit, Philadelphia, Chicago, Cleveland, and New York.[33] Calling themselves New Negroes, some migrants adopted a more militant approach to resisting discrimination and advocating for "the race." While some black vaudevillians offered audiences new visions of black modernity, many black performers were forced to wear blackface masks and provide audiences with well-worn derogatory performances of Uncle Tom, Zip Coon, and Mammy. Jim Crow also crept its way on to the stage, where anxiety over interactions between black men and white women led many theater managers to forbid them from appearing on stage together.[34]

As fair-skinned workers and their darker-skinned counterparts competed for housing, jobs, recreational space, and racial dominance, by the

1920s a new form of racial logic began to emerge. Realizing they had more at stake in maintaining the black/white racial divide than they did in subdividing European races, Americans increasingly assigned everyone to one of two racial categories based on "visual cues."[35] Thus, over time this new racial logic had the effect of whitening once foreign interlopers, while those with even "one drop" of "Negro blood" stayed black.[36] From the 1890s through the 1920s, then, a new racial binary evolved which designated virtually all Americans either black or white. This logic never reflected reality, however, and vaudevillians that performed as racially ambiguous characters exposed large cracks in this flawed racial reasoning.

New Women, newly whitened European immigrants, native working and middle-class Americans, and New Negroes all patronized the vaudeville theaters of American cities. When they saw the names of famous celebrities light up the newly electrified signs outside their neighborhood theaters, they flocked to watch performances in which they saw themselves. Because they dramatized unfolding technological, economic, social, and cultural changes, vaudeville performances offer a fitting setting for investigating and contextualizing the discord surrounding race and gender in early twentieth-century America.

――――――

This book focuses on four vaudevillians who provided audiences with complex race and gender bending performances between 1900 and 1930. These performers started their stage careers at young ages, escaping from working and middle-class families to New York, Chicago, or Boston to launch their careers on the vaudeville stage. Eva Tanguay (1879–1947), Julian Eltinge (1881–1941), Lillyn Brown (1885–1969), and Sophie Tucker (1884–1966) became beloved international celebrities. With the exception of Brown, whose race kept her from the most lucrative roles, they were some of the highest grossing acts in American vaudeville. As visible cultural icons, they reflected and shaped turn-of-the-century gender and racial upheaval.[37]

Tanguay, Eltinge, Brown, and Tucker represented qualities as diverse as their audiences, yet several common themes link them together. They each enjoyed longer-than-average stage careers, finding success on both sides of the Atlantic within and outside the field of vaudeville, starring in films, Broadway musicals, cabarets, and nightclubs and, in some cases, recording songs Americans could play on their phonographs or hear on the radio. Billed as "coon shouters," "wild girls" and "gender impersonators," each became famous as a specific type of novelty act, distinguishing themselves by highlighting their most unique and particular traits. However, performers who billed themselves as gender impersonators made race as much a part of their performance as gender, and fairskinned coon shouters like Tucker crossed gender boundaries as often as they crossed racial ones. These performers gained notoriety and success because they adopted behaviors and appearances associated with races and genders that were off limits to them. Just as P.T. Barnum's ambiguously titled "What is it?" exhibits invited patrons of dime museums and freak shows in the nineteenth century to question the race, gender, and humanity of his spectacles, these four vaudevillians left audiences curious, confused, and captivated.[38] Audiences questioned the authenticity of what they saw and heard, and were left to ponder the ways in which gender and race were made rather than born.

Race and gender benders begged audiences to take a second and third look—to listen and to stare—and finally, to turn their gaze inward as well. Rooted in anxieties over interracial relationships, mannish New Women, and effeminate men, vaudeville managers frowned upon representations of racial, gender, and sexual ambiguity. Yet, race and gender benders solicited just such interpretations in their performances. As one critic said of Eltinge, they "provided a new topic for conversation" and knew "the exact pulse" of the public, which told them "just how far to go in everything."[37] Indeed, Tanguay, Eltinge, Brown, and Tucker thrilled American audiences just short of offending them; in the process, they complicated, disrupted, and sometimes reinforced evolving racial and gender binaries.

Because vaudeville performers sometimes communicated worrisome messages about the future of the American race, the task of carefully monitoring representations of gender and race became increasingly urgent. As Jim Crow put definitive physical space between those with fair and dark skin, Tucker's performances embraced a cultural kinship between the two. Likewise, Tanguay's performances represented a dangerous new hybrid—a light-skinned, savage white woman—a mercurial, manly predator, who was egotistical and aggressive. While critics fretted over the mannish New Woman, Eltinge embodied the stunning, hyperwhite Victorian woman on stage and the rugged outdoorsman off stage. As a fair-skinned African American who could pass for white, Brown put a modern face on the cosmopolitan black dandy.

At the same time these performers offered audiences coping mechanisms, they also appeared to threaten the fruition of a perfect, modern American civilization by dramatizing the convergence of genders and races for all to see. Through the light-skinned cosmopolitan dandy, the hyper-white Victorian lady, or the well-tanned outdoor ranchman, they linked definitions of gender to race in contradictory ways, using race to both uphold and undermine gender norms at different moments. At times, these performers encouraged critics to make connections between their on-stage performances and their off-stage lives; on other occasions, they insisted on their separateness. They showed Americans that gender and race were bendable; they were what you made of them and they could not be disentangled from each other.

––––––

Though this book is primarily a work of social and cultural history, it draws upon several lines of interdisciplinary scholarship. It responds to the call feminist scholars began issuing in the 1980s for more rigorous interdisciplinary work that examines the intersectional nature of gender and race.[39] Following their lead, this book takes an intersectional approach, which assumes that gender and race are historically contingent, mutually constitutive categories that find their meaning through each other. They are social constructs, imposed, resisted, and reinforced, but reliant on each other.

In recent decades, gender and queer theorists have usefully explored the unstable, performative nature of gender. Judith Butler profoundly influenced this field by arguing that, rather than existing as an "interior essence" linked to sex, gender is anticipated, produced, and reproduced through performed rituals.[40] All gender is, therefore, a social performance and a form of "persistent impersonation that passes as the real."[41] What is remarkable about vaudeville, then, is that race and gender bending performers showed audiences the performative, artificial nature of these constructs nearly a century ago.

Butler acknowledged that race and gender "always work as background for one another, and they often find their most powerful articulation through one another."[42] More recently, queer race theorists have explored the knots that bind together race and gender, criticizing how previous scholars have analyzed gender, sexuality, and race as if they were somehow separate and unrelated entities.[43] According to Siobhan Somerville, the "challenge is to recognize the instability of multiple categories of difference simultaneously rather than to assume the fixity of one to establish the complexity of another."[44] In this same vein, this book examines how race and gender found their meaning through one another on the stage in the early twentieth century. The vaudeville stage was not simply a place where performers winked at current events and rehashed well-worn comedic tropes. At the same time eugenicists, sexologists, legislators, and pundits told audiences that gender and race were biological facts, vaude-villians nudged audiences to reconsider what was real or counterfeit, fixed or fluid, ancient or modern, human or animal, man or woman, black or white. As the voice of the city and the people's art, vaudeville was a criti-cal cultural site for performers and audiences to reinscribe, modify, and challenge existing discourses about gender and race.

Scholars who have studied theatrical performances of race have in-fluenced my understanding of vaudeville's race and gender benders. Many scholars have assumed that the practice of blackface and the use of racial dialect were inherently derisive and exploitative, allowing performers who adopted racial disguises to laugh with the audience at the Other, further whitening themselves in the process.[45] However, race bending performances were not a one-way street. In the tradition of Eric Lott's work on American minstrelsy, I argue that these performances often conveyed mixed messages about the multiply-dimensioned, artificial nature of race. Likewise, vaudeville audiences expressed a range of con-tradictory responses to these performances, often feeling both desire and derision.[46] These performers bent, borrowed, and stole from genders and races that were purportedly not their own, but they did so in ways that did not necessarily assure their own advancement. Rather, they risked being perceived as sexual inverts and racial outsiders.

A number of important works on vaudeville and theatrical perfor-mance have also help lay a critical foundation for this work.[47] Recent scholars have looked to vaudeville to uncover signs of feminist conscious-ness, the agency of minorities as they resisted relentless discrimination, and acrimonious debates over the nature of high and low art. While each of these accounts has informed this book, *The Prettiest Girl on Stage is a Man* attempts to tell a different story.

Though three of the four performers examined here have been ex-plored elsewhere, no scholar has used a nuanced intersectional analysis to illustrate the interdependency of race and gender in their performances or in vaudeville more broadly. By placing these performers in dialogue with Brown, a black male impersonator who has not previously received critical consideration, I hope to recuperate the career of a forgotten fig-ure while highlighting how race as much as gender shaped the meanings of each of these performances. Structured around four comparative case studies, this book uncovers important conversations about race in un-expected places, finding racial discourses in popular culture where most scholars have focused on gender, and vice versa. This approach also dif-fers from previous studies of gender performance by considering gender impersonations not as distinct forms of grotesquerie or signs of sexual subversion, but as subtler yet no less potent cultural markers of race. By analyzing an array of primary sources, I attempt to recover and unpack their careers, while ultimately revealing the inseparability and instability of gender and racial constructs in America more broadly.

If only because of their enduring success, these performers raise legitimate questions about typicality, and I do not intend to suggest that they represent all vaudevillians. Rather, they are a small sampling of performers, many of which regularly blended race and gender bending identities in their performances. While other performers came and went, Tanguay, Eltinge, Brown, and Tucker stayed relevant, adapting to the desires of fickle American audiences for over twenty years. Over and over again, audiences chose to patronize specific headliners because they provided them with something desirable—vivid illustrations and playful manipulations of encroaching racial and gender changes.

This study relies heavily on primary sources located in several archival collections.[48] My analysis draws from close readings of professional photographs, sheet music, phonograph records, and theatrical advertisements. I contextualize these documents with hundreds of newspaper articles and critical reviews, published by over forty black and white-owned regional and national presses primarily between 1900 and 1930.[49] Contemporary theater and performance-oriented periodicals and magazines such as *Variety* and *Green Book Magazine* also provide important resources. Though these sources do not reveal the motives of performers or the extent to which their performances were shaped by managers and agents, reviews tell us the ways in which their performances inspired both unease and pleasure in audiences and critics.

Several memoirs and autobiographical essays written by vaudevillians, including Sophie Tucker, Eva Tanguay, Joe Laurie Jr., and Ethel Waters, also provide a comparative perspective.[50] However, I approached these as self-consciously produced texts, which reflect the performers' attempts to control their reputation and legacy as much as to document lived experiences. Caroline Caffin's, *Vaudeville: The Book* and Charles Stein's collection of essays, *American Vaudeville as Seen by Its Contemporaries* also provide further context. I compare these with critical reviews and scholarly works on other contemporary performers who experimented with notions of race and gender, including May Irwin, Gladys Bentley, Alberta Hunter, Anna Held, Eugen Sandow, Bothwell Browne, George Walker, Jack Johnson, and the Gordon, Whitman, and Boswell sisters. Finally, correspondence with one of Brown's former drama students, Robert Kya-Hill, filled informational gaps about her performances.

In an effort to highlight change over time, the four case studies in this book appear in chronological order. Although each of these performers was active between 1900 and 1930, this study begins with Eva Tanguay, whose career was the first to self-destruct in the 1920s. Scholars of American history and popular culture have only begun to fully examine Tanguay's significance, and have virtually ignored the role of race in her performances, perhaps because she rarely resorted to obvious racial tropes such as wearing blackface or speaking in dialect. However, Tanguay was an enormously successful provocateur, whose career provides insight into the ways in which gender and racial ideologies were messy and malleable. At a time when over-civilized white men desired, but could not maintain, a monopoly on modern primitiveness, Tanguay boldly suggested that white women could be more manly and primitive than their animalistic male counterparts. In Chapter One, I argue that her popularity reveals the extent to which modern Americans were excited and entertained by the prospect of blurring the unstable meanings of whiteness with Otherness, manliness with femininity, and savagery with civilization.

In Chapter Two, I analyze the career of vaudeville's most renowned female impersonator, Julian Eltinge. By presenting audiences with a fair-skinned Victorian lady through the body of a white male, Eltinge played a distinct role in negotiating popular meanings of race and gender. He published a women's magazine and sold his own brand of whitening beauty products, offering fashion tips to women who hoped to emulate his hyper-white femininity. His on and off-stage performances demonstrate the centrality of whiteness to femininity, providing important opportunities for analyzing contemporary understandings of gender and racial norms at the turn of the century. Ultimately, this chapter suggests both how popular constructions of whiteness were deeply gendered and how race could be used as a tool to neutralize gender transgressions.

Chapter Three brings attention to the scholarly silence surrounding black male impersonators and examines the role of race in gender impersonation more broadly. As a biracial woman who portrayed the cosmopolitan, modern black dandy but sang about an antebellum southern past, Brown offered black and white audiences starkly different visual and aural messages about gender and race. Her willingness to continue impersonating men when she was nearly eighty years old, long after the supposed obsolescence of the respectable male impersonator, illustrates the inadequacy of current scholarship on male impersonators. This chapter also suggests that black male impersonators viewed their work with far less reticence than did white gender impersonators.

The final chapter focuses primarily on the first twenty years of Sophie Tucker's long professional career, tracking her reception along racial and gendered lines. In her autobiography, *Some of These Days*, Tucker proudly recollected that her performance was so authentic that she had difficulty convincing her audience she was not a Southern black girl. She claimed that doing so necessitated removing one of her black gloves to reveal her pale hand. Chapter Four interrogates Tucker's claim, arguing that close analysis of her early career demonstrates that blackface and dialect—acting black—did not always help a performer become white. For Tucker, sound, size, sexuality, and style were all mitigating factors in the performed negotiation of race and gender, and—to the delight of her audiences—each provided a space within which to resist the tidiness of unfolding racial and gender categories.

These performances could ultimately be liberating, opening up new possibilities of expressing and understanding gender and race. But they could also serve to reinforce existing norms and help enforce conformity. The performers that are the focus of this study were not equally transgressive; each reflected and revised how contemporary Americans understood race and gender in contradictory ways. Yet, together, their successes demonstrate that the development of gender and racial binaries was neither as inevitable nor as neatly distinct as scholars have previously thought. On the contrary, self-conscious audiences and discerning critics were titillated by the notion of purposely blurring and contradicting those developing boundaries at the same time they sought to confirm them. Figures like Tanguay, Eltinge, Brown, and Tucker, help us retrace connections between gender and race for Americans—both the performers who entertained their audiences, and the people who spent time and money watching contested representations of the fundamental, but slippery, concepts that shaped their lives.

THE PRETTIEST GIRL ON STAGE IS A MAN

CHAPTER 1

SEX, SAVAGERY, AND THE WOMAN
WHO MADE VAUDEVILLE FAMOUS

*I*t is no coincidence that the curious appellations and adjectives heaped upon Eva Tanguay during her long, record-breaking career in American vaudeville could have aptly described a wild animal. Tanguay evoked animality not simply in how she moved or what she sang, but *how* she sang. For example, after seeing Tanguay perform for the first time in Buffalo, New York, in 1912, one critic commented: "Miss Tanguay's voice contains no more music than a buzz saw, she has no more repose than a mad dog fleeing before a mob of small boys."[1] And in what he intended as an insult, but Tanguay probably welcomed as a compliment, one critic described her voice as "the wail of the prehistoric diplodocus."[2] Tanguay encouraged such comparisons by singing songs like "Someone Left the Cage Open and I Walked Out" and "I'd Like to be An Animal in the Zoo" (see Figure 1).

By wearing costumes made of feathers and furs and singing seemingly autobiographically-themed material about her primitive nature and animalistic aspirations, Tanguay became "The I Don't Care Girl," who was beloved for her defiance of Victorian expectations of white feminine decorum. In her own time, such conduct made her a household name, sealing her reputation as a popular provocateur and distinct symbol of early twentieth-century American conflicts over the unstable and tangled meanings of gender and race. Using vaudeville as her medium, Tanguay

Figure 1. "I'd Like to Be an Animal in the Zoo" Sheet music, Jerome H. Remick and Co, 1910. (Historic Sheet Music Collection, University of Oregon Libraries, Music Services).

gave live audiences a preview of the kind sensationally primitive per-formances African American entertainer Josephine Baker would become famous for in the 1930s. Clad in feathers and fruits, Baker seemed to echo Tanguay when she told the press, "People have done me the honor of believing I'm an animal."[3] But as a fair-skinned white woman, this conduct made Tanguay a household name beginning in 1903. Tanguay linked white womanliness to animalistic savagery at a time when both racial and gender ideologies were under considerable reconstruction. In doing so, she presented audiences with a new ideal of racialized masculine femininity.

From 1903 through the 1920s, magazines and hundreds of daily newspapers regularly published Tanguay's photograph and reported on her performances, fashions, backstage antics, and personal life, once devoting an entire article to the secret of her shiny hair (fittingly, it was champagne).[4] This intense level of coverage afforded Tanguay the status of a national celebrity. To her supposed chagrin, a reported 517 professional imitators and impersonators, both female and male, made successful careers mimicking the songs, dances, and costumes she made famous.[5] Scores of photographs, critical and autobiographical essays, original sheet music, and even a feature film in which she starred as a cross-dressing, wild gypsy, reveal the life and work of a unique and certainly not well-behaved woman—a woman who both reflected and challenged popular beliefs about gender and race in turn-of-the-century America.

Within the past few years, renewed popular interest in Tanguay has inspired her first full-length biography, a feature article in *Slate,* and comparisons to Madonna, Lady Gaga, Katy Perry, Sarah Silverman, and even Kim Kardashian.[6] Though a number of scholarly books feature Tanguay on their cover or interior pages, she has yet to make more than a few appearances in their indices.[7] The few scholars who have examined Tanguay have remarked on the surprising lack of scholarly attention paid to this successful, yet elusive, figure in American popular cultural history.

This chapter expands on the work of other scholars by utilizing a wide variety of archival material, including the recently organized Eva Tanguay Papers at the Henry Ford Museum. It examines this material through the revealing lenses of race and gender. The chapter also contextualizes her life and work within dominant cultural themes that shaped turn-of-the-twentieth-century America, including the conservative values endorsed by President Theodore Roosevelt and the writings of prominent intellectuals such as G. Stanley Hall and George Beard. Such men were concerned about "race suicide" and the epidemic of nervous exhaustion known as neurasthenia, thought to be infecting white American New Women in particular. The nature and reception of women's performances in popular theater reflected anxieties emerging about the New Woman, who attended college, rode bicycles, and sometimes turned her back on marriage and children in favor of education and work.[8] Unlike some New Women, Tanguay did not pursue a college education, work in a settlement house, or campaign for women's suffrage. Yet she played a distinct and highly visible part in major cultural shifts, using the stage to exploit and experiment with changing, interdependent notions of gender and race. Tanguay linked her transgression of gender norms to racial ideologies by connecting both to her supposed savage primitivism. In offering modern audiences the primitive savage in the body of a white woman, Tanguay provides an important case study of how gender increasingly took on racially-specific meanings in the early twentieth century.

Pinning down the precise meaning of primitivism is challenging in part because, as Marianna Torgovnick argues, "the needs of the present determine the value and nature of the primitive."[9] By the turn of the twentieth century, the savage primitive had long been a figure of fascination in American popular culture. In the mid-nineteenth century, P.T. Barnum exhibited the racially exotic savage through the "freak show" in dime museums and circuses. Most famously, he showcased the long-haired Davis brothers, billed as the "Wild Men of Borneo," the bushy-haired "Circassian Beauty," and the "Missing Link" between man and beast.[10] In the late nineteenth and early twentieth centuries, racial ideologies were particularly fragile and primitivism could cast an even wider net over groups with little in common aside from their Otherness. Within American borders, African Americans, Native Americans, Asians, non-Nordic European immigrants, the poor, and men and women of any race or class who did not fit prescribed gender norms could all represent the savage primitive.[11]

In the 1880s racial segregation dramatically expanded and black men, in particular, were vilified as primal beasts with a penchant for raping white women.[12] In the 1890s, entrepreneurs continued to capitalize on American fascination with the backwards dark savage in other arenas. American businessmen contrasted their modern technological inventions and architectural accomplishments with dark-skinned, half-naked Dahomeys at the World's Columbian Exposition.[13] In the nascent film industry two decades later, black men were portrayed as primitive rapacious beasts in W.D. Griffith's *Birth of a Nation* (1915) by white male actors in blackface masks and wooly wigs.[14]

At the same time that black men were being vilified in popular culture, the rising tide of immigration from southern and eastern Europe and widespread nativist sentiment made white Americans, particularly those of northern and western European Nordic descent, anxiously view themselves with new urgency as the civilized superiors of racial Others. Indeed, as American readers learned of President Theodore Roosevelt's African safaris and Edgar Rice Burroughs's literary fantasies about a young man named Tarzan who was reared by apes in Africa, they harnessed the concept of the pre-capitalist, un-Christian savage with special relish.[15] As a white woman, Tanguay immersed herself in this popular primitive discourse. Through her vaudeville performances she presented herself as an animalistic, racially ambiguous, manly female belonging to another time and place. In doing so, she contrasted herself with white New Women and overly civilized white men striving to recover their manliness by living the strenuous life. In short, she offers an important case study of the complex racialization of gender.

RECOVERING THE RACE THROUGH THE STRENUOUS LIFE

Tanguay was born in 1878, when the first generation of New Women began to open settlement houses, attend women's colleges, and form activist groups. By the early twentieth century, many believed that New Women were not fulfilling their duty to reproduce the white race because they had become distracted by these other endeavors. Public figures like Theodore Roosevelt openly expressed their fear that old-stock Americans of Anglo-Saxon Protestant descent would soon lose political and cultural control of the nation to the children of foreigners. Tanguay was an apt model for such trends; throughout three failed marriages, she never had any children. Indeed, the changes associated with the New Woman gave white American men reason to worry about the masculinization of women and the feminization of men. Thus, near the turn of the new century, many men became particularly invested in the notion of reasserting their virile (and later, specifically heterosexual) masculinity.[16]

In 1899, when Tanguay was twenty-one years old, President Theodore Roosevelt famously coined the phrase "the strenuous life." He originally used the phrase to advocate an aggressive American foreign policy in Puerto Rico, Cuba, and the Philippines.[17] In a culture increasingly dominated by Darwinian ideas about the survival of the fittest, Roosevelt believed that a Spanish-American and Philippine-American war would provide a "longer term solution to modern civilization's seemingly dangerous tendency to make young, middle class, and wealthy men, soft, self-seeking, and materialistic."[18] In other words, war would help a new generation of men, lacking the martial experience their fathers earned in the Civil War, maintain gender boundaries against the challenges posed by New Women.

After the Spanish-American and Philippine-American wars ended, Roosevelt's phrase continued to connote "a virile, hard-driving manhood."[19] In his 1898 speech, "The Duties of a Great Nation," he advocated the strenuous life as both a national and personal lifestyle: "Greatness means strife for nation and man alike. A soft, easy life is not worth living, if it impairs the fibre [sic] of brain and heart and muscle. We must dare to be great; and we must realize that greatness is the fruit of toil and sacrifice and high courage."[20] Two years later, Roosevelt further expounded on this belief, asserting "men who have made our national greatness are those who faced danger and overcame it, who met difficulties and surmounted them, not those whose lines were cast in such pleasant places that toil and dread were ever far from them."[21] Most of all, Roosevelt detested men who led a comfortable "sedentary life," the polar opposite of the strenuous life.

While white American men like Roosevelt imagined themselves reclaiming their primitive manly sides through imperialist wars, hunting trips, boxing matches, and collegiate sports, middle-class women were simultaneously encouraged to lead a sedentary lifestyle. This feminine ideal was most aptly demonstrated by the widespread use of the "rest cure" as the premier treatment for neurasthenic women. The rest cure, famously described in Charlotte Perkins Gilman's autobiographical story "The Yellow Wallpaper," "grew from the concept that the mental and physical work associated with new social, educational, and occupational roles for women led to depletion of nerve force."[22] The rest cure mandated that affected women be "relegated to complete bed rest in a recumbent position for approximately one month."[23] Silas Weir Mitchell, a physician and practitioner of the rest cure, insisted on complete confinement and immobility: "I do not permit the patient to sit up, or to sew or write or read, or to use the hands in any active way except to clean the teeth."[24] To ensure limited movement and expense of nervous energy, early in the treatment, women were even spoon-fed milk by attending nurses.[25]

In the following years, the phrases "the strenuous life" and "the sedentary life" continued to take on gendered and racial meanings characterizing levels of physical exertion. Although Roosevelt was the most visible icon of this trend, many Americans came to believe the strenuous and sedentary lifestyles had the potential to preserve or destroy the potency of manhood, womanhood, and the white race. Roosevelt spoke plainly over what he perceived to be the urgency of appropriate gender roles in preserving the so-called Anglo-Saxon race. He proffered, "the woman must be the housewife, the helpmeet of the homemaker, the wise and fearless mother of many healthy children." In addition, he said, "When men fear work or fear righteous war, when women fear motherhood they tremble on the brink of doom."[26] Here, Roosevelt made a not so subtle allusion to race suicide.

If the role of the white woman was to bear children and maintain the home, and the role of man was to labor and fight, Tanguay had it exactly backwards. One could hardly find a more apt example of the antithesis of "the sedentary life" than her, as she traveled the country performing energetic dances, living primarily out of hotels and suitcases for more than twenty years. While Tanguay playfully sang about Roosevelt on stage in a song called "When Teddy is a Partner of Mine," Roosevelt likely saw her as the embodiment of the worst kind of New Woman.[27] Because Tanguay shrugged off the roles of housewife, helpmeet, and homemaker, she was a dangerous role model: if all American white women conducted themselves as she did, the race would indeed commit a kind of suicide.

In 1904, Tanguay described her performances in words that would have pleased Roosevelt if they were uttered by a white man. "The work is strenuous," Tanguay said, "but I like action and do not mind it: excitement agrees with my health. The constant rush does not tire me in the least." Demonstrating what a poor patient she would have been for the rest cure, Tanguay explained: "I could not be still if I wished. My temperament is not one of repose."[28] Instead of attributing to her the grace and beauty of other female performers, critics described her astounding feats of athleticism and strength. Writing under the pseudonym "Gussie Gusher," in 1912, one interviewer fantastically described Tanguay's unrivaled energy noting that she first "ran nine times around the lobby" going about 60 mpg. She then stopped before "she jumped over the clerk's desk and back eight times." He reported that after she whirled around she "reached the street and went south a mile a minute" going so "fast and looked like a bear being chased by the Indians."[29] Other critics more explicitly noted their delight (or perhaps betrayed their disappointment) that "Mistress Eva had bitten no one."[30] Such tongue-in-cheek stories corresponded to others the press printed about her, satirizing both her and the appeal she held for her audience.

In shaping her public image, Tanguay attributed her success to her willingness to assert herself physically. In an ostensibly autobiographical essay entitled "Success," published in *Variety* in 1908, Tanguay described a philosophy that sounded much like one of Roosevelt's speeches: "Obstacles of all sorts were put in my way to prevent my success, but I started to fight and discovered I had a temper that had been given to me to carry me through life." She continued, "You see, obstacles force us to assert ourselves."[31] In recalling "starting to fight," Tanguay was speaking literally. In addition to her temper, she claimed to carry with her hatpins "to defend myself should anyone attack me."[32] Tanguay's words are striking for a few reasons. She self-consciously explained an ethos of assertiveness and physical aggression. In an age when masculinity meant defending one's honor and facing down tough obstacles, the philosophy she endorsed was impossible to divorce from its masculine connotations. This passage demonstrates that Tanguay wanted readers to believe she felt unconstrained by Victorian expectations of white feminine decorum, which dictated that "a middle class American woman earned admiration by providing loyal support to her husband, rearing moral children, and superintending an orderly household."[33] Alternatively, she deliberately aimed to violate expectations of white femininity—to fight to make herself more visible than other female performers who were already violating those expectations simply by appearing on stage.

Tanguay not only failed to abide by prescribed roles for the Victorian American woman by staying married to one man and reproducing many healthy white children, but she also personally embodied all that threatened the virility of the white American male. By failing to show deference to anyone and insisting on a public role, not of maternal softness and self-sacrifice, but of unapologetic self-aggrandizement, she behaved as only white men should. Yet the more she acted like a man, the more financial success and adoration she received from her loyal public, to the perplexity of many seasoned theater critics. Newspaper articles repeatedly commented on the frequency with which her performances sold out and the array of flowers thrown on stage at the conclusion of her performances. One writer observed that Tanguay's "popularity offers the deepest riddle that any public performer ever suggested." Appreciative audiences crowded into theatres night after night, and when Tanguay appeared on stage, "there was the satisfied feeling that an audience indicates when its favorite is there before it."[34] In assessing Tanguay's enigmatic popularity, another critic quipped that to admire her "is quite the regular thing. Everybody's doin' it. I admit that I am."[35]

As her celebrity profile became more visible, Tanguay continued to emphasize her strenuous lifestyle as she embodied the picture of health, vitality, and strength. If, as historians have argued, the "new corporate industrial order massively assaulted" both "manly pride and brotherhood" among American men, Tanguay's status as a prominent, wildly successful, athletic, unmarried, wealthy white woman further undermined this manliness.[36] To those fearing race suicide, her performances should have been as troublesome as they were entertaining. Yet nearly all critics expressed more awe than dismay over her energy.

Fears of the declining energy and feminization of white men manifested themselves in medical diagnoses of neurasthenia, or nervous exhaustion, in white New Women. In 1881, George M. Beard published his most influential work, *American Nervousness: Its Causes and Consequences*. In it, he explained that nervous exhaustion was caused by "excessive brain work, intense competition, constant hurry, rapid communications, the ubiquitous rhythm and din of technology."[37] In later works Beard explained manifestations and varieties of the disease, such as hysterical, traumatic, digestive, cerebral, and sexual neurasthenia. Beard had a diagnosis and neurasthenic category for everything ailing late nineteenth and early twentieth-century Americans, from sleeplessness to indigestion. He defined neurasthenia as "a chronic, functional disease of the nervous system, the basis of which is impoverishment of nervous force; deficiency of reserve, with liability to quick exhaustion... 'Nervousness' is really nervelessness."[38]

In a culture of nervelessness, even critics who disliked Tanguay remarked upon her impressive vitality and endless supply of nerves, of which middle and upper class white men in particular were supposedly in such dire need. In contemplating her popularity, one critic charged, "on every ground this feeling is wholly incomprehensible to the ordinary theatergoer. Apart from her great industry and constant movement there is no feature of the singer which is in the slightest degree out of the ordinary. She is a hard worker. At times she was breathless from her exertions. She makes no claim to beauty." The writer grudgingly conceded: "If there be one artistic lesson to be learned from the popularity of this singer it is to be found in her conscientious devotion to duty. She never relaxes in her efforts for a minute."[39] In language revealing the racial implications of Tanguay's gender transgressions, another reviewer wrote: "before her turn was half over she was bathed in a sheet of perspiration comparable only to the proverbial Ethiopian on the day of exercising suffrage."[40] Addressing the concerns undergirding the dilemma of neurasthenia, another critic was awed by the abandon with which Tanguay "wasted energy with an extravagance that indicated the supply was unlimited."[41]

Such a response indicates that Tanguay's popularity stemmed, in part, from her apparent endurance and the degree to which her critics were perplexed that a white woman was capable of giving such a performance. In a newspaper article Tanguay explained the secret of her "perfect health... 'Moderation in diet, cold tubs in the morning, plenty of exercise in the open air. . . This is the secret," she added, "of what people... call my marvelous vivacity. I never get tired, and I have never been seriously ill in my life, which I enjoy to the extreme limit."[42] Newspapers also reported that in her spare time she became one of the first women to soar "500 feet above the ground in a balloon. She has hunted big game and she has whipped insolent stage hands."[43] Reporters also boasted she was "an expert swimmer and high diver. Her highest dive was from a height of 50 feet."[44] The press documented Tanguay's every strenuous move, positioning her as the opposite of the neurasthenic woman. In doing so, they helped make her an uncomfortable anomaly as a savage white woman.

GENDER BENDING THE WHITE NEW WOMAN

While women like Tanguay defied convention on and off stage, contemporary artists such as Charles Dana Gibson prescribed the visual fit and form for New Women to follow with the creation of their iconic pop culture counterpart, the Gibson Girl. Artists like Gibson portrayed the ubiquitous Gibson Girl flying a kite, going for a stroll outdoors, or even playing golf. But rarely was she seen breaking a sweat or seriously exerting herself. In the era of the companionate marriage, the Gibson Girl was consistently situated in heteronormative contexts, often on a date with her similarly-complexioned beau (see Figure 2). The Gibson Girl was young, modern, active, stylish, and irreproachably white. Though she flirted with athleticism and had a more public role in life than her Victorian mother, she maintained a demure, rigidly upright posture, and was generally bedecked in full-length skirts and long sleeves; her mouth was closed, her lips pursed, and her hair neatly piled on top of her head in an elegant chignon. Most importantly, she was a generic icon of modern white femininity. Besides her supposed newness, there was almost nothing particular about her; as female impersonator Julian Eltinge would show, she could be anyone anywhere so long as she had the right clothes and the right complexion. In short, she was trussed up in a seemingly new, but ultimately unthreatening, package.

The Gibson Girl starkly contrasted with the likes of Tanguay on a visceral level. Unlike the Gibson Girl's chic up-do, Tanguay's uniquely untamed hairstyle struck critics and fans as a metaphor representing, not only her unruly personality, but also the ways in which she did not fit neatly into contemporary gender and racial paradigms. In 1914, Caroline Caffin described Tanguay's appearance in terms that highlighted her betrayal of conventional gender aesthetics, devoting an entire paragraph to her hair. "Your eye is arrested by the wild mop of stiff, tousled blond hair, which seems so charged with electric vigor that no amount of combing or brushing could alter its assertive unruliness. It seems as if the exuberance of her intense vitality radiates through this raffish aureole, setting the surrounding atmosphere agog with vivacity." Caffin continued, "Every inch of her, from the topmost spike of yellow hair to the tip of her never-resting toe is alive, nervous, vital."[45] Another critic more curtly likened Tanguay's hair to "the mane of a badly trimmed poodle."[46]

Figure 2. Charles Gibson's rendering of stylish turn-of-the-century New Women, titled "Picturesque America, anywhere in the mountains." Although the illustration attempts to show the active side of New Women, it is noteworthy that the women are, in fact, sitting and, as the illustration's title indicates, they are located in a generic setting. Originally published in *Life*, May 24, 1900, 442-43. (Cabinet of American Illustration, Prints and Photographs Division, Library of Congress, LC-DIG-cai-2a12817).

Just as her indefatigable energy suggested a gender Otherness to contemporary observers, critics may have supposed that Tanguay's "stiff," "unruly," "wild," utterly un-Gibson-like hair also betrayed an ambiguously non-white ancestry. In a similar fashion, the most famous actress of the nineteenth century, Sarah Bernhardt, explained in her memoir that a hairdresser tasked with taming her curly locks once exclaimed, "What hair!... It might be the hair of a white negress!"[47] In the same decade in which one anthropologist published a study featuring "a photographic chart of hair samples intended to indicate degree of intermixture" between blacks and whites, and self-made millionaire Madame C.J. Walker sold hair-straightening solutions to black women hoping to conform to white middle-class standards of beauty, photographs suggest Tanguay

Figure 3. Tanguay's open mouth
and hair like that of a "badly
trimmed poodle" convey her
irreverent performance persona
and gender and racial Otherness.
(Strauss Peyton Studio, c. 1921.
Photographs, Professional, 1921–
1939, Box 3, Eva Tanguay Papers,
Benson Ford Research Center, The
Henry Ford, Image ID: THF116220).

was attempting to exaggerate the ways in which her hair appeared to both unfeminine and racially-Other (see Figure 3).[48]

In attempting to make her hair both bigger and frizzier, Tanguay recalled the exotic incongruity of the Civil War era freak show known as "the Circassian Beauty." Despite her pale skin and supposedly pure white racial ancestry, the Circassian Beauty's most recognizable feature was her bushy, afro-like hair. This was an effect Tanguay extended efforts to call attention to, even singing about rumors "that my hair with rats is stuffed."[49] In the fifth set of extra verses of her theme song "I Don't Care," Tanguay also sang: "They say my hair's in silly style, But I don't care. . . You see my hair with me's a fixture." Emphasizing her authenticity, Tanguay continued, "And its color's not a mixture."[50]

Though Tanguay's conspicuous hair and perpetually open-mouthed expressions readily distinguished her from Gibson Girls and perhaps aligned her more closely with nineteenth-century freak show performers, her eccentricities reached far beyond her appearance. While the Gibson girl made women's gentle flirtation with athleticism fashionable, Tanguay took this to an extreme. She built a reputation as a highly physical performer whose career was her first priority. She freely argued with her male and female coworkers about stage time and billing order, cultivating an increasingly aggressive personal and professional ethos. This persona made her a perfect fit for the vaudeville stage. According to one scholar, vaudeville audiences expected "a visceral, fast-paced, direct, physically demonstrative and sometimes violent style of comedy."[51] In a genre that emphasized live interaction between the audience and the performer, successful female vaudevillians such as Fanny Brice, May Irwin, Trixie Friganza, Marie Cahill, and Sophie Tucker relied on their bodies to carry off performances that emphasized dance, costume, and self-referential commentary. Other performers, including Anna Held, Lillian Russell, and Florenz Ziegfeld's bevy of chorus girls made their beauty a central part of their acts. In both types of performances, the white female body played a central role.

Yet unlike many other white female vaudevillians, Tanguay's performances of white womanliness were more bizarre than beautiful. On stage, she was known as the "The Cyclonic One" and the "Queen of Perpetual Motion"; indeed, her signature move was to spin violently across the stage like a tornado.[52] In attempting to describe her unique style of dancing, in 1913 *The Evening American* said her "savage gracefulness and her untrammeled hair form a series of most entrancing pictures."[53] According to Jane Westerfield, for the duration of one play, Tanguay's dance routine was so strenuous that "every night [she] sought relief from the problem by having the property man beat the backs of her legs with barrel staves."[54] From this visceral image Westerfield concludes, as have many others, that Tanguay "had a powerful physique and very few people chose to argue with her."[55] This last assessment is of particular interest because it highlights the ways in which Tanguay was the essential anti-neurasthenic. Not only did she make a living by her physical labors with exhaustive performances, but she also played an active role in building her reputation as a highly physical performer who did not hesitate to protect her livelihood with that same physical strength.

In 1911, *The Washington Post* published a peculiar story that demonstrates the connections between Tanguay's aggressive physicality and her gender and racial bending. The story reported that Tanguay "was not an easy patient for the dentist. Seven husky men had to hold Eva down while the dentist went after the molars. They rubbed rosin on their gloves to give them a good grip."[56] The sensational anecdote exaggerated Tanguay's unnatural strength, apparently equal to that of seven men. Though the did not identify the race of the "husky" men, non-white men would have been strongly discouraged from laying their hands on a fair-skinned woman. In this scenario, then, Tanguay overpowered the white race and the male sex, suggesting that as a fair-skinned woman, she was a gender and racial anomaly. Interestingly, one year earlier, another newspaper reported Tanguay's height and weight as only five feet and one and one half inches tall, weighing 139 pounds; not a slight build for a woman of that height, but certainly no match for "seven husky men."[57] Heightened by the need of the men to wear gloves with rosin, these images described a small, but dangerous, creature to be handled with care. Like white men on an African safari attempting to wrestle with lions and crocodiles, Tanguay had to be tamed by white men. Such tales about Tanguay's strength would have had racial implications for turn-of-the-century audiences, who long equated superhuman strength and indelicacy with men or non-white women. Historian Jennifer Morgan has convincingly argued that early white settlers of the "New World" perceived black women as categorically different from white women, attributing to them almost unnatural strength that allowed them to toil in the field the same day they gave birth.[58] As Laura Briggs has argued, even obstetricians writing in the early twentieth century believed that "black women could feel little, even being somewhat exempt from pain."[59]

Perhaps more than other vaudevillians, Tanguay likely played an active role in crafting her image as an aggressive beast who was immune to pain. Biographer Andrew Erdman suggests she had several people helping her project such an image. She was a close friend (and alleged lover) of C.F. Zittel, a journalist who effectively functioned as her publicist by frequently writing about her in his weekly column on vaudeville in *The New York Journal*.[60] In 1907, Zittel even wrote the words and music to one of Tanguay's songs, "Nothing Bothers Me," which was essentially a sequel to her theme song "I Don't Care."[61] With the complicity of members of the press, Tanguay seemed to take pleasure in hyperbolizing stories about her own savagery, portraying herself as a merciless brute. Her active role in retelling these stories helped distinguish her from other female leads who likely would have been appalled at being cast in such an unfeminine and distinctly un-white light.

With help from many others, Tanguay portrayed herself as not only a nuisance, but as a dangerous threat. According to composer Isidore Witmark, in 1903 Tanguay nearly choked him to death.[62] Isidore was standing "when Eva came up behind him, and, standing on the step above him, put her arms around his neck." Then suddenly "Eva shrieked with laughter and without realizing it, tightened her arms around Isidore's throat in a grip of steel," and Isidore bit her. "Eva drew back in shock and rage, about to attack him, when he all but collapsed."[63]

Like most stories about Tanguay, this one smacks of sensationalism, but because it furthered her notorious reputation, Tanguay probably would have approved of its telling. Witmark's story highlights her physical potency on two levels. First, her ability unknowingly to nearly choke another person in a "grip of steel" spoke to her supposedly bottomless strength. In this anecdote, like an animal, she was unaware of the depths of her strength and the harm she was capable of inflicting merely by "shrieking." Second, the anecdote further emphasizes Tanguay's physical prowess by virtue of the fact that her victim, in this case Witmark, was an adult male. While the veracity of this anecdote is difficult to ascertain, its accuracy is of little consequence, because the story aptly demonstrates the sensationalism surrounding Tanguay and her manly acts, embellished in typical Tanguay fashion. Published by Witmark many years after Tanguay's death, the story also indicates that some of Tanguay's friends and compatriots, especially those whose success was tied to her own, were complicit in her efforts to fashion an image of gender transgression.

Countless other examples demonstrate her willingness to betray gender conventions by using aggression and violence on behalf of her career (or at least that was the rationale she and others offered). Vaudeville scholars Charles and Louise Samuels assert that, when asked by a stagehand what she would do if a fan flirted with her, Tanguay yelled, "'Watch!' Supposedly, she then picked [the stagehand] up and threw him against a wall, knocking him unconscious."[64] Allegedly the stagehand then had to be taken to the hospital and eventually won a civil suit against Tanguay for one thousand dollars, an event on which newspapers across the country eagerly commented. Here, again, her victim was male. In describing the incident, *The New York Times* reported that the arrest followed an altercation "in which George Rough, the property man for the company, and Clarence Hess, a stagehand, came together because Hess did not get out of the way when Miss Tanguay rushed from the stage to her dressing room." *The Times* further reported that, in doing so, Tanguay pushed Hess down a flight of stairs. "Rough came near being mobbed by the other hands and Miss Tanguay slapped right and left to protect her champion." The story continued, "Hess appeared exhibiting the wounds which he says the actress gave him, swore out a warrant for her arrest on the charge of malicious assault."[65] Despite her status as a white woman, *The Times* described Tanguay as both the aggressor and paternal protector. Utilizing her strength, she came to the rescue of her male property manager, saving him from a mob of stagehands. Here, again, it is worth noting that the victim she "saved" was a man.[66] At the turn of the century, such a move from a young white female, and an unrepentant explanation, was startling.

Such well-publicized narratives solidified Tanguay's reputation as a stalwart and temperamental bully, making it clear to audiences, performers, stagehands, and managers alike that she would willingly cross gendered fault lines and use her physical strength to protect the exclusive property rights of her act. Each incident and its publication simultaneously violated gender and racial ideals about the delicacy and passivity of white women. Given Tanguay's reputation and the predominance of gender impersonators in vaudeville, it is perhaps not surprising to learn that Tanguay took at least one turn as a male impersonator. What is most noteworthy, however, is that her male impersonations were far less transgressive than her performances as herself. Reviewers of her male impersonations noted that Tanguay looked like "a little boy" and her "male attire does not interfere with the display of her charms."[67] Unlike Julian Eltinge and Lillyn Brown, gender impersonators who offered convincing performances that attempted to temporarily deceive the audience, Tanguay did not convince critics she was actually a man. Like many other white male impersonators, her male characters were quaint and unthreatening. It is perhaps ironic, then, that audiences perceived Tanguay to be most ladylike when she was dressed as a man, yet her performances as herself threatened to undermine gender and racial norms more than her attempts at cross-dressing did.

SELF-MADE MEN

Tanguay's gender bending performances both on and off stage provide examples of what queer studies scholar Judith Halberstam has called "female masculinity." Halberstam focuses on masculinities contained within the queer female body, arguing that masculinity "becomes legible as masculinity where and when it leaves the white male middle-class body."[68] But Tanguay embodied a particular brand of racialized female masculinity that was neither male nor queer. Though scholars often couple lesbianism with conceptions of masculinity, Tanguay's contemporaries did not link her actions to sexual inversion and they never seemed to agree on whether she was sexy or unattractive as a white woman. Thus, as a woman who had romantic relationships with men, she provides a striking early example of an "alternate masculinity" located outside of both the white male and queer female body.[69] In Tanguay's case, gender and racial norms provided her with tangible boundaries against which she transgressed and thereby secured her fame. In short, without the chaste, delicate, white Gibson Girl, there would be no boundary for Tanguay to push against. Her subversiveness did not, at first glance, appear as visceral as vaudeville's professional gender impersonators and acts like "lady boxers." Yet by repackaging dominant racial ideologies about the savage primitive, Tanguay became a race and gender bender who challenged norms embodied by the generic white New Woman.

Much like Halberstam reads masculinity outside the white, male, middle-class body, historian Gail Bederman has examined how, as an African American athlete and celebrity, boxer Jack Johnson "played upon white Americans' fears of threatened manhood by laying public claim to all three of the metonymic facets of manhood—body, identity and authority."[70] Johnson was as famous for his flamboyant irreverence and conspicuous consumption as he was for his boxing skill; he took pains to assert his success as a "self-made man...who dressed his beautiful blond wives in jewels and furs and paraded them in front of the press."[71]

Though scholars have spilled much more ink on Johnson's flamboyant transgression of gender and racial decorum, he provides a useful model demonstrating the performance of manliness at the turn of the twentieth century. Like Johnson, Tanguay also violated prescriptive gender and racial codes, becoming a literal and figurative outlaw by proclaiming superior physical strength, an aggressive attitude, and a self-aggrandized sexual identity the prerogatives of a white woman.

As critics did with Johnson, both Tanguay and her critics made much of her self-made financial success. In autobiographical essays, she boasted of giving a substantial amount of her wealth away to those less fortunate than her.[72] Although giving her money away could be considered an act of maternal selflessness, Tanguay did this loudly and immodestly. She demanded credit, thus, counteracting the perceived feminine quality of such charitable gestures. Belying one scholar's claim that "no one but Tanguay cared how much she made," the press closely documented Tanguay's astronomical salary, spending habits, and extravagant lifestyle.[73]

In 1909, the year the Lincoln penny replaced the Indian head cent, Tanguay wore one of her most famous vaudeville costumes, a forty-pound dress "covered with [4,000] bright Lincoln pennies"[74] (see Figure 4). Like a peacock asserting his sexual prowess to potential mates, Tanguay sang "Money," and literally wore her wealth, to the delight of audiences and the bemusement of critics everywhere. The act involved throwing "real money into the audience to be carried home as souvenirs," causing "a general scramble" in which one newspaper reported that "a fat woman in an end seat was bowled over into the aisle."[75] This act made a lasting impression on Tanguay's fans, who wrote her fan letters to express their delight. While one wrote to thank her for her "two cents," another described how one of her pennies "struck me on top of the nose when you performed."[76] This unconventional behavior betrayed the quiet modesty that white women were expected to espouse as mothers, daughters, and wives. Instead of being repelled by such flagrant transgression of these expectations, though, audiences were quite pleased to be hit on the head by them.

In his lengthy profile of her in *Green Book Magazine*, Rennold Wolf emphasized the importance of Tanguay's self-made success, arguing that

Figure 4. Tanguay pictured in 1912 in her famous penny dress, which she claimed was made of 4,000 pennies and weighed forty pounds. While performing in this dress, she held a purse filled with pennies she threw to the audience. (Eva Tanguay Papers, Benson Ford Research Center, The Henry Ford, Image ID: THF116219).

her professional progress is best shown by recording the development of her earning ability which was $8 a week when she was a child. Since then, her weekly "salary has grown as follows, $20, $30, $35, $50, $75, $150, $300, $500, $600, $1,000, $1,500, $2,000, $2,500, $3,500."[77] Wolf also noted, "within the week Miss Tanguay has presented to a friend within the vaudeville field a motor launch that cost her $4,000" and described her extensive collection of diamonds, which had "an aggregate value of $75,000."[78] Rivaling her forty-pound penny dress, Tanguay flaunted her wealth by making another costume out of "one, five, ten, and fifty dollars bills that she had sewn together."[79] Beginning in 1913, Tanguay found new ways to enhance her wealth by managing and heavily promoting her own vaudeville company. Becoming her own boss her offered the opportunity to boost her salary even more and afforded her power and independence rare among her female counterparts.[80]

Although motherhood continued to take on significance as the most honorable role for Progressive Era women, Tanguay continued to shrug off the roles of wife and housekeeper, with three failed marriages (the last to one of her employees, more than twenty years her junior), none of which produced any offspring.[81] Instead, Tanguay lived in her ostentatious home with an unnamed companion, and in 1908 defended her alleged decision to reject the rumored marriage proposal of female impersonator and fellow vaudevillian Julian Eltinge: "'It would be folly for me to sacrifice my independence by marrying anyone. Not even a millionaire could supply me with any comforts that I can't secure alone with my salary.'"[82] Though reporters spilled much ink envisioning the race and gender bending nuptials of a savage white female and a convincing hyper-white female impersonator, nothing came of the publicity stunt.

Tanguay continued to flirt with the idea of marriage as a way to elicit more publicity. In 1915, she made an even more brazen suggestion about marriage when, in song, she promised a "50-50 division of the receipts" to "some man—be he old or young, lanky or dumpy."[83] Although she was already married at the time, Tanguay advertised for a kept man whose affections she could buy. When Tanguay divorced in 1917, newspapers covering the divorce proceedings quoted her stating, "I've worked hard all my life, and I can't be annoyed by having a man to support. I bought his clothes and his meals and paid all his bills."[84] By purporting to share her personal life with the press, Tanguay enhanced her image as a self-made, independent success. Like popular male performers, she boasted of her success while giving fans the illusion of intimacy by inviting the press into her lavishly appointed home to take photographs that showcased her wealth.

Like Tanguay, African American boxer Johnson used his home to declare his irreverence towards social conventions. Despite the racially discriminatory practices of real estate agents, in 1912, Johnson put forth an image of self-made success and insolence when he asserted his right to move into an all-white middle-class suburb, to the dismay of its current inhabitants.[85] Wealth gave both Johnson and Tanguay the means to ignore the conventions others were forced to follow and to fashion identities as autonomous individuals, despite the obstacles posed by their gender and race. Although the vast majority of contemporary black men and white women living in Jim Crow America lacked the socio-economic and legal means to assert such an identity, Tanguay and Johnson proved to be highly visible, flamboyant exceptions. Wealth gave Tanguay the means to ignore the conventions others were forced to follow, allowing her to fashion an identity as a gender and race rebel. In doing so, she playfully co-opted the archetype of the male patriarch who functioned as protector and provider.

Johnson and Tanguay both courted the attention of the press and openly displayed their contempt for the law. Johnson "treated minor brushes with the law—his many speeding tickets and automobile violations—contemptuously, as mere inconveniences which he was man enough to ignore."[86] After 1905, Tanguay became known for her theme song, "I Don't Care!," the lyrics of which aptly described her irreverence: "They say I'm crazy, got no sense, But I don't care, They may or may not mean offense, But I don't care, You see I'm sort of independent, Of a clever race descendant, My star is on the ascendant, That's why I don't care."[87] To put a quick end to a squabble when the police had been called, Tanguay once "produced a roll of bills and cried: 'Take it all and let me go for it is now my dinnertime.' Incredulous, the police captain told Tanguay that he was not in the practice of selling releases and that her bond (two hundred dollars) would be arranged."[88] According to another source, "it was a famous Tanguay gesture that she often carried five to fifteen thousand-dollar bills in her purse and to settle [a] dispute, she simply peeled one off her roll."[89]

In addition to pure physical power, deep financial pockets, and a commanding sense of authority, sexual prowess was another key component of twentieth-century manliness that Tanguay eagerly asserted. Johnson made sure he appeared adept in this regard as well by demonstrating his conquest of prized white beauties, parading his three white wives in front of photographers. To illustrate his prowess even more viscerally, "during his public sparring matches, Johnson actually wrapped his penis in gauze to enhance its size. Clad only in his boxing shorts, he would stroll the ring, flaunting his genital endowments for all to admire."[90] He also asserted his manly prerogative by treating his wives as his personal property, emotionally and physically abusing them, while Tanguay similarly assaulted fellow performers and stagehands.

Like Johnson, Tanguay wore provocative costumes she designed herself "and they are, of course, original, that is, what there is of them."[91] In 1909, the *Kansas City Times* reported that she was arrested "because she wore a costume (mostly tights)" which a Detective McVeigh "didn't consider street clothes" and that "Miss Tanguay made such a noise about being arrested that the act following hers had to be stopped. Miss Tanguay finally consented to put on clothes that the detective considered proper for her to go to the Rockaway Police Station in."[92] The newspaper emphasized Tanguay's willful reluctance to comply with contemporary standards of white feminine modesty by stressing her insistence on the right to adorn (or lay bare) her body as she saw fit.

Tanguay's music and lyrics often confirmed this theme of sexual autonomy through the lens of primitivism. She explicitly affirmed her sexual assertiveness in songs with primitive allusions such as, "I Want Someone to Go *Wild* with Me," "Caveman," "Hottentot," and "The Big Amazon."[93] Whether she was dressed as a peacock, a swan, or a leopard, when Tanguay "glided into view, the audience had to hold its breath. What there was of her costume fitted splendidly, but there was not much."[94]

The connection Tanguay made between sex and primitivism was particularly significant because white contemporaries associated strong sexual appetites with men and non-white women. Sexual hygienists believed most American men harbored animal instincts and needed their better halves to restrain and purify their lust: "Purity came natural to her, whereas a man constantly struggled to subdue his animal instincts."[95] Likewise, experts asserted that "'savage' women… were hypersexual."[96] Just as assumptions about black women's supposed strength and immunity to pain did not end with the abolition of American slavery, belief in non-white women's hypersexuality persisted as well. While modern medical texts argued that white women were supposedly uninterested in sex, black women (and men) were believed to be naturally lascivious creatures.[97] Although birth rates were declining across all races, obstetrical medical literature in the late nineteenth and early twentieth centuries insisted that the fertility rates of nervous white women were in sharp decline, while non-white women continued to be excessively fecund.[98]

Tanguay's racially-Other sexual prowess and strength were contained within the body, the central site where manhood could be displayed, observed, admired, and feared. In his 1909 defeat of the reigning (white) world boxing champion, Johnson clearly established the superiority of his body and skill for the manly art, to the dismay of many white Americans enraged by the seemingly grave racial implications of his victory. The violent race riots that followed his triumph attest to the degree to which many American white men felt imperiled by the specter of the superior black male body. By defeating the reigning white champion, Johnson single-handedly threatened the status of the white male body in a very public way.

Perhaps taking a cue from Johnson, Tanguay claimed the masculine right to ownership even more forcefully than many of her male contemporaries, making clear that her music, signature style and even her look were *her* property. Despite consistent criticisms and the self-deprecating songs she sang about lacking beauty and any real talent for singing or dancing, she became one of the highest-grossing and most oft-imitated performers of her time. Just as professional athletes like Johnson encouraged challenges from contenders, but promised to squash all competition, in 1910, Tanguay sang a song called "Give an Imitation of Me," daring professional Tanguay imitators to continue emulating her style. Likewise, she took out a large newspaper advertisement to warn imitators that "no further imitations"of her singing and style "would be tolerated."[99]

The press helped sensationalize this confrontational approach. One lengthy profile of Tanguay even cast Tanguay opposite Johnson, stating that she had an "ambition to be the stage's Great White Hope. For among Miss Tanguay's other assets is a right-hand punch which is said to rival in destructive force the kick of an army mule."[100] The racial undertones and animalistic dimensions of this comment are not incidental; other pundits often reiterated these themes throughout her career. Another reporter linked Tanguay more directly with Johnson, suggesting she "bears the reputation of being an 'a la Jack Johnson,' when it comes to protecting what she believes to be her rights."[101]

While little has been written about the public challenges that early twentieth-century female American performers made to each other, historian John Kasson contends that "formal challenges," which included standing and published offers to best all comers "gave working and middle-class men occasions to participate vicariously in dramas of strength, courage, and honor." Kasson continues that such "challenges, borrowing elements of the aristocratic duel, gave working and middle-class men occasions to participate vicariously in dramas of strength, courage, and honor."[102] These challenges were particularly important for vaudeville strongmen like

Eugen Sandow and prizefighters like Johnson. The significance of Tanguay's public challenges to stop her imitators functioned in a similar way. (Not incidentally, her warnings to stop imitating her were also aimed at female impersonators as well). By taking out a large advertisement she hoped would reach fans, competitors, and critics alike, Tanguay loudly declared her manly right to body, identity, and authority and, of course, simultaneously advertised her new song, "Give an Imitation of Me."

While Johnson inflamed white expectations and fears of the ape-like, virile black rapist brought to the silver screen in films like *Birth of a Nation*, Tanguay trounced expectations of white feminine civility. Although both figures did not hesitate to bend gender and racial boundaries, white audiences celebrated Tanguay's transgressions while denigrating Johnson's. Transgressive or not, as a fair-skinned woman, audiences found Tanguay far less menacing than the first black heavyweight-boxing champion, whose triumph sparked race riots around the nation, just as Tanguay's career peaked on the vaudeville stage. In short, Tanguay's transgressions were tolerated—even celebrated—while Johnson's were toxic. While Tanguay acted manly, she was still a fair-skinned woman, but Johnson's blackness would always be "unforgivable."[103]

SAVAGERY, CIVILIZATION, AND *THE WILD GIRL*

Just as Tanguay linked her subversion of gender norms to primitivism, she simultaneously evoked and manipulated racial ideologies to elicit publicity through the lens of savage primitivism. Prominently featuring nudity, betrayal, and violence, the biblical story of Salomé provided her with the perfect opportunity to do just that. Beginning in 1908, vaudeville fans developed an appetite for the sensational story of Salomé, which was en vogue thanks to Oscar Wilde's controversial work of the same name.[104] In fact, so many actresses and female impersonators portrayed Salomé that critics suggested audiences had caught a case of "Salomania."[105] According to historian Susan Glenn, Salomé "was a symbol, a role, and a mask for women." Much like Tanguay, "she was a sign of what society found both terrifying and exciting. She was a figure to be watched and those who seized the image were inviting the public to look at them in new ways."[106] Portrayed by Gertrude Hoffman, Maude Allen, and a slew of female impersonators including Eltinge, Salomé impersonations were so widespread that many vaudevillians offered their own rendition of the story.[107]

In the penultimate scene of the play, Salomé "fondles the severed head of John the Baptist whom she ordered decapitated because he spurned her advances."[108] While most vaudevillians placed a white papier-mâché head on a platter to enact this scene, Tanguay was determined to make her performance more sensational than that of her competitors. Instead, she chose to use a "Negro boy."[109] Pleased with her own innovation, Tanguay bragged that she "did something else that no one else had thought of. Instead of dancing around holding the papier-mâché head I hired a Negro boy with big eyes. I sat him on the side of the stage, all covered up. As I began to dance, I uncovered his head which, to the audience, appeared to be resting on a silver tray. As I moved about the stage his huge eyes also moved, following me."[110] One reviewer quoted Tanguay: "I sang as I danced and dropped one veil after another." While in the audience, Tanguay's sister, Blanche Gifford, was reportedly "convinced that Eva would be arrested for indecent exposure."[111] Tanguay claimed that her audience "was electrified. But when the Mayor of New York heard about the dance, he sent word to me to put some clothes on or he'd close the show."[112] Indeed, reformers across the country took issue with many renditions of Salomé, banning the performance in several states.[113]

Just as Johnson paraded his white girlfriends in front of the press, the image of a barely clad white woman slowly removing her clothing in front of a wide-eyed black male must have incited anxiety over miscegenation, the social and sexual mixing of the races which fixated on lascivious black men preying upon chaste white women. Tanguay presented these performances during the nadir of race relations as the Ku Klux Klan was growing in numbers, race riots erupted across the country and Southern mobs lynched record numbers of black men accused of failing to keep their distance from white women. On stage, theater managers discouraged plot lines that cast white women opposite black men. Allegedly, black comedian Bert Williams even had a clause written in his contract stipulating that he would not appear on stage at the same time as white chorus girls in Florenz Ziegfeld's famous *Follies*.[114] Yet Tanguay deliberately violated these conventions in order to draw out the rapt attention of audiences and critics. The explicitly sexual tone of Tanguay's Salomé performances reveal a modern fascination with blurring boundaries on stage, in ways that were forbidden off stage. The success of these performances demonstrates that theater-going Americans were excited by depictions of cross-racial sexual encounters; further, they supported acts showing white women actively *seducing* black men by attending such performances in record-breaking numbers. Audiences received Tanguay's performances with unprecedented enthusiasm, adding significantly to her star power and her pocket. It is telling that her salary reached its zenith of 3,500 dollars per week (over 70,000 dollars today) when she was performing as Salomé.[115]

Turn-of-the-century audiences often made connections between what they saw on stage and assumed about a celebrity's personal life. Tanguay was no exception. One source claimed rumors persisted that Tanguay "had black lovers."[116] It is plausible that this rumor was fueled by Tanguay's casting choice for her Salomé performance, but such gossip may also have been rooted in truth. George Walker (one of the first black stars to perform on Broadway) had a reputation as a philanderer, and according to several sources, Tanguay was rumored to have been one of his mistresses.[117] Whether or not the rumors were true, their existence did not damage Tanguay's career and she succeeded in making her rendition of Salomé stand out from the rest, heightening her visibility and power in the process. Her alleged dalliances with Walker and her casting of a black male seemed to suggest that she had to venture beyond her race in the pursuit of sexual satisfaction. As a result, she once again defied convention and audiences understood her performances as emblematic of her own race-crossing passions. While theater managers hoped performances would sell tickets by appealing to audiences seeking to shore up unstable racial and gender identities, Tanguay became even more popular by making their instability the crux of her performances.

Throughout her career on the vaudeville stage, male performers such as Al Jolson and Eddie Cantor often included skits featuring the blackface mask, while it was not uncommon for female performers to speak in dialect or bill themselves as a coon shouters.[118] Many of Tanguay's most successful peers, including May Irwin, Stella Mayhew, Nora Bayes, and Anna Held, used what they termed "niggar dialect" to sing "coon songs" that purported to represent black culture. As Chapter Four will explore in detail, Sophie Tucker started her career in blackface and spoke in dialect, effectively co-opting the archetypal figure of the oversexed black female as a way to sanitize her frank discussion of sex. Yet the extent to which Tanguay did *not* use explicit tropes of black sexuality to broach the topic of sex and female desire is notable.[119] With the exception of her Salomé performances, which relied on representations of the exoticized Oriental Other, Tanguay did not employ specific ethnic stereotypes commonly used as a tool for safely broaching the topic of female desire. Nor did Tanguay couch her discussion of sex in maternal tones by evoking the stereotype of the overweight Mammy.

Though Tanguay did not wear blackface or use dialect, she did use pre-existing racialized understandings of the generic, non-white primitive who was as much animal as human. She tapped into contemporary

Figure 5. Tanguay in her peacock costume, Baker Art Gallery, c. 1921. (Box 3, Eva
Tanguay Papers, Benson Ford Research Center, The Henry Ford, Digital ID: THF116224).

racial undercurrents through her self-representation as an animalistic,
savage, pseudo-primitive who was emotionally and sexually volatile. One
of her earliest performances was as "Coloma, the Hoo-doo, a bare-footed
Fiji Islander with a flimsy voile slit skirt,'" a character who suggested
a "certain kind of colonial sexual allure."[120] Tanguay emphasized this
theme in her costumes, which often included the feathers and furs of
exotic animals. One dress "worked out in gorgeous spangled design two

Figure 6. Tanguay dressed as a swan in one of her many animal costumes, 1921. (Strauss Peyton Studio, Box 3, Eva Tanguay Papers, Benson Ford Research Center, The Henry Ford, Image ID: THF116214).

peacocks, their bodies joining a sweep of real peacock feathers which form the back of the skirt"[121] (see Figure 5). Another notable costume appeared to channel a swan (see Figure 6).

Tanguay incorporated this primitive, animalistic theme in one song by riffing on a sensational news story about a French doctor who allegedly gave his patients organ transplants from monkeys.[122] In "When the Doc Makes a Monkey Out of Me," Tanguay wryly sang: "Have you heard the rumor, some sort of gland or tumor will make us live a thousand years or more." By invoking an animal thought to be the distant ancestor of mankind at a moment when Americans feared they might be a species endangered by race suicide, Tanguay suggested that as a human-monkey hybrid, she could live forever. She further sang: "I've got to get a gland that comes from a monkey. The change should be an easy thing for me."[123] By implicitly calling herself a monkey, Tanguay adopted a racial epithet to describe her own white female body, urging audiences not only to raise an eyebrow at her whiteness and womanliness, but her humanity and mortality. At the same time Tanguay sang about her similarities to monkeys, contemporary physicians' claimed that "African, indigenous and other colonized women had wide pelves [sic], more like that of the female gorilla than like those of European females."[124] Likewise, eugenicists argued that "the skulls of 'lower races' are closer in cranial shape to 'the low-browed ape.'"[125] In one song, then, Tanguay simultaneously primitivized herself through intersecting popular, political, and scientific racial discourses.

Tanguay used both aural and visual means to encourage audiences and critics to link her to animals. In addition to singing songs like "I'd Like to Be an Animal in the Zoo," at an animal exhibition at Coney Island, Tanguay arranged to have a photographer capture her posing with a variety of lions. Extant photographs show Tanguay with three lion cubs wrapped in her arms, while another illustrates her hoisting up a much larger lion from behind (see Figure 7). Allegedly, the lion trainer suggested "that she pose in a den of ferocious tigers. Impulsively she agreed," springing into the den "and there she stood motionless while a less brave photographer from a place of safety 'took' her again and again."[126] While this phrasing sensationalizes Tanguay's bravery in comparison to the weak-willed photographer who accompanied her, these photographs do not suggest a "motionless" Tanguay. Rather, they show an eager woman with hair in her eyes and a maniacal grin on her face seizing a rather reluctant lion. Such vivid photographs appear almost comical when compared to the staid illustrations of the Gibson Girl, and they demonstrate Tanguay's attempt to visually embed herself in a primitive past linked to dangerous exotic animals. These images complement the nicknames the press heaped upon her, like "Mother Eve's Merriest Daughter" which also evoked a primitive, pre-industrial past.[127]

It is not surprising that such images seemed to leave critics perplexed. In fact, Tanguay's performances, personality, and pictures were so evocative of Otherness that critics turned to science in an effort to make sense of her.[128] In an era when social Darwinist theories shaped

Figure 7. Tanguay holding a young lion, most likely at Coney Island's Dreamland animal exhibit, c. 1925 (Photographs, Professional, 1921-1939, 2 of 2, Box 3, Eva Tanguay Papers, Benson Ford Research Center, The Henry Ford, Image ID: THF116216).

the thinking of many intellectuals and critics, Rennold Wolf explained Tanguay's wild persona through her heritage: "Perhaps Miss Tanguay's peculiar temperament can be explained in a measure by her ancestry. Her father was a Parisian, and her mother Canadian French. Four generations back on her mother's side was an American Indian and Miss Tanguay suspects that therein the blood of her savage great-great grandfather runs in her veins."[129] The search for "savage" blood in Tanguay's family indicates that critics could not accept that a white woman (not to mention the daughter of a doctor, a fact the press rarely mentioned) could act the way she did without a viable racial explanation. Tanguay's active role in this search suggests that she was very different from vaudeville's cross-dressers who claimed to hate their work and did it only because audiences and managers demanded it. By self-identifying her so-called savage ancestry and saying she'd like to be an animal, Tanguay embraced rather than resisted her stage role as a racial inferior.

To explain her gender bending, critics felt compelled to scrutinize her race and Tanguay helped them to do it. This makes sense given that racial explanations lay at the heart of contemporary scientific theories such as phrenology and eugenics. Tanguay purposefully evoked such a rationale herself when she discussed her alleged ancestry with journalists, telling them, "as early as she could realize anything about herself she knew that she was an exotic."[130]

According to experts, this supposedly savage and exotic ancestry would have helped explain Tanguay's transgression of gender norms. In his influential work on neurasthenia, neurologist George Beard claimed that race played a pivotal role in making one either susceptible or immune to nervous exhaustion: "nervous disease of a physical character, scarcely exists among savages or barbarians, or semi-barbarians or partially civilized people."[131] Echoing the theories of contemporary obstetricians, he argued that "woman in the savage state is not delicate, sensitive or weak. Like man, she is strong, well developed, and muscular, with capacity for enduring toil." Beard noted that "[t]he weakness of woman is all modern and it is pre-eminently American."[132] Beard juxtaposed modern, nervous American white women with "female Indian squaws" who are "so different from the tender and beautiful women of the white races that they seem to belong to *another order of creatures.*" Specifically, he detailed a young Apache wife who, having quarreled with her husband, "seized him by both ears and the hair" and then "threw him on the ground, and raising his head with her hands, beat it upon the hard ground until he begged for his life."[133] Beard also described how a woman belonging to the same tribe served her husband a delicious dinner and disappeared into the woods to give birth to a newborn, returning in less than an hour "dressed in the finest apparel and ornaments, as lively and strong as though nothing had happened."[134] Beard's descriptions starkly contrasted with the expectations imposed upon supposedly fragile, middle-class white women, who were encouraged to lead a quiet, sedentary life, free of mental and physical labor.

In his treatise on neurasthenia, Beard also maintained that nervous men and women were consumed by too much worry and forethought, a quality integral to civilized life that did not impede the savage. Forecasting "is the very essence of civilization as distinguished from barbarism, [it] involves a constant and exhausting expenditure of force."[135] In contrast, Tanguay sidestepped such worries. Even the lyrics and title of her theme song, "I Don't Care!" and her nickname, "The I Don't Care Girl," described her naked irreverence.

Given the racial implications of her supposedly primitive qualities, it is noteworthy that Tanguay originally sang "I Don't Care!" in a musical comedy conspicuously titled *The Sambo Girl*, in which she played the starring role. As 19-year-old American dancer, car racer, and muse, Carlotta Dashington, Tanguay did not don blackface, although "My Sambo" was considered a coon song.[136] Like many of Tanguay's roles, her character's irreverent persona was once again tied to a fuzzy racial Otherness. Tanguay took an active role in attempting to highlight the unique racial origins of her character herself, telling a reporter that, in response to many inquiries from fans as to what a "Sambo" was, she was "thinking of printing a standardized reply postcard" that would read "Mr. Webster defines 'The Sambo Girl' as the 'offspring of a dark person and a mulatto. And I may add, in conclusion, that the term is of East-Indian derivation.'"[137] Tanguay wanted audiences to know that the irreverence and child-like abandon she portrayed as Dashington (and, in most of her roles) was best embodied by non-whites, be they Native American, African American, East Indian, or the taboo product of miscegenation.

In contrast to the worries plaguing civilized people, Beard also argued that the open expression of emotions and personality was an essential element of savagery. "Laughter and tears are our safety valves; the savage and the child laugh or cry when they feel like it—and it takes but little to make them feel like it; in a high civilization like the present, it is not polite either to laugh or cry in public." However, Beard added that constant inhibition "is an exhausting process, and to this process all civilization is constantly subjected."[138] By this logic, Tanguay lived outside the confines of white civilization as she sang "I Don't Care!" (1905) and "Nothing Bothers Me!" (1907). If not to the savage, Caroline Caffin's firsthand description of Tanguay's performance likened her to another under-developed form of civilization, a child. Tanguay's voice "shrieks. The steps make no attempt at rhythmic movement," Caffin said. And her dancing, she continued, is "just the undirected romping of a healthy, restless, child. And naively, childishly, self-conscious are her songs—if we can call them songs."[139] While vaudeville's other race and gender benders exploited the discord between seemingly incongruous racial and gendered sounds and sights, Tanguay consistently used both her voice and costumes to secure her image as a gender and racial outsider.

In perhaps an attempt to cultivate her position just outside white, properly gendered and raced civilization, in 1917 Tanguay starred in a movie called *The Wild Girl*.[140] This feature film, written expressly for Tanguay, "exhibited her gyrational dancing and revealing costumes," casting her as "an iterant gypsy girl" who "lived in the wild and was in touch with nature."[141] Like all her business endeavors, this production of The Tanguay Film Corporation was primarily a self-promoting feature meant to showcase her talents and profit from her celebrity status.[142] Along with a few new gimmicks, the film combined the most sensational themes of Tanguay's stage performances. The plot "begins with a dying stranger abandoning a baby girl in a 'gypsy camp,' with a note explaining that when the child turns eighteen, she is to inherit a 'Virginia estate.'" The chief of the gypsies has instructed the tribal matron to "dress and rear her as a boy."[143] Years later, the gender of the now-grown girl, called Firefly, is discovered by the rest of the tribe and one of its members demands to marry her, though Tanguay's character refuses this proposal. To Tanguay, playing a gender bender and racial Other who shirked civilized life must have seemed the role of a lifetime. Unsurprisingly, advertisements for the film show Tanguay's hair teased to suggest a texture contemporaries associated with non-whites.[144] Here, again, Tanguay's gender bending was facilitated by the racialization of her character.

While Beard and Roosevelt viewed Native Americans as an inferior race far below whites and close to blacks on a hierarchical scale measuring stages of civilization, the physical prowess they attributed to black and Native American women embodied the strenuous life they sought to recapture for degenerating American white men. This lifestyle recalled a mythical past when Americans lived on the untamed, unending frontier, bore ten children, faced danger daily, withstood disease, and fought off savages. Yet, as an urban white woman, Tanguay encouraged audiences to draw connections between her gender bending and the belief that racially Other women possessed animal-like strength.

Tanguay led a strenuous, primitive lifestyle, as she slammed men's heads, stabbed stagehands, and nearly strangled an adult man. She performed fearless acts of athleticism, requiring a regular assistant to beat her calves to bring back the feeling in her legs after a rigorous performance. One reviewer used language which would have struck George Beard as eerily similar, saying that Tanguay "is remindful of nothing so much as the war dance of an *apache* or the fetish of a South African *savage*."[145] Tanguay was, in essence, not a white woman, but the remarkable, semi-barbaric creature Beard imagined and fetishized. She was half animal, half human—a female Tarzan.

Tanguay's foray into film and, more importantly, her unprecedented success in musical comedy and vaudeville, raise the question of why the image of a wild white woman so resonated with early twentieth-century urban Americans inundated with messages about Darwinian hierarchy, neurasthenia, race suicide, and the need for dangerously soft white men to recover their manhood by leading a strenuous life. Tanguay offered working and middle-class audiences a vacation from their modern, mechanized city lives. She provided a refuge for those whose "units" of energy were surreptitiously siphoned out of them by nervous energies and taxing intellectual exercises. She was not alone in this endeavor. Other high profile actresses cross-dressed, spoke in ethnic dialect, donned blackface, and evoked animals in their performances, while popular dances such as the Turkey Trot, the Grizzly Bear, and the Monkey Glide allowed whites to access their inner animals.[146] But on the vaudeville stage, Tanguay offered audiences a safe space in which they could experiment with the conundrum of a savage, sexual white woman—a surprisingly appealing icon. Tanguay offered modern American audiences a coping mechanism for the present, and a visceral glimpse of what they imagined their former, more primitive selves looked and sounded like. In doing so, she provided a kind of provocation of concerns about which early twentieth-century Americans were already thinking. Indeed, in speculating about the cause of her popularity, as so many bemused critics did, Caffin captured Tanguay's appeal: "She has indeed caught something of the elemental dynamic buoyancy that enables mankind to over-ride disaster and, having caught it, is radiating it upon a nerve-wracked world."[147] As she sang about how a monkey's gland would make her live forever, Tanguay helped a wrist-watch wearing people worry just a little less about their numbered days as a declining race. In 1915, she eerily promised them in song, "A hundred years from now, Tanguay will be 'running' still." And she was right.

CONCLUSION

Although she was one of the most frequently photographed and highly-paid stars in vaudeville, Tanguay largely remains a quirky and misunderstood anecdote in the history of American popular culture. As Susan Glenn contends, Tanguay was one of many contemporary female performers who, by making spectacles of themselves, loudly claimed a new space for women on stage.[148] Yet Glenn also argues that Tanguay never "transcended the cultural paradigm which situated female humor in the framework of comedic sacrifice of normative femininity and beauty."[149] But as this chapter has attempted to demonstrate, norms of beauty, femininity, and female behavior were inextricably entangled with racial ideologies from which they cannot be separated. In fact, Tanguay's aggressive behavior, self-aggrandizement, and persistent claims to primitive savagery were the means by which she put herself outside the confines of normative *white* femininity.

Other scholars argue that Tanguay's gender transgressions were nullified by her tempestuous personality and her so-called overweight figure that supposedly made her unattractive and grotesque—even seemingly insane—to her audience.[150] For instance, Robert Allen describes Tanguay as "the only female performer to achieve stardom in big-time vaudeville with an act structured around sexual transgression." But he adds that she "succeeded only by virtue of that transgressiveness being channeled through and contained by the grotesque." And concludes that "her sexuality was not so much that of a siren as a mad woman. As such it could not be taken as 'seriously' transgressive but only as comically grotesque."[151]

Tanguay best addressed this claim herself when she wryly asked her audience "why, if they thought she was crazy, they paid to see her when there were so many public institutions where the insane could be viewed for nothing."[152] Like the three other performers examined in this study, Tanguay gave her fans what they wanted by demonstrating the flexibility of the boundaries that organized their lives. These performances walked a fine line between gender bending and gender perversion, and were deeply entangled with generic allusions to animality and racial Otherness. Such a path allowed her simultaneously to take hold of the privileges of primitive manliness without fully losing her status as a white woman. Tanguay tread this line deliberately, as she made clear in a 1914 interview: "there's more money in making people believe [I] am made mad, at a big salary, than there is in slaving in a laundry."[153] She self-consciously joked about this in front of her audiences when she wryly sang, "There's a Method to My Madness."[154]

Tanguay was acutely aware of the sensibilities of her audience. "There is a deep scheming method in her charming madness," *The Daily News* reported in 1913, adding "Eva knows just how sane she is and how bright her audiences are to applaud her joyful antics."[155] Like many of vaudeville's race and gender benders, she gained notoriety and success because she simultaneously adopted behaviors and appearances associated with a race and gender that society deemed off limits to her. Her success demonstrates the nature of unfolding gender and racial binaries and illustrates that these ideologies were not distinct.

Tanguay boldly suggested that white women could be more primitive than their animalistic male counterparts, who desired but could not maintain a monopoly on modern primitiveness. However, to many social critics, the newly feminized American white man presented a more immediate danger than the adventurous New Woman. The following chapter examines Julian Eltinge, vaudeville's most renowned female impersonator, who was forced to contend with fears of the feminized American white male. Though they were two of the highest paid vaudevillians of the early twentieth century and were once rumored to be engaged, Eltinge used the vaudeville stage for very different purposes than Tanguay, ultimately amplifying the whiteness of the women he impersonated while distancing himself from the effeminacy of which he and his peers were accused. Just as it was for Tanguay, race was a critical component of these gendered performances.

CHAPTER 2

"MAKING A WOMAN OF HIMSELF"

JULIAN ELTINGE AND THE HYPERWHITE LADY

In 1904, the same year in which Eva Tanguay described her work as a constant, strenuous rush, America's foremost female impersonator, twenty-year-old Julian Eltinge, told the press, "It takes me two hours to transform myself into a woman but it has taken me six years to learn how to do it."[1] Unlike Tanguay, whose off-stage antics and interviews with the press suggested she was simply portraying herself on stage, Eltinge tried to convince critics that he was nothing like the female characters he portrayed. Most importantly, he desperately tried to convince American audiences that gender impersonation, at which he excelled, did not come naturally to him, nor was it a pleasurable practice. Indeed, Eltinge's career hinged on what Marjorie Garber has called "the progress narrative," which rationalized and normalized cross-dressing through "a story that recuperates social and sexual norms."[2] For over twenty years, Eltinge was able to situate himself within these norms by convincing audiences of vaudeville, Broadway theater, and film that becoming feminine was a laborious and distinctly unpleasant process. His success in doing so helped make him the most respected female impersonator of the early twentieth century in a line of work many Americans considered freakish.

Women were Eltinge's most ardent fans and considered him a leading expert on turn-of-the-century American women's fashion and beauty culture. One reviewer argued that "Julian Eltinge is an amazing mirror in which we see ourselves, not, unfortunately, as we all are, but as we all want to be." The reviewer added, "Women should be grateful to Mr. Eltinge, for showing them themselves as they ought to be."[3] Eltinge offered himself as an elegant model of white womanhood and his own magazine boldly declared him, "The Prettiest Girl on the Stage."[4] He entertained working girls, middle-class housewives, New Women, and middle-aged ladies, as well as bachelors, husbands, fathers, and sons at a time when the meanings of femininity and whiteness were highly unstable. He claimed his performances provided "a help to womankind," offering a revised model of femininity, an updated version of the Victorian woman. By presenting himself as an industrious, upper-class, rugged man with an unusual talent for creating the illusion of beautiful white womanhood, he uplifted female impersonation into the realm of art.

While the performances of female contemporaries like Tanguay and Tucker emphasized themes of personal liberation, racial Otherness, larger than life personalities as well as social and sexual rebellion, Eltinge promoted hyper-white Victorian grace and femininity, ideals to which white women could aspire and white men could admire. In doing so, he exaggerated conventional perceptions of the nature of manliness and femininity and reinforced existing gender and racial norms more than he undermined them. As performers like Tanguay became famous for failing to be a lady, Eltinge became an icon of refined white ladyhood. As a highly visible icon of turn-of-the-century popular culture, his performances provide an amazing mirror in which we can see the interconnected and dynamic constructs that shaped identities in modern America.

Contemporary critics closely documented Eltinge's female impersonations for over two decades, leaving behind rich records of his career. Although Eltinge's life continues to generate popular interest, like Tanguay, scholarship on the historical significance of his performances has been limited by a singular focus on gender or sexuality.[5] Scholars most often argue that Eltinge was a closeted gay man, whose unusual career as a cross-dresser helps us understand what it meant to be a gay American male in the early twentieth century. While such studies have been illuminating, this chapter adds a new dimension to existing work by illustrating how Eltinge's performances both reinforced and modified images of womanhood and manhood through race in the fracturing world of turn-of-the-century urban America. This work considers Eltinge in the context of existing scholarship on whiteness, suggesting how popular constructions of whiteness were deeply gendered at the turn of the century. In fact, Eltinge's use of whitening powder was such an important aspect of his female impersonations that, in 1910, he established his own line of whitening beauty products, sold through *The Julian Eltinge Magazine and Beauty Hints*.[6] Eltinge's on- and off-stage performances demonstrate how race could be used to uphold existing gender norms and temper gender bending performances. His career illustrates the role one highly visible man played in conflating whiteness and femininity, providing important opportunities for analyzing the relationship between gender and racial norms at the turn of the century.

MANUFACTURING WHITE MANLINESS

Born in 1884 in the mining enclaves of Butte, Montana, Eltinge was the grandson of Irish immigrants. His father, a miner, allegedly had financial problems that forced the family to move to Boston when Eltinge was a teenager.[7] Historians know little more about his origins, but the real story about his family reveals less about contemporary gender and racial norms than the fictions he sought to propagate. The contradictory stories surrounding his entrée to female impersonation blur myth with fact, revealing much about his efforts to create a respectable, fixed sense of self. They also more broadly illustrate gender ideals in turn-of-the-century America. In his many interviews with the press, Eltinge fashioned a history that separated him from disreputable female impersonators by making sure his audience believed he had been forced into female impersonation.

Early in his career, perceptions of class played an important role in helping Eltinge distinguish himself from other impersonators and secure his status as a normal white male. To project an image of refined, white, American manliness, he invoked the image of a college boy, preempting questions about his breeding, education and wealth. One reviewer approvingly said that Eltinge was "a university graduate, with quite the best characteristics of his kind. And this is perfectly compatible with his performance, which is just a clever, innocent, and wholly inoffensive bit of mimicry."[8] In a lengthy profile, a journalist characterized him as "the son of wealth, his father being a mine owner."[9] *Green Book Magazine* noted: "Eltinge is in every way normal, rational and serious minded. In private life he is a neatly dressed young man whom one might mistake for a bank teller."[10] Still another critic quipped that when Eltinge's Boston aunt "found out that her nephew, William Julian Dalton, and the chap called Julian Eltinge on the stage were one and the same individual, she wept, fainted, and her blue Boston blood boiled."[11] The writer's alliterative turn-of-phrase revealed that many perceived female impersonation as shameful, and therefore attempted to persuade readers and critics of Eltinge's enviable origins.

In the "College Boy as a Chorus Girl," a female commentator on women's fashions and beauty culture circulated another narrative about Eltinge's early theatrical career, suggesting that he made his first stage appearance as a college student with Harvard's Hasty Pudding Club theatrical troupe.[12] Among a crew of oarsmen and football players, Eltinge was supposedly chosen by members of the all-male club to play the female lead. When his peers insisted he take the female role, Eltinge "produced a big, black cigar and said he'd die for his college and his country, but any man, woman or child would have to give him chloroform first." The writer added, "these insults brought on immediate warfare, for Julian is something of a boxer and won't stand for everything." When he finally "condescended to talk on the subject without bloodshed," his peers deprived him of food and spent two days "getting the unwilling gentleman into stays." The article noted that crowding "a fine, husky large No. 7 man's size into a cute little dainty high-heeled girl's No. 4 took the combined strength and argument of half a dozen students."[13]

Indeed, early in his career, Eltinge himself claimed that he moonlighted as a female impersonator while still a freshman at Harvard.[14] Yet the *Quinquennial Catalogue of the Officers and Graduates, 1636–1930* of Harvard contains no record of him having attended or graduated.[15] As one of the whitest and most androcentric places in the country around the turn of the century, Eltinge could not have chosen a better setting than Harvard to situate his backstory. Perhaps with the help of the press, he invented a Harvard identity just as he invented his stage name to sever connections with his real past and lend credibility to the image he tried to cultivate of a normal, intelligent, young man, bred in an upper-class white family. This revision of Eltinge's origins effectively highlighted, not only his reticence to dress as a woman, but the primitive physical nature of his revulsion against the work. Due to Eltinge's will power and physical strength, it took six young Harvard men to force him into women's clothing.

The description of Eltinge being held down by six men paralleled a rumor newspapers circulated about Tanguay, discussed in Chapter One. Emphasizing her manly physical strength, in 1911 one newspaper described the need for seven men to hold her down while a dentist attempted to clean her teeth.[16] Both Eltinge and Tanguay displayed manly behavior in these scenarios, although his bravado conformed to prescribed gender ideals for white men, while hers comically transgressed those for white women. Eltinge's story assigned to him other explicitly gender specific qualities, including cigar smoking (a "big, black cigar," no less) and a violent temper which necessitated treating him like an untamed animal, chloroformed and deprived of food and drink. [17]

Unlike Tanguay and Tucker, who belabored and exaggerated their working-class roots, Eltinge claimed an upper-class identity. Though both Tanguay and Eltinge infused their performances with seemingly auto-biographical material, Eltinge did so only in the masculine parts of his stage performance, sometimes appearing at the end of his performances as a "college boy." Yet while Tanguay's seemingly autobiographical per-formances recast the French-Canadian daughter of a doctor as a gendered oddity and member of a racial underclass, Eltinge's self-presentation cre-ated a more respectable past and simultaneously upheld existing norms linking whiteness to femininity. In this sense, at least, Eltinge was far less transgressive than Tanguay.

In an entirely contradictory story, again reflecting Marjorie Garber's progress narrative by emphasizing his lack of initiative playing women's parts, Eltinge claimed that his female dance teacher pushed him into fe-male impersonation. Suggesting the low esteem in which he held this line of work, in this version, Eltinge maintained he was pursuing his aspiration to be a blackface comedian. Having arrived early one day for his cakewalk lesson, Eltinge observed eight girls rehearse ballet, noticing that one was particularly ungraceful: "After they left I gave a burlesque of the large girl for [my teacher's] benefit." This story suggested that Eltinge intended to parrot the mocking tone of female impersonators who used blackface to comedic effect in minstrel productions. But to his surprise, Eltinge claimed his teacher "suggested then and there I go in for female impersonations, and predicted that I would make a hit. The idea had never occurred to me, and I did not take kindly to it at first." [18] After his teacher convinced him to give one performance "in skirts," Eltinge "worked hard for three hours a day for weeks at a time."

He carefully explained that the accuracy of his impersonations did not result from any unnatural gift or intuition; rather it was the product of study and hard work, requiring that he unlearn how to be a man. "Al-though [my teacher] had said I carried my hands and arms well, I had a great deal to learn in this respect. Then, my feet! I persisted in toeing in, as men do. A woman, you know, toes out; she stands more gracefully, with one foot a little in advance of the other, and when she walks her toes take an entirely different angle from those of a man." [19] Eltinge em-phasized this training involved rigorous work, "hours of daily practice," art lessons, consultations with his mother, and an apprenticeship at a clothing store to learn the finery of fabrics—all knowledge that did not come naturally to a "regular fellow."[20] Alone, he could not intuit the subtleties of womanhood; only biologically female advisors could provide such instruction.

As in countless other interviews, Eltinge called attention to supposedly innate differences between white men and women, including the shapes of their fingers, the cadence of their walks, the grip of their handshakes, and the shape of their eyes. One lengthy article detailed the behind the scenes aspects of Eltinge's male to female transformation, explaining how he selected and styled his feminine wigs, corsets, dresses, and high heeled shoes.[21] Most Americans considered a lack of visually-identifiable differences between men and women an attribute of savage non-white races.[22] Thus, Eltinge's emphasis on these supposedly natural differences between white men and women helped him claim the privileges of white manhood off stage and the highly evolved nature of American men and women more generally. However, in highlighting these differences and explaining how he overcame them, he divulged how any man or woman might replicate his results. In doing so, Eltinge ultimately suggested that the differences between men and women were learned and malleable.

Once his career began to take off, Eltinge's wealth and success continued to provide solid evidence of his white manliness. Just as Tanguay bragged about her salary and ability to provide a luxurious lifestyle for those around her, Eltinge advertised his wealth, inviting *Architectural Digest* to feature a spread of his Spanish-inspired palatial home and *House and Garden* to photograph his landscaping.[23] Fans seemed fascinated by his exorbitant salary, which critics favorably compared to that of President William H. Taft; one essay, titled "Who Would You Rather Be?" even suggested that, of the two, Eltinge had the more desirable job.[24] Although unmarried, Eltinge made clear that he used the profits from his career to fulfill his manly duty to provide a lavish lifestyle for his mother.[25] Audiences understood that the "kind of character required for economic success was not just virtuous, but manly."[26] Modern success in the corporate order required white men to cultivate industrious habits, self-discipline, ambition, and perseverance. One male reviewer admitted, "Many of us would, no doubt, be willing to wear skirts for two hour and a half each day for that tempting sum."[27] Another posed the question directly to readers: "Would you wear corsets for $12,000 a week?"[28] While discussion of her salary made Tanguay seem immodest and unfeminine, such publicity helped Eltinge normalize cross-dressing as a viable way for a white man to make a prosperous living.

In contrast to Tanguay's relationship with the press, Eltinge used his own magazine to help tame what was otherwise a transgression into a neutral professional practice. In 1912, Eltinge's own periodical, *The Julian Eltinge Magazine,* asserted Eltinge is "a husky young man of 29, agreeable, manly and without the slightest trace of the sissiness one might expect to find in the nature of a man who impersonates a woman. Rapidly, and with all the commonplaceness of a mechanic putting on his jumper and overalls for a day's work, Eltinge strips" and begins his transformation.[29] In another issue of his magazine, Eltinge claimed: "I study the fair sex as the electrical engineer studies the complicated switch-board in the power plant, or the bridge specialist the latest example of the cantilever."[30] Comparing himself to a mechanic and engineer masculinized an act otherwise deemed peculiar. In an age obsessed with expertise, professionalization, and mechanization, this passage positioned Eltinge as a methodical, manly professional.

Eltinge also showed how he reversed this transformation backstage to further reassure his readers that once he exited the stage, any semblance of feminine decorum vanished completely. He used props of masculinity to communicate this message. One critic observed: "By way of seeking relief, his first act when he comes off the stage is to light a thick, black cigar, and this he smokes even before he has taken off his feminine garb. It is a funny spectacle to see this stunning figure in Nile green décolleté and rigged in a gown that would be good enough for a queen's reception, puffing away at a cigar, and cursing heartily over the discomfort of the stays."[31] Whether or not he was ever a member of Harvard's Hasty Pudding Theatrical Troupe, Eltinge used many of the same strategies to sanitize his impersonations as did members of elite university theatrical troupes that specialized in cross-dressing. In 1915, *The New York Times* reported that female impersonators at Columbia and New York University were excellent athletes, including one who "'puffed on a cigar' and 'uttered several expletives'" during his interview.[32] Like boxing and time spent outdoors, cigars in particular, became potent symbols of manliness. It is a curious turn of events then, that while Eltinge used his fame as a female impersonator to endorse commercial products like corsets, high heels, and makeup, Tanguay lent her name to the Eva Tanguay Cigar Company.[33]

Eltinge's fear of not being considered "one of the guys" motivated him to project an off-stage image of a successful, hyper-masculine white man. In contrast to his impersonations, he probably intended to project his public persona toward male audiences and other male performers whom he feared might otherwise ostracize him. A writer for the *Indianapolis News* posited that Eltinge's "appeal is to the sex he impersonates—to such an extent that it would seem every block would boast an imitator of Eltinge to reap the feminine favor lying in wait. To be sure, mere man goes to see Eltinge, too. Often he is dragged thither." But, the writer concludes, once there, the man remains "complacently tolerating the affable idol of his partner's gaze."[34] If men were not the target audience of Eltinge's on-stage performances, most of his publicity interviews were conducted backstage by male reporters as American manly conversations held over cigars. A writer for *The New York Star* claimed Eltinge "outrivals Douglas Fairbanks in his breezy, democratic, dyed-in-the-wool, American manner."[35] This homosocial white masculine framework undoubtedly shaped the tone of published interviews with Eltinge, enabling other white men to accept him as a man out of corsets and an artist—or at least a professional—in them.

Critics rarely mentioned Eltinge's Irish ancestry and he seemed to enjoy the privileges of white manliness with relative impunity. However, as a white man who earned his salary impersonating women, Eltinge must have found it increasingly difficult to maneuver successfully the contested terrain of modern gender and racial norms. Of the Progressive Era, Peter Filine argues, "the concept of manliness was suffering strain in all its dimensions—in work and success, in familial patriarchy, and in the area that Victorian Americans did not often discuss aloud, sexuality."[36] In an era often characterized by a major crisis over shifting gender roles, Eltinge's simultaneous attempts to masculinize his own image off stage, distinguish himself from supposedly sissified female impersonators, and promote himself as the preeminent model of white feminine beauty appear to be at cross purposes. But in fact they were dependent upon each other. Because critics of female impersonation were not in short supply, masculinizing his image, often in racial terms, was critical to his ability to produce his particular vision of hyper-femininity. If, as Filene argues, the turn of the century marked a crisis of manliness, the hyper-masculine image Eltinge convincingly exhibited off stage partly explains his popularity. One perceptive reporter unambiguously explained, "one of the reasons for Eltinge's immense popularity, both on the stage and non-professionally, is his thorough manliness."[37]

Although it is difficult to determine exactly how much influence Eltinge or his manager had in shaping press coverage, the stories circulating benefited not only him, but also writers, readers, and audiences. Despite their different settings and circumstances, each narrative insisted on Eltinge's normal, healthy, white American manly inclinations. Each emphasized his lack of initiative in becoming a female impersonator, while highlighting his current wealth and success. Such stories helped to sanitize cross-dressing on the vaudeville stage, lending an air of the ordinary to those who patronized and praised female impersonators. By suggesting he cross-dressed only unwillingly or as a means to achieve upward mobility, rather than for pleasure, Eltinge's narrative essentially upheld existing male female norms.[38] And because these stories simultaneously upheld his status as a modern white, regular fellow, they distinguished him from other female impersonators, who were unable to convincingly sell the progress narrative to their audiences.

"IS IT ART?" THE FAIRY AND THE FEMALE IMPERSONATOR

In 1905, after establishing himself in the United States, Eltinge embarked on his first European tour. By 1907 he boasted of performing in London, Paris, and Berlin. Later, he toured Japan, China, Australia, and New Zealand.[39] Throughout this period, he promoted himself as an international performer and artist, infusing sophistication, cosmopolitanism, and a bit of the exotic into the work-a-day world of the average theater-goer. Eltinge was the first modern female impersonator in America to graduate to the Broadway theater and, in 1912, became the first gender impersonator to have a theater named after him.[40] By 1917, he had imitators around the world and critics even dubbed Cha Pih Yung "The Julian Eltinge of China."[41] To their own bemusement, many critics found themselves commending Eltinge for his ability to make the shameful work of cross-dressing respectable and artistic.

Montgomery Phister tried to explain the rationale behind Eltinge's enigmatic success: "It may be the success of curiosity, but whatever it is and upon whatever grounds it is to be explained, it is far beyond the ordinary that it is only to be defined as a furore [sic]."[42] *Variety* claimed, "His popularity is at a point that whatever he attempts is accepted without the slightest sign of disapproval in quantity of applause."[43] Other critics advised: "late comers will not be able to obtain admission to the theatre this afternoon and tonight at any price" because "Eltinge has certainly broken all local records for 'repeat' engagements."[44] In the field of female impersonation, such mainstream approval was unique.

At the apex of his fame, Eltinge boasted that requests for photos "average three hundred a day." In *The Julian Eltinge Magazine and Beauty Hints*, which he edited, published, and distributed with manager A.H. Woods at his performances, Eltinge published a "sample of one [photo request] from two *society ladies* in Chicago."[45] The request came in the form of a three stanza-rhyming letter allegedly written by a fan. The likely fictional letter emphasized the education and respectable tastes of the society ladies to whom Eltinge's upper class feminine beauty and grace appealed. Without explicitly saying so, it also implied their whiteness. Such testimonies from fans helped Eltinge dispute the assumption that female impersonation appealed only to those harboring abnormal, low tastes, especially male inverts.

In the same issue of his magazine, Eltinge included a brief and highly complimentary passage meant to illustrate the breadth of his fan base. Signatories supposedly included an "American citizen," "Irate Englishman," "Soldier," "Rich Man," "Sailor," "Poor Man," "Beggerman," "Judge," and "Car Conductor."[46] The list indicates that Eltinge hoped to market himself as having a diverse demographic appeal on both sides of the Atlantic, and it specifically implied a cohort of enthusiastic and virile male fans, both rich and poor, to complement his well-known base of female admirers. Similarly, a brief column in *Vanity Fair* emphasized: "the applause which greets this female impersonator comes from *both* sexes."[47] The persistence with which such comments appeared in reviews suggest that Eltinge, his manager, and the press worked collectively and constantly to frame his performances as respectable artistic entertainment, appropriate for the co-mingling of properly gendered men and women from all classes.

As early as his first year of professional impersonation, Eltinge made countless statements to the press that he would soon quit this line of work to take on romantic leading roles in legitimate theater. One report claimed, "Within the manly chest of Julian Eltinge there dwells an ambition that will some day [sic] take him into the classics." Further, the report said his female impersonations "have merely caused a hiatus in his career and he expects within a few years to realize his youthful ambitions."[48] Claims that Eltinge aspired to be a more traditional artist were well-received by the public and made him more likeable to critics. One reviewer commented in 1907, "One can't resist congratulating Julian Eltinge for his determination to get away from female impersonation as a means of livelihood."[49] Whether or not these intentions were genuine, Eltinge and his publicity agents asserted them for twenty years, repeatedly claiming he was on the verge of retirement from female impersonation and preparing to take on male roles. In making such claims, Eltinge showed a keen awareness of popular concern that impersonating women on the stage for too long might somehow turn a man into a woman off stage. If not already manifest elsewhere, this belief was codified in 1915 when *The New York Times* reported that a dean at Yale instituted a new rule barring members of Yale's Dramatic Association from impersonating females for more than one consecutive year because continuous cross-dressing would eventually render the impersonator effeminate.[50]

Despite his protestations, though, Eltinge stuck with cross-dressing. In Broadway, musical comedy, and film, the plots of his productions provided explicit justification for his cross-dressing, often relying on a variation of the same stale formula.[51] These storylines typically found Eltinge dressing as a woman to right some wrong, but they were loosely organized around a heterosexual romantic theme, which culminated in a happy and coupled conclusion. In 1911, Eltinge celebrated manly heroism and self-discipline in the musical comedy *The Fascinating Widow*, and in later musical comedies, sacrificed his pride by wearing women's clothes for the sake of justice. In the guise of a woman, Eltinge played a Robin Hood-like character who stole from the rich and redistributed wealth to the poor, conveniently winning his true love in the process.[52]

In his Broadway productions, Eltinge also appeared as a man to offer his audience an immediate and contrasting masculine image. Referring to his first major musical comedy effort outside vaudeville, Eltinge said, "The thing I like most about my present play is that I am not compelled to try and convince the public that I am a woman. The public is always wise to deception, only the persons in the play being ignorant of the true state of affairs. Even in the play," Eltinge continued, "two of my chums are 'on,' and when I am alone with them I assume masculine airs in the feminine garb." Though the appeal of such acts lay in the comic incongruity of a character assuming "masculine airs in feminine garb," Eltinge expressed discomfort at the prospect of audiences mistaking his "true" gender. Reinforcing his lack of pleasure in female impersonation, he concluded, "I love those scenes in which I am at liberty to 'put across' male comedy."[53]

In these parts, Eltinge played a self-reflexive role, trying to provide the public with a palatable representation of himself—a man, forced (as he insisted was true in his own life) by circumstances beyond his control to impersonate women while making good in the process. In short, like the hyper-white Victorian lady he portrayed on stage, Eltinge impersonated a sanitized version of himself. Most of these roles were written specifically for Eltinge; he and his manager were probably influential in their creation, hoping they would reflect well upon him as a normal, even admirable man who shared the same values as the average white American man.

Despite his popularity and the reassurances of those who attested to his off-stage manliness, Eltinge's stage work potentially exposed him to serious criticisms to which even he was not impervious. In response to one of his most successful plays, one reviewer objected, "The sight of these men with pinched-in waists, high-heeled slippers, silk stockings and fluffy lingerie is not calculated to inspire respect for either them or their profession." Such indictments against female impersonation had ramifications far beyond individual impersonators. Critics could hardly ignore the thousands of loyal fans who made Eltinge rich by paying to see him perform, buying his photographs, sheet music, magazines, and the products he endorsed. "In justice to themselves," this critic continued, "I sincerely hope another season will find [female impersonators]...in wholesome dramas... instead of pandering to the abnormal tastes of commonplace theater-goers." However, chalking up Eltinge's appeal to the so-called abnormal tastes of vaudeville patrons could not easily explain his cross-gender, cross-class appeal, or his ascension from vaudeville to Broadway. In fact, vaudeville audiences were a mix of both working and middle class, native and immigrant, men and women. They were, then, not abnormal or low, but the average urban American. Nonetheless, this writer concluded his invective by comparing Eltinge to "the men with painted faces and other visible evidences of the pathetic decline of the human race."[54]

The general disrepute in which female impersonation was held and its categorization as a symptom of the decline of the human race continuously urged Eltinge to distinguish himself from fellow impersonators. Indeed, he did so with considerable success. One skeptical reviewer grudgingly conceded that Eltinge was "not as repugnant as those others of his *tribe*. He contrives at intervals to let his masculinity shine through his assumed character, and make plain that the effort is a part of his acting method, which partly takes the curse off the whole affair."[55] The writer's categorization of Eltinge as belonging to an entirely different tribe alluded to the perceived existence of a third intermediate sex, understood by psychologists as inverts. Reviewers distinguished Eltinge from other fellow impersonators by remarking that he "made the 'stunt' less freaky than any man who has ever attempted it because his work is always smooth, neat and never vulgar, even in lines and situations that are highly suggestive."[56]

Behind references to tribes, critics conveyed that their concerns over female impersonation were rooted in anxieties over the decline of American civilization. As a man who wore women's clothing and was occasionally genuinely mistaken for a woman, Eltinge obliterated the separate spheres supposedly occupied by American men and women and threatened their physical containment within the body. The erosion of the differences between the way men and women dressed, talked and walked threatened to turn civilized Americans into the so-called savages of Africa and Asia.[57]

To many, female impersonation and the unprecedented success of individuals like Eltinge inspired uncomfortable introspection, forcing audiences and critics to question their own complicity in such supposed perversions. As the nation's premier female impersonator seemed to lead America away from the civilized, respectable society it believed itself to be, some critics "feared that American manhood was going to hell in a wig, dress, and high-heeled shoes."[58] In one of Eltinge's first published reviews (unequivocally titled "A Disgrace to Vaudeville"), one critic sarcastically remarked, "Isn't it sweet, exquisite, touching and soulful!" And then continued, "Isn't it a fine thing to know that the simpering Julian Eltinge is likely to be on the same program with you any week? When, oh, when will these female impersonators be driven from the stage! When! Perhaps the S.P.C.A. [Society for the Prevention of Cruelty to Animals] will answer the question some day."[59] Published in September 1904, seven years before Eltinge reached the peak of his fame, this review is pointedly critical of Eltinge as "simpering," a contemporary barb used to describe effeminate men known as "fairies."[60] Such criticisms demonstrate why he was obliged to make his off-stage white manliness just as seemingly real as his hyper-white feminine characterizations on stage.

To uphold his own work as art, Eltinge distanced himself from the camp sensibility used by other female impersonators, which played on "irony, incongruity, theatricality, and humor to highlight the artifice of social convention, sometimes exaggerating convention to the point of burlesquing it, sometimes inverting it to achieve the same end."[61] Confirming his lack of camp, critics commented that Eltinge's "girl imitation" was "entirely different from anything else of its kind, inasmuch as he uses no falsetto voice, jeweled pins or spangled gowns."[62] Unlike most female impersonators, Eltinge also did not alter his voice when he sang as a woman. Though his singing talents were limited, critics praised him for using his voice skillfully to sustain the illusion that he was a woman. Just as they praised male impersonator Lillyn Brown, critics claimed "the illusion is only deepened when Eltinge sings a song, as he has a deep throaty voice of a sweet timbre, just what one would expect from a strong, powerful woman."[63]

His performances of white womanhood were reportedly so realistic and artistic that the press sensationalized moments of genuine confusion over his gender. Just as audiences were sometimes confused about the race of Tucker and bemused by the eccentricity of Tanguay, first-timers at Eltinge's performances may have felt uncertain about whether they were watching a female impersonator or a female singer. Critics labeled him a "'Real' Woman Impersonator," speculating that Eltinge "is chuckling over the results of his singing 'I'm Looking for a Sweetheart.'" They noted that "he received so many mash notes from the Johnnies that there was no room on the mail rack for anything else. Even when Eltinge removes his wig he finds it hard to dispel the illusion."[64] Eltinge even reportedly received marriage proposals from his fans.[65] His talent for fooling audiences allegedly found a home in Europe as well. When he first performed in Germany, "he was not advertised as a man and for two weeks fooled the oldest theatergoers into believing he was a woman." He received "letters, notes, flowers and gifts of all kinds, including invitations" from men of Hamburg "who found La Belle Eltinge wholly adorable."[66] The realness of his female characters offered audiences an intellectual exercise that asked them to untangle authenticity from illusion; they came back again and again to determine if this artist was a man or a woman. Even after they realized he was a man, they kept coming back for a closer look so that they might marvel at how he accomplished the illusion.

In the field of female impersonation, Eltinge's only significant rival in popularity was Bothwell Browne, who, like Eltinge, worked with George Cohan's minstrels. Yet Browne's impersonations received scathing criticism for their vulgarity and explicit eroticism. His attempts to transition to Broadway and film were resounding failures.[67] Sharon Ullman concludes that Browne failed to achieve mainstream success because his acts were too erotic, specifically citing his "Serpent Dance," which featured a live snake.[68] Yet Eltinge performed similar, equally erotic dances. In 1909, he began to follow his "incense act" with "The Cobra Dance," a "slow and sensuous rhythmic dance" which sounds strikingly similar to Browne's "Serpent Dance."[69] In this performance, Eltinge explicitly evoked the primitive animality of Tanguay's signature style. But instead of condemnation and disgust, Eltinge's erotic performance inspired reverence. Critics noted that "If all women dancers who delve into the realms of the Far East for subject themes kept within the same bounds of real art that Mr. Eltinge does, the stage to-day would be the richer therefor [sic] and the present day fantasy for sensationalism and vulgarity would not be so apparent."[70] This comparative criticism of both female impersonators and female performers was ironic because Eltinge borrowed ideas from others.[71] Not only did critics find Eltinge more tasteful than his male and female competitors, they also considered him more beautiful. Writing for *The Seattle Post-Intelligencer*, one critic went so far as to say that Eltinge's inimitable femininity made "some of his fair associates in his vaudeville revue seem almost gross."[72] Despite his suggestive costumes and movements, critics explicitly invoked Eltinge as a model of white femininity that showcased artistic beauty far better than women and other female impersonators ever could.

Despite critics' favorable observations that he never performed vulgar acts, like Tanguay, Eltinge also performed as Salomé. In doing so, he recalled being "barelegged and barefoot; and more embarrassed than ever."[73] One year after introducing his rendition of Salomé, Eltinge debuted a new "Hindoo [sic] dance" called "The Goddess of Incense, incorporating special scenery and electrical effects."[74] *Dramatic Mirror* gave a detailed description of this act: "He appears as a beauty of the Orient, in a clinging white décolleté garb of the Far East, bare feet, jeweled head dress, breast plates and ornaments." Further, "The burning incense, the vases, shrines and other properties of the setting" all give "a more artistic result."[75] Yet again, several of these acts were unmistakably sensual. Of his "bathing girl routine," one critic even boldly claimed "the less [Eltinge] has on, the more attractive he is. We recommend the bathing song number for corroboration of our statement."[76] Clearly, a pale face, a big budget, and a manly persona off stage were key ingredients to creating an artistic female impersonator.

While the perceived effeminacy of other female impersonators prevented them from achieving similar success or enjoying a reputation as respectable artists, Eltinge boasted that he was asked to perform for such notables as King Edward VII, who rewarded him with the gift of a bulldog.[77] Because he was viewed as a manly man, audiences believed his realistic performances required so much painstaking effort that they had to be art. To separate himself from other female impersonators, Eltinge also claimed that his peers disgusted him. He expressed his disdain for the work and its repute claiming, "I have been at the theatre and seen female impersonators that have made me rather disgusted with the whole business." Eltinge added, "I would prefer some other line of work, but no matter where I go they want the specialty by which I am best known."[78] In short, Eltinge pacified his critics by seeming to agree with them. Critics conceded that he was unique. *Stage Pictorial* frankly stated "he is not like the ordinary female impersonator. If he were, there would be no place for him in these pages."[79]

In many ways, the gender impersonations audiences witnessed performers like Eltinge portray on the vaudeville stage were analogous to the popular drag balls of Harlem and Greenwich Village. Between 1890 and the onset of World War II, drag balls, where upper-class urbanites often came as spectators, played an important role in fostering a collective gay identity. Overlapping with Eltinge's career, drag balls "created

liminal cultural spaces in which people could transgress—and simultaneously, confirm—the social boundaries that normally divided them and
restricted their behavior."[80]

As a *New York Herald Tribune* article from 1934 makes clear, at drag
balls, inversions of race and class were at least as central as experimenta-
tions with gender: "Caucasians came disguised as Orientals. Mongoloid
individuals blackened their faces and appeared as Ethiopians. Negroes
powdered their skins and dressed as Scandinavian villagers. College boys
masqueraded as hoboes." And, of course, "Men danced with women in
men's clothes. Women danced with men in women's clothes."[81] Such
dramatic inversions of class, race, and gender norms bore a striking resem-
blance to Eltinge's whiteface gender impersonations. For some, attending
his performances might have served residents of smaller cities as a working and middle-class alternative to drag balls. Reflecting on drag balls
he attended, Howard Raymond recalled that crowds of people, including
fashion designers, attended the balls for previews of the latest fashions.
"'What we wore to the ball one year," Raymond reported, "you'd see offered in the best shops the next season.'"[82] Similarly, Eltinge claimed
the inspiration for his costumes came from traveling abroad; he boasted
that he single-handedly introduced new European fashions to America
and subscribed to "all of the French and American fashion magazines"
because, he said, "I watch the styles more closely than the average mo-
diste."[83] Both Eltinge and organizers of the drag balls boasted that they
were major trendsetters in turn-of-the-century New York fashion.

Although attendees at drag balls often wore costumes similar to those
regularly seen in vaudeville, they were increasingly falling under closer
critical scrutiny and were just the sort of activity from which Eltinge
strenuously labored to distance himself. As early as the late nineteenth
century, those attending masquerade balls called them "drags" but neither Eltinge nor his reviewers used this language to describe his work.
Instead, critics described him as a female impersonator or "Delineator
of Female Types."[84]

As a regular performer in New York City, Eltinge had the opportunity to participate in this subculture, but only at the risk of losing his
credibility as an artist, as well as his broad audience appeal. At worst,
he could have been accused of being a fairy, something he worked hard
to avoid.[85] His attendance at drags would have insinuated that he took
pleasure in dressing as a woman and this was something he could not
risk suggesting. In fact, several articles about Eltinge detail his adamant
refusal to appear off stage in women's clothing. When interviewed,

Eltinge explicitly asserted that the stage was the only setting in which he could be compelled to dress in women's attire.[86]

While drag balls were understood as a larger-than-life articulation of gay subculture, it remains unclear what gay men thought of Eltinge's camp-free depictions of white womanhood. Although one historian suggests that Eltinge "attracted a large following... among male homosexuals," contemporary observers sensationalized incidents involving suspected fairy fans only to suggest how they repulsed Eltinge.[87] According to one scholar, "fairies were known as female impersonators." Regardless of sexual preference, "in the right context, appropriating even a single feminine—or at least unconventional—style or article of clothing might signify a man's identity as a fairy."[88] Fairies were expected to adopt "effeminate dress and mannerisms, they were thus often called inverts (who had 'inverted' their sex and were thus inwardly female) rather than homosexuals."[89] Similarly, Eltinge's on-stage appropriation of feminine dress would have been enough evidence for contemporary audiences to classify him as a fairy—they need not believe he had sex with other men. Yet for most of his career, Eltinge's off-stage manly image and insistence that his work was art helped mainstream audiences to accept him as a regular fellow.

Eltinge also distanced himself from unsavory associations with fairies by insisting that he aimed his performances at women. Although evidence suggests women only constituted one-third of vaudeville audiences in 1910, they increasingly entered the public sphere as spectators and consumers, and since the 1880s, vaudeville managers such as Tony Pastor actively solicited their patronage by banning alcohol and promoting Ladies' Nights.[90] Such efforts helped Eltinge argue that his performances were inoffensive, performed for the benefit of women and children rather than the vulgar perversions of male fairies. "I never play to the men; I never see them in my audiences. It is the women I want to impress—they are the ones who observe the finer details," Eltinge claimed. "More than anything else, I play to the middle-aged woman," he continued. Adding, "I must not burlesque in setting or costume, for it would," he insisted, "eliminate the effect of any serious bit of business."[91] Whereas some critics accused female stage stars who performed as Salomé of degrading themselves and white women generally because their performances seemed to excite male audiences, critics were more likely to accept Eltinge's performances because he claimed to aim them at women.

As his career progressed, race played an increasingly important role in Eltinge's artistic depictions of New Women. Early in his career, he

presented audiences with exoticized, racially-indistinct female characters but these were his least popular acts. They enjoyed much briefer
rotations than his supposedly more realistic portrayals of fashionable
white women. When his beautiful performances of white womanhood
uncomfortably mixed with the racial exoticism of his costumes, music,
and scenery, critics were less impressed. Rather than watch another salacious Salomé impersonator or "Hindoo" dancer, Americans preferred to
see Eltinge as an attractive, whiter, refined version of themselves, decked
out in an expensive wardrobe with an enviable complexion.

In the same act in which he portrayed Salomé, Eltinge also performed
as a woman alongside another popular minstrel player, George "Honey
Boy" Evans, singing "Oh, You Coon," appearing this time in blackface.[92]
He performed a duet opposite Evans who played a "mischief-making
coon" in "The Belle of the Barber's Ball."[93] In this way, he began his
career not unlike Tucker, who claimed she was forced to perform in
blackface at the beginning of her career because managers thought she
was too ugly. But reviewers dedicated comparatively little ink to discussing Eltinge's blackface performances, exhibiting a clear preference
for his white American beauties.[94] In another act, Eltinge portrayed "the
Gibson Girl of high-toned colored society."[95] This time, he burlesqued
the Gibson Girl in light blackface in a song called "The Sampson Girl."[96]
The Sampson Girl was a light-skinned comic figure much like the hybrid
character portrayed by Tanguay in *The Sambo Girl*. While the Sambo
Girl was an irreverent, racially-Other character who allowed a white
female performer to act irreverent herself, Eltinge's Sampson Girl was
a throwback to nineteenth century minstrel players who cross-dressed
and race-crossed at the same time.

Of course, in the countless illustrations iterating this new vision of
femininity, both the New Woman and the Gibson Girl were never portrayed as black, biracial, or from an immigrant background. Instead, they
were ivory white Nordics. Because most white audiences, including an
increasingly heterogeneous group of white and near-white immigrants,
felt ideals of feminine beauty did not apply to black women, audiences
likely perceived these performances as comedic burlesques rather than
art. And since serious portrayals of hyper-white women on stage were
critical to his perception as an artist, the Sampson Girl would not last
long as one of Eltinge's girl types.

F. Michael Moore argues that Eltinge's blackface productions flopped
because "blackface entertainment was on the decline."[97] Yet Eltinge appeared as the Sampson Girl in 1908, while other performers continued
successfully to perform in blackface through the 1920s.[98] Even when

white actors stopped using burnt cork, they did not altogether abandon blackface performance styles, including speech patterns such as dialect and nostalgic plantation-style, Southern songs. Rather, Eltinge's blackface act failed because vaudeville audiences wished to see him represent a type of upper-class, respectable beauty exclusive to unimpeachably white women. In stark contrast to most of Eltinge's female characters, women like Tanguay wore tights over visibly bare legs, embraced shorter skirts, sang with sexual innuendo, posed with their mouths open, literally let down their hair and invoked the racial Other. They were seen less as artists than as spectacles. Both Tanguay and Tucker were even threatened with legal charges for including obscene content in their performances. While Tucker and Tanguay helped audiences laugh at the antics of the Other, only Eltinge invited women to look adoringly upon a bleached out version of themselves.

Clearly, the combined illusion of upper-class whiteness helped Eltinge's performances appear to be real art. As Linda Mizejewski has demonstrated of Florenz Ziegfeld's chorus girls, though they were scantily clad and sometimes even semi-nude, they were considered artistic because their bodies were extremely pale and their costumes were elaborate and expensive. By contrast, successful black Broadway productions were considered representations of natural black energy and entertainment.[99] Whether on the vaudeville or Broadway stage, Eltinge's elaborate sets, costumes, and white face makeup encouraged critics to suggest his work was art rather than low-brow entertainment.

In addition to the whiteness of his female characters, Eltinge's ability to convincingly assert a masculine persona off stage also distinguished his performances as art. One reporter claimed, "Mr. Eltinge is so manly that, unlike other impersonators in that line, you never forget he is a man."[100] In 1916, a review of Eltinge explained: "He is the one man who can wear skirts without offense, and perhaps the secret of his success lies in the fact that he is always ready with a wink for the spectators, a wink which says, 'You know I hate this because I'm a regular fellow, but I do it just to give you a good time.'" Such interpretations implied that Eltinge sacrificed his pride only for the sake of his art and his audience, a truly gentlemanly gesture.[101] Eltinge reminded the press, "You know a husky brute like me doesn't squeeze himself into those confounded things [corsets] for the fun of it."[102] Sacrificing his comfort for a hefty paycheck, the admiration of his audiences and, ultimately, the sake of art, however, was a different story.

Eltinge's enormous success sparked interest in the history of cross-dressing and contemporary newspaper columnists often invoked the antiquated practice of British cross-dressing on the legitimate stage to sanitize a practice many Americans enjoyed, yet still considered a bit unseemly.[103] They recalled that, until the nineteenth century, women were generally forbidden to appear on stage and young men routinely played Shakespearean characters such as Desdemona, Ophelia, and Juliet.[104] Just as Eltinge claimed he hoped to do, critics noted that past cross-dressers such as Edward Kynaston, Gathalial Pavy, and Stephen Hammerton successfully "graduated from these feminine characters and achieved what we would call stellar success in this day in many of the more robust male roles." They recalled that Sarah Bernhardt, the most famous late nineteenth-century actress, achieved critical success portraying Hamlet.[105] Eltinge claimed that, unlike his predecessors, he had not yet graduated to male roles because his managers and audiences were so fiercely loyal to his female impersonations that they simply would not accept him in any other role. Nonetheless, situating Eltinge among a pantheon of well-respected white actors helped further establish him as an artist, not an invert.

Ultimately, Eltinge's artistic performances endorsed rigid gender conventions more than they mocked them. In portraying graceful white society women, he offered himself as an icon for women aspiring to an Anglo-centered image of upper class beauty and grace. Despite his more sensual performances, Eltinge evoked a demure and restrained sense of feminine decorum. One reviewer suggested "Mr. Eltinge is considered the most artistic impersonator of women we have upon the stage, and his work is refined and graceful throughout."[106] Still another insisted, "in the finer work of Eltinge, there is not a suggestion of burlesque or farce. It is his aim to look exactly like a cultured and refined woman."[107] Because Eltinge primarily emulated refined white women and maintained his manliness off stage, he dignified female impersonation into a respectable profession and art.

EMBODYING THE MODERN WHITE MAN AND WOMAN

While his negotiations with the press were crucial to uplifting Eltinge's performances out of the realm of farce and into the world of art, Eltinge used his body with efficacy on stage and off to dramatize the spectacle of gender in modern America. Historian John F. Kasson has written persuasively about the ways in which early twentieth-century American men such as Theodore Roosevelt, strongman Eugen Sandow, and magician Ehrich Weiss (better known as Houdini), turned images of strong white masculinity into popular spectacle. In fact, Kasson argues that "crucial to Roosevelt's success was his ability to turn prized characteristics of manliness into spectacle, literally to embody them."[108] In an increasingly visual culture, public icons such as Roosevelt, Sandow, and Eltinge provided Americans with a template for how the white male body could successfully adapt to new challenges posed by changing gender ideologies.[109] Eltinge stands out among such men, however, because he provided working models of gender for both white women and men.

Off stage, Eltinge's biggest struggle remained convincing Americans that he was just as manly as men like Eugen Sandow. At the turn of the century, popular magazines described the physique of the contemporary hero as "'in every way a large man—large in build, in mind, in culture. He is nearly six feet high, and with a kind of stately bulk which turns the scales at something like 250 pounds,' a man with 'steel blue eyes,' jaws wired with steel,' 'shoulders of Hercules,' 'tremendous even gigantic physical endurance.'"[110] Vaudeville audiences celebrated the sculpted, bulging muscularity of men like Sandow, billed as "The Most Powerful Man on Earth," photographing him nearly nude in "primitive" costumes to highlight his well-defined muscles.[111] Sandow even sold how-to-become-manly guides, including *Body Building or Man in the Making: How to Become Healthy and Strong* (1904) and *Strength and How to Obtain It* (1897).[112] One image used to market his vaudeville act showed Sandow in a revealing costume lifting "the human dumbbell," filled with two comparatively child-sized white men fully clothed in modern suits.

Eltinge tried to emulate Sandow by publishing similarly styled, heavily-edited photographs depicting his own version of the human dumbbell. Unfortunately for Eltinge, however, his frame did not match this new aesthetic definition of white manliness (indeed, the "steel blue eyes" reveal the presumption of whiteness). He stood 5'8" and was relatively fleshy, qualities that allowed him to squeeze into a corset without appearing conspicuously tall or broad shouldered. He lacked Sandow's muscular frame; his figure was round at the waist and full in the chin and cheeks, a shape that, dressed as a woman, hinted at voluptuousness but avoided suggesting vulgarity. The press noted, "his only unmasculine feature is his lack of muscular development," which he explained is something he had to cultivate. He added, "it was the biggest sacrifice I had to make."[113] Just as he defended his bachelordom by suggesting that he could not be a proper husband to any wife while in show business, Eltinge suggested that only the demands of his career prevented his body from looking like that of Sandow.

In one sense, Eltinge shared more in common with vaudeville's irreverent Tanguay than with men like Sandow. L. Wolfe Gilbert, the "dean of Tin Pan Alley," said of Eltinge, "he was known to have beaten up many a tough long-shoreman and hoodlum. I know he was truly a 'he-man.'"[114] To the press, both Tanguay and Eltinge conveyed the ready willingness of a white man (infused with just the right dose of primitivism) to fight anyone who besmirched their honor. *The Cincinnati Times Star* took care to report that some confused Eltinge with "Fireman" Jim Flynn, "The Great White Hope" of heavyweight boxing.[115] Early in his career, one reviewer claimed that "any one [sic] who doubts that when at Cambridge he was an athlete of some pretensions can get all the proof he wants by stirring up a little row with him. Two or three stage hands, mistaking the feminine figure all made up for the performance as the kind of easy mark that could readily be guyed, had a rude awakening in the shape of beatings."[116]

As with Tanguay, exaggerated narratives of gendered violence had an important role to play in his career. Eltinge's efforts to perpetuate rumors that he never hesitated to take part in a physical altercation paralleled Tanguay's well-publicized fights with stagehands, managers, and other female performers. Columnists and reviewers often exaggerated Tanguay's violent temper and physical prowess, adding to her notoriety and popularity by sensationalizing her life both on and off stage. Witnesses and victims of her violence told such tales as often as she did. In doing so, they amplified her gender transgressions through the lens of race. Perhaps because Eltinge's gender bending performances were already suspect and white men were already concerned with appearing to be too civilized, the press was complicit in his efforts to fashion himself as a manly virile American man, whose lifestyle fell within white gendered norms.

Eltinge offered evidence of his manly body by boasting that he could not long be contained by a woman's corset; he claimed they fit him so poorly that he broke an average of 3,000 a year.[117] Observers explained that Eltinge's appearance "gives every indication of having absorbed all the strenuous exercises that college life gives to a young man" and a "systematic course of gymnasium work and *outdoor* exercises keeps him in fine robust appearance."[118] This enthusiastic endorsement of Eltinge's outdoor manliness and strenuous lifestyle reveals the persistent need for reassurance that Eltinge was a "man's man."

Eltinge presented himself as an athlete who could compete with professionals, and in one interview, explicitly compared the preparatory work for his stage performances to training for a boxing match: "Sometimes before a show I am obliged to get rid of from 17 to 20 pounds of superfluous flesh. It's like training for a prize fight more than anything else, except that I labor under difficulties that the prize fighter knows

Figure 8. Julian Eltinge (left) boxing with an unidentified man, possibly former champion "Gentleman" Jim Corbett, 1918. (Billy Rose Theatre Division; New York Public Library for Performing Arts; Astor, Lenox, and Tilden Foundations; Record ID: 1866140).

nothing of."[119] To help readers envision him as a rugged athlete, Eltinge posed for newspapers as he labored outdoors, swam in lakes with his bulldogs, and posed in full boxing regalia, pretending to spar with contemporary boxers (see Figure 8).

It is no coincidence that Eltinge repeatedly mentioned his talent for boxing to convey a vision of primitive white manliness that was beyond reproach. The sport reached the height of its popularity in the early twentieth century and many American men saw boxing as a way for overly-feminized urban white men to restore their lost virility.[120] Eltinge was frequently quoted recalling his mythical boxing days at Harvard, ruefully bemoaning the fact that his work in female impersonation demanded that he refrain from too much exercise, lest he lose his ability to emulate feminine figures.[121] Eltinge also used his brief acting roles as a man and his public appearances off stage to create a stark and exaggerated contrast to his corseted feminine figure.[122] Once again pointing to the performed nature of gender, he candidly admitted that it was his habit to sport a mustache and "a walking suit which made me look six times as large as I really am."[123]

In the years preceding Eltinge's whiteface female impersonations, historian Frederick Jackson Turner announced the closing of the American frontier and Teddy Roosevelt went west to test his mettle as a ranchman. As the Wild West disappeared into settled cities and urbanization and immigration continued to crowd more people into less space, the degeneracy of white males seemed to loom on the horizon. In this context, Eltinge's well-publicized purchase of a large farm signified his efforts to stay connected to untamed land and the rough outdoors.[124] Eltinge explained that he spent his summers working outdoors at his large farm on Fort Salonga, Long Island (see Figure 9). After interviewing and photographing him at work on his farm, critics advised: "the actor who would be healthy and handsome should wear overalls in private life and roll up his shirt sleeves. That is the gospel of Julian Eltinge, whose mind turns to farming and his mother when the business hours of the theatre are ended." Originally published in *The Boston American* in 1912 and proudly reprinted in Eltinge's own magazine, the article revealed an acute awareness of the suspicion surrounding his gendered behavior: "You may not think that Mr. Eltinge is an honest-to-goodness farmer when he is at home," the writer began. "I had doubts about it myself—but he exhibits photographs to prove it, so there can be no further argument."[125] Eltinge further suggested to the author that if he dropped around "anytime during the summer, you undoubtedly will find me up to my knees in rough, *outdoor* work." Eltinge added, "I am strongly inclined to turn farmer for the rest of my life."[126] In other interviews, Eltinge would have made Roosevelt proud, claiming, "I can hardly wait for the week to end" because "I'm dead anxious for a good hunting and fishing trip."[127]

Comparisons of Eltinge's public appearances as a man and woman reveal his efforts to reinforce a binary gender system; masculinity and

Figure 9. Out of his corset, Eltinge is pictured in overalls with his shirtsleeves rolled up, feeding chickens on his farm. Pictures from this photography session were featured in an article titled, "The Sort of Fellow Julian Eltinge Really Is." *Green Book Magazine*, Nov 1913. (Billy Rose Theatre Division; New York Public Library for Performing Arts; Astor, Lenox, and Tilden Foundations; Image ID: th-10448).

femininity were mutually exclusive opposites. Yet because his female impersonations were more feminine, whiter and curvier than the average cross-dresser, his off-stage manly image had to overcompensate with more visible difference. To make sense of these opposites existing in one body, Eltinge had to be a hyper-feminine, hyper-white woman and hyper-masculine man, each with conspicuously gendered clothing, complexions, and suitable settings.

While Eltinge's statements to the press often reinforced and pushed traditional gender conventions to their Victorian extremes, he sometimes sent modern female readers ambivalent messages. These messages blurred traditional distinctions between appropriate practices for men and women. Although Eltinge used boxing as a metaphor to shore up perceptions of his own white manhood, in 1912 he publicly endorsed boxing as a sport for women. In his self-promotional *Julian Eltinge Magazine and Beauty Hints*, he assured his readers, "Any woman can be strong who wishes to be. And to be fashionable she must be strong." He continued, "Boxing is an excellent exercise to correct one of the primal weaknesses of women." Eltinge argued that women were "the only being of the female sex in the scale of creation who are slower than the male." For example, he noted that male lions and tigers were the faster sex and fiercer opponent. Boxing, then, could teach American women to access their animal natures and "take a defeat in a manly fashion." Boxing would help develop "the arms, the shoulders, the chest, the parts of the body in which women are defective." Furthermore, it "teaches the pupil to 'drop a masher with a punch,' to protect herself in crowded streets, or to defend herself and her home against an invading burglar."[128]

Endorsing boxing for white women was a bold move. As Eltinge's own boxing-related publicity stunts demonstrate, by the first decade of the twentieth century, boxing had become the quintessential masculine, working-class sport, notorious for its excessive violence and bloodshed. In 1894, Charlotte Perkins Gilman, one of the most prolific and influential contemporary feminist writers, declaimed boxing as a symbol of the decay of white civilization, invoking a popular racist trope by describing a prizefight as "a scene of savagery which would not have been out of place in the heart of Africa."[129] The same year Eltinge urged women to box, Congress even outlawed violent films depicting boxing in the aftermath of black boxer Jack Johnson's defeat of Jim Jeffries and the ensuing race riots.[130] Whether imagined in the "heart of Africa" or a professional ring in urban America, boxing was a thoroughly manly and primitive pursuit.

Boxing, then, should never have been an activity for white, fashionable Gibson Girls and New Women. This contemporary icon of white womanhood, graphically illustrated by artist Charles Dana Gibson, was often pictured playing golf, croquet, or leisurely riding a bicycle, but she did not get dirty, break a sweat, or bleed.[131] She represented new female freedoms, but in reality, her independence "did not go much beyond playing sports, wearing comfortable clothing and looking self-reliant."[132] In other words, the Gibson Girl was modern but ultimately not threatening. The prospect of advising women to box, especially ivory-complexioned Gibson Girls, must have seemed outrageous to many.

Yet the outrageousness and incongruity of women boxing was the core of its appeal. At the same time Eltinge encouraged female readers of his magazine to take up boxing to "correct" their "primal weaknesses," "lady boxing acts" became popular on the vaudeville stage.[133] Performers like the Gordon Sisters, who the *Boston Sunday Journal* described as "Amazonian athletes" who possessed "scientific knowledge of boxing" and "other 'mannish' sports," toured the vaudeville circuit for over ten years.[134] Though such performers billed themselves as "scientific" "bag punchers," much like Tanguay, their performances sensationalized the manly transgressions of pale white women.

By encouraging women to box, Eltinge suggested women improve themselves by making their bodies more like men's. His advice prescribed a new set of rules and roles for both genders: women should be tough enough to beat a man (as Tanguay repeatedly did) and men should look at such women, in Eltinge's words, "with surprise and respect."[135] Had critics paid closer attention, they might have responded to Eltinge's advice with alarm. Lady boxing on the vaudeville stage was one thing, but, as a white man, Eltinge encouraged the women in his audiences to adopt manly behavior in the real world. Just as Tanguay boldly laid claim to the privileges of primitive white manhood, Eltinge encouraged his female readers of both middle and working-class backgrounds to do the same. Instead of relying on husbands, brothers, or fathers, he urged women to protect their own property against invasion and to physically defend their honor against the untoward advances of barbarous men.[136] This advice was particularly striking in the context of continued worries about the rising effeminacy of men, the masculinity of the New Woman, and the ensuing degeneracy of the white race.

In the same issue of his magazine in which Eltinge encouraged women to box, he explicitly prescribed gender roles for men and women by listing attributes of the ideal husband and wife. Although this was not his own fate, he suggested the ideal goal for contemporary men and women was to marry. For the American wife, the most important qualities were "health, frankness, common sense, humor, a great conception of the universe and humanity, radicalism." He added that the ideal wife should be a suffragist and who possesses "courage, sympathy, patience." His requisites for the ideal husband differed only slightly, including "health, a great aim in life, belief in woman's suffrage" combined with "confidence and frankness" and "a sacred regard for womanhood and motherhood."[137] Like his promotion of boxing for women, his endorsement of both male and female support for suffrage is striking. Many men vehemently argued that suffrage would distract women from more important domestic and maternal duties, leading to physical illness and crippling reproductive problems by sapping them of limited nervous energy. But Eltinge endorsed a fusion of values both Victorian (a "sacred regard for womanhood and motherhood,") and modern (an independent political identity, partnership in a companionate romantic relationship). Instead of viewing the political involvement of women as physically and mentally debilitating both to women and the white race, Eltinge suggested that political activism was part of a healthy lifestyle.

Taken together, Eltinge's messages about modern New Women seem at odds. While he advised women to learn the "gentle art" of boxing, seize the right to vote, and even praised their athleticism in a song called "The Modern Sandow Girl," he also published an article in his magazine by British writer Marie Corelli, disparaging the New Woman.[138] According to Corelli, "by the ever-excess of their *outdoor* sports," New Women are "gradually doing away with their originally intended shapes and becoming as flat-chested as jockeys under training. No flat-chested woman is pretty. No woman with large hands, large feet, and the coarse muscular throat and jaw developed by constant bicycle-riding, can be called fascinating," Corelli said, adding that "Men's hearts are not enthralled by a Something appearing to be neither man nor woman. And there are a great many Somethings about just now."[139] Historian Gail Bederman has argued that contemporary Americans identified "advanced civilizations by the degree of their sexual differentiation. Savage (that is, nonwhite) men and women were believed to be almost identical, but men and women of the civilized races had evolved pronounced sexual differences." Americans believed that savage men "even dressed like women, in skirts and jewelry."[140] Thus women who appeared "to be neither man nor woman" also appeared to threaten the future of the white race. Despite his suggestion that boxing could correct women's defective aspects, Eltinge seemed to agree with Corelli; the attractive, feminine figure he modeled was never flat-chested, nor did she have large hands or feet. And she was always unquestionably white. Eltinge took great pains to whiten his face and minimize the size of his feet and hands, once demonstrating the obvious differences between men and women's feet by posing for photographers, modeling a larger, wider left foot in men's shoes and pants while his right foot appeared smaller in hosiery and tiny heels.[141]

The contradictory statements and images within the pages of Eltinge's magazine suggest he was aware of the danger of whole-heartedly embracing the more radical aspects of the New Woman. While maintaining his manliness off stage by posing as a boxer and farmer, he sought to temper the New Woman with Victorian beauty and decorum on stage. Above all, she had to remain white and distinctly different from modern men. Though his magazine suggested the New Woman exercise her body and her political prerogative, she must never *look* like a man.

BUYING WHITE BEAUTY

Eltinge transformed his body to provide patrons with a cleaner, whiter version of the New Woman than a real woman ever could. By embracing Victorian conceptualizations of feminine beauty and styles of clothing, namely heavy, floor length gowns shaped by corsets thick enough to restrict movement, Eltinge's vision of the New Woman highlighted the supposedly natural physical distinctions between men and women.[142]

Critics praised the perfect ladies Eltinge presented, referencing their whiteness and wealth by calling them "pedigreed" and "thoroughbreds."[143] When impersonating such women, along with the expensive gowns and statuesque carriage that signified their upper class origins, Eltinge made the whiteness of his Gibson Girl's skin a key element of his act. One reviewer saw Eltinge as an emblem of upper-class white beauty, predicting that "many a rich society queen would give half of her fortune, or all of it, to be endowed with such exquisitely molded arms and shoulders, chest and back, with such a graceful neck and classic head, or to possess the *superb whiteness* of the velvety skin."[144] Another backstage observer described Eltinge's male to female transformation, commenting: "the healthy outdoor color of the skin on his face and neck was slowly being changed into a dead-white as he rubbed on a liquid preparation."[145]

The reporter's choice to linger on the "superb" and "dead" whiteness of Eltinge's female persona is particularly telling given the rising popularity of sunbathing. In fact, tanning was so common that Florenz Ziegfeld paid his pale, leggy chorus girls bonuses at the end of the summer for not getting a tan.[146] Recasting women as indoor ornaments to be tucked away from the elements yet publicly displayed on stage, Eltinge and Ziegfeld's efforts demonstrate the work American men performed in maintaining interdependent racial and gender boundaries in the early twentieth century. As the manliness of overly-civilized, soft American male urbanites came increasingly in to question, the excessive paleness of women became ever more important.

Racial and gendered ideologies about American beauty had long been connected to class, as laborers were more likely to work outdoors and be leaner than the middle and upper classes, whose lifestyles and ample diets enabled a paler complexion and fuller figure. Swarthy complexions and dirty faces were often attributed to Jewish, Irish, and Italian immigrants, regardless of actual complexion. However, Eltinge's vision of manliness depended on this darker complexion. Out of makeup, critics noted his "dark brown hair and dark eyes" complemented the healthy hue of his natural complexion, which, taken together, provided physical evidence of the manly hours he spent laboring outdoors on his farm.[147] In this new context, pale skin no longer denoted wealth for men, but signified a questionable distance from the strenuous life outdoors. A tanned complexion, then, provided evidence of masculinity earned outdoors.

In contrast to Eltinge's bronzed and rugged outdoorsman, the women he portrayed stayed indoors and when they did go outside, they gestured toward the Victorian era by carrying a parasol to protect them from the sun. But most importantly, Eltinge emphasized that the effect of the pale white lady could be achieved through the use of beauty products. Sensing the curiosity of his fans, Eltinge confided to one backstage observer, "The fair, soft feminine skin... the difference between mine and the real thing is that mine comes from a bottle and is applied when needed." Eltinge told *Theatre Magazine* that he covered his arms, neck and shoulders with "a white liquid of my own preparation" and that "the result is the brilliant white for which I strive."[148] Such statements emphasized a concrete *racial* difference between women and men, while suggesting that Eltinge could only conceal his natural manly hue through the application of makeup.

The backstage invitations Eltinge gave to reporters revealed his efforts to emphasize the laborious process this transformation necessitated and to stress repeatedly the differences between male and female skin. Witnessing Eltinge whiten his skin backstage, this same reporter explained: "Upon request he volunteered the information that his 'skin' consisted of several ingredients, including zinc ointment to give the needed whiteness."[149] By inviting reporters to witness and record this transformation and by highlighting the necessity of physically whitening up, Eltinge underscored the fact that hyper-whiteness was a female virtue that, like corsets, heels, and hairstyles, did not come naturally to him.

Eltinge knew that female fans eager to shore up their own claim to white femininity would be deeply interested in the ingredients he used in his whitening solution. Historian Kathy Peiss argues that "the ideal face, defined by pale skin and blushing cheeks, remained remarkably constant for most of the nineteenth century" and as early as 1849, cosmetics manufactured in America reached 355,000 dollars in sales.[150] In fact, in the nineteenth century skin whiteners were the most popular of all cosmetic products, used by women of all races, ages, and classes.[151] As the commercialization of cosmetics expanded at the turn of the century, however, whiteness became increasingly manufactured. Women paid their local druggists to concoct special mixtures, and turned to mail-order cosmetics firms. Whiteners were usually made from ground starch, rice, or chalk, but often contained toxic levels of mercury, lead, and arsenic, causing permanent scarring and even death for some users.[152] Many women willingly took such risks because a hyper-white complexion "asserted bourgeois refinement and racial privilege."[153]

Peiss argues that "notions of Anglo-American beauty in the nineteenth century were continually asserted in relation to people of color around the world" so much so that "travelers, missionaries, anthropologists, and scientists habitually viewed beauty as a function of race."[154] Beautiful white skin on women, therefore, demonstrated the advanced state of American civilization. But wearing too much makeup also posed potential dangers. For much of the nineteenth century, Americans associated painted faces with prostitutes. By the turn of the twentieth century, however, working and middle-class women could artfully apply makeup and create a natural white look, implying sexual, social, and racial respectability in the same way Eltinge did on stage.

Not only could the average woman carefully apply whitening powder, lipstick, and blush without inviting doubts about her character, but many working immigrant women in Eltinge's audiences would have also viewed whitening up as a matter of professional and social prudence. In his seminal work on the construction of whiteness, David Roediger recalled W.E.B. DuBois's argument that even white workers who "received a low wage [were] compensated in part by a… public and psychological wage."[155] Roediger argues "the pleasures of whiteness could function as a 'wage' for white workers. That is, status and privileges conferred by race could be used to make up for alienating and exploitative class relationships."[156] Through his beauty products and magazine, Eltinge propagated a hyper-whiteness that not only paid himself a substantial wage, but could provide a pleasurable feminized whiteness for women with few resources.

Such whiteness gave women access to an elusive brand of hyper-white femininity while evoking civilization and upper class status.

Eltinge's use of makeup to impersonate women was the fundamental ingredient in demonstrating that properly gendered modern men and women should possess different shades of skin color. In an interview, he explicitly explained the logistics of switching from male to female (and thus darker to lighter) roles within the same play: "When I first makeup I apply that of the girl and over it I add a darker, more flesh-like tint belonging to the boy. Thus when I am ready to make my appearance as the widow, I can remove the boy makeup very readily."[157]

In 1909, a photograph accompanying one reviewer's profile of Eltinge viscerally makes clear the gendered nature of whiteness (see Figure 10). Eltinge peers at the camera, holding the whitening product in his left

Figure 10. Dressing room picture of Eltinge with half of his face made up. *Green Book*, Dec 1909, 8. (Billy Rose Theatre Division, New York Public Library for the Performing Arts, Astor, Lenox and Tilden Foundations, Image ID 5126407).

hand, with the left half of his face painted a distinctly feminine hyper-
white. Conversely, the right side of his face exhibits a strikingly dark
"healthy, outdoor color." From the neck up, he is half man, half woman,
exhibiting two starkly different degrees of whiteness, using color to signify gender unmistakably. This photograph highlighted Eltinge's ability to embody, but differentiate, between the sexes simply through the
visual cues of complexion. Such images recall nineteenth-century minstrel playbills, which "paired pictures of the performers in blackface
and without makeup—rough and respectable, black and white."[158] One
minstrel player gained fame solely for "being able to change from black
to white and back in seconds."[159] Although he once claimed it took him
years of study and practice to do so, Eltinge, too, highlighted the speed
with which he eventually executed this change. *The Boston Daily Globe*
even timed one of Eltinge's transformations, reporting that he managed
it in as little as 3 minutes and 34 seconds.[160] While David Roediger has
argued that blackface minstrels were "the first self-consciously white entertainers in the world," as a white man further whitened-up in women's
clothing and makeup, Eltinge was perhaps one of the first self-consciously
masculine white entertainers. If blacking up showed that whiteness really mattered, then Eltinge's whitening up and cross-dressing highlighted
the intimate connection between gender and race.

In *The Color of Race in America,* Matthew Guterl explains that in
1900 (at the beginning of Eltinge's career) Americans read race through
language, religion, nationality, class status, and color.[161] However, over
the next forty years, race came to be recognized almost solely for its "optical qualities," making it "possible for anyone who spoke English, looked
'white,' and subscribed to state patriotism" to therefore "lay claim to the
civic privileges of Nordicism. This new sense of race was not just rooted
in science, not just in an evolving political economy of racial difference,
but also in a new visual sense of what race looked like."[162] Guterl concludes that "the story of race in modern America is far messier, and far
less inevitable, than previously supposed."[163]

Yet the "story of race" is even messier than that. Eltinge contributed
to Americans' visual understanding of race, but for readers of playbills,
photographs, and advertisements, he neatly captured readily identifiable
contrasts not only between shades of white, but male and female bodies.
Eltinge's photographs and explanations of how to transform from male to
female demonstrate that he simultaneously highlighted the performative
gradations between the two, rendering gender and race related matters
of self-definition and presentation. They show that colored codes of race
were the means through which Eltinge performed gender. Ultimately,

his self-transformations suggested, not only that "outdoor" "healthy" whiteness was manly and indoor hyper-whiteness was womanly, but the two were oppositional and interdependent.

Though scholars such as David Roediger readily acknowledge constructing whiteness was a "gendered phenomenon," gender was bound with race in ways that we have not yet fully appreciated.[164] Whitening products like Eltinge's made the illusion of hyper-white femininity more accessible, helping immigrants and working women to feign or solidify their tenuous grasp on whiteness. To different groups of women, Eltinge conveyed the message that differences in skin tone perceived among immigrants were not as important as those differences among men and women. Yet, in doing so, Eltinge drew attention to the fact that both race and gender were artifice—unstable constructions that could be adopted, adapted, and appropriated by anyone. The real trick was remaining respectable in the transformative process, something only men like Eltinge, who reinforced gendered norms through performing tan, outdoor manliness off stage, could do.

Eltinge and his manager saw an unprecedented opportunity in audiences' interest in how he achieved his enviable stage complexion. Around 1910, at the height of his popularity, they began selling hyper-white skin formulations to women by the bottle, providing access to a white complexion to countless women for as little as twenty-five cents (see Figure 11).[165] In explaining the origins of his line of beauty products, Eltinge claimed: "thousands of ladies throughout the country have written asking me what facial preparations I use to transform myself from a man to a woman. The letters have been so numerous that I have decided to establish The Julian Eltinge Preparations Company."[166] Another magazine advertisement offered "A Chance for Every Woman to Be as Beautiful as Julian Eltinge," confirming that many women insisted he "give them the secret for his exceedingly beautiful complexion."[167]

More pointedly, a four-page advertisement in his magazine insisted "many women envy Mr. Eltinge's beautiful white arms and shoulders, made so by his own recipe of whitening and powder." And that it "has often been said that the handsomest woman on the stage is a man, meaning, of course, Julian Eltinge. If his various preparations make him so, what will it do for the ladies?"[168] The advertisement concluded by warning readers: "the woman who prides herself on being as nature made her is very apt to be unnecessarily ugly."[169] To bolster sales of his products, Eltinge and his managers portrayed the use of whitening makeup as a normative, respectable and judicious feminine practice and (anticipating later commercial efforts) shamed women who failed to use such products.

Julian Eltinge Delights the Fair Ones

Thousands of ladies throughout the country have written asking me what facial preparations I use to transform myself from a man to a woman. The letters have been so numerous that I have decided to establish

The Julian Eltinge Preparations Company

Manufacturing the following articles that make me

"THE FASCINATING WIDOW"

The

Julian

Eltinge

Cold

Cream

The
Julian Eltinge

LIQUID
TOILET
POWDER

The
Julian Eltinge

FACE
POWDER

Every lady should write for a jar of the JULIAN ELTINGE COLD CREAM, the cream with a face value. A series of six large photographs, 11 x 14 inches, of Julian Eltinge is published, showing him as

Bride, Bathing Girl, Society Woman, Dressing for the Stage, Widow and Himself

Any of these beautiful pictures will be mailed free with every jar of cold cream

Prices, 25c, 35c, 50c, and 85c

ADDRESS

The Julian Eltinge Preparations Company

17 East 17th Street, New York City

Figure 11. "Julian Eltinge Delights the Fair Ones," an advertisement from *The Julian Eltinge Magazine and Beauty Hints*, c. 1912, 57. (Townsend Walsh Collection, New York Public Library for Performing Arts).

In doing so, he reinforced the on-going commodification of racialized American beauty culture and its intimate connection with immigrants' efforts to assimilate into American society.

Eltinge and his manager, A.H. Woods, were masters of integrated product placement. They produced a variety of promotional ephemera, including 11 by 14 inch photographs of Eltinge in costume that consumers could display at home and postcards they could keep or send to others. On postcards, Eltinge advertised his cold cream and simultaneously promoted his latest musical comedy *The Fascinating Widow* (see Figure 12). The image juxtaposed Eltinge as himself, standing while paddling in a canoe as he was surrounded by superimposed images of some of his most popular female types. The types featured including a blushing bride, a bathing girl carrying a parasol to block the sun, and a woman in a white wig, who looked like an imitation of Marie Antoinette. Both the bathing girl and the woman in the white wig serve as ultimate icons of feminine hyper-whiteness. In case female consumers did not already get the message that this beauti-

Figure 12. Promotional advertisement for Eltinge's musical comedy *The Fascinating Widow* and his line of beauty products. As a bonus, this card may have been mailed out to customers who purchased his beauty products, c. 1911. (Billy Rose Theatre Division; New York Public Library; Astor, Lenox, and Tilden Foundations; Digital ID: th-10458).

ful feminine whiteness was for sale, the top of the card boldly claimed in red ink, "The Julian Eltinge Cold Cream makes me look like these." The open-ended use of "me" may have referred to Eltinge, but more importantly, it also invited female consumers looking at the card to imagine themselves transformed into his hyper-white female types as well.

Eltinge not only sold beauty products, but thoughtfully provided his readers with a detailed set of instructions for replicating his white results. Advertisements instructed women to use the Julian Eltinge Face Powder and "Julian Eltinge Cold Cream, which he applies all over his face, and then, as he has a very strong, dark beard, he uses a grease paint of delightful youthful tint, which he spreads on very thickly, and then works it in most carefully." By emphasizing the dark, manly beard he had to conceal, readers were reminded of Eltinge's masculine virility. Readers were further instructed: "the neck and shoulders are then carefully whitened with the Julian Eltinge Liquid Powder." Thus, if a woman wished to "make the best of the features nature has given her, will but study her face as carefully as Mr. Eltinge does his, she can decide just what may be changed to advantage and what may be left alone."[170] Such statements confirm that Eltinge did not consider skin color an unchangeable feature.

On the eve of the twentieth century, an increasingly visible coterie of female celebrities became important models of self-presentation for New Women. For reference and inspiration, many women stored pictures of celebrity faces in their photo albums alongside family and friends.[171] As a pervasive presence in popular culture and an active agent of publicity, Eltinge made certain that women could acquire his photos and postcards for this same purpose. Indeed, Eltinge was not the only performer to hawk whitening products to women. Anna Held, wife of Florenz Ziegfeld and the original "Ziegfeld Girl," also lent her name to a brand of whitening products.[172] One advertisement featured Held presenting readers with a powder puff, offering "a utopian promise" that would "beautify as well as whiten and homogenize different, dark, rejected or ordinary looks."[173] Just as the press described the ingredients Eltinge used to create his whitening products, critics sensationalized stories about Held, claiming she achieved her remarkable ivory complexion by bathing daily in milk.[174] It is not incidental, then, that Eltinge included an impersonation of Anna Held in his performance repertoire. The Irish-American Eltinge and the Polish-Jewish Held became paragons of hyper-white feminine beauty and spokespersons for face powders, whitening products, and corsets. Held reached an even wider audience than Eltinge, writing a syndicated newspaper column dispensing beauty advice to eager readers.[175]

F. Michael Moore notes that famous actresses such as Nora Bayes and Lillian Russell, who performed in the same era as Eltinge, also used their fame to profit from endorsing beauty products. Yet these women were considered so naturally beautiful that others less well-endowed likely felt they could make only futile efforts to emulate their complexions. On the other hand, when a man like Eltinge endorsed his own line of makeup and beauty products, he convinced the average woman that she too could achieve the near-magical results he accomplished as a man.[176] Aware of the power of such appeals, Eltinge explicitly argued: "with me a great deal depends upon my 'make-up' box, therefore I will never be without the... preparations."[177] As a tanned male, "so leathery that his impersonations offer the strongest contrast between the man and the part he assumes," Eltinge was uniquely well-positioned as a persuasive spokesman for such products.[178] Although it remains unclear how many women bought these beauty products and believed in their transformative power, Eltinge and his manager thought his vision of white beauty had enough influence upon the urban American female consumer to make such a commercial venture profitable.

Though the growing consumer culture of which women were an integral part worried some Progressive reformers, Eltinge's advertisements and performances largely upheld traditional, respectable images of white womanhood that few considered objectionable. By watching his performances, reading his magazine, purchasing the corsets and heels he endorsed, and buying his line of whitening beauty products, Eltinge offered his fans the opportunity to simultaneously purchase upper-class whiteness and femininity. At the same time, he also shored up his own tanned manliness and distance from the fairy. Compared to the efforts of contemporary female vaudevillians, he ultimately offered audiences conservative ideals to live by.

CONCLUSION

In the 1920s, Eltinge traveled and performed in "Eltinge's Revue with the Julian Eltinge Players," reviving the fifteen-minute vaudeville set in which he played four different female types.[179] But over the next ten years, as he aged, critics remarked that Eltinge had gained too much weight and his looks had become matronly. To make matters worse, in February 1923, Eltinge was found in possession of sixteen quarts of liquor and was arrested for bootlegging in violation of the Volstead Act.[180] A few years later, the press reported a notorious collision with a police car. The bad publicity resulting from both incidents marred his reputation as an icon of artistic respectability.[181]

Other forces were also at work that made the end of his career seem inevitable. As Eltinge aged, fewer audiences continued to see female impersonation as an innocuous act and more cities began to outlaw cross-dressing in all forms. With the onset of the Great Depression and World War II, and the return to more rigid gender roles, tolerance for visible gender inversion waned.[182] A new cadre of experts and sexologists turned their attention to homosexual inversion and sexual deviance. As a healthy, wealthy, educated, adult white man at the top of the Darwinian racial and gender scale, Eltinge's failure to demonstrate his sexual interest in women while continuing to dress like them made him a source of discomfort. In 1940, Eltinge attempted to perform his old act at a Los Angeles nightclub called The Rendezvous. However, city laws against transvestitism compelled him to undergo a psychological examination before providing him with a permit which only allowed him to appear in a tuxedo, standing next to a rack of his former costumes.[183] This performance marked the dim finale of a once celebrated international star. Later that year, rumors of his alcoholism and kidney problems circulated widely and, in 1941, his weight at an all-time high, his looks long-gone, and his career at a stand-still, Eltinge died of a cerebral hemorrhage at the age of fifty-seven.[184]

"Nothing will ever completely erase the slur from female impersonation," reflected *The Chicago Daily Tribune* on the occasion of Eltinge's death, "but Julian Eltinge came as close to lifting it as any man ever had." He was so close "that he suffered very little during his lifetime from the taunts of either the rough or the simpering and light-minded play followers of his time."[185] Unlike nearly all other female impersonators of his era, the public accepted Eltinge as a charmingly peculiar phenomenon who posed no serious threat to the established order and should therefore be tolerated, even celebrated, rather than ostracized.

But race was critical to enabling him to normalize perceptions of his gender and sexuality; it was the means through which he tempered the threat cross-dressing posed. By enhancing his self-presentation as a physically powerful, rugged, tanned outdoorsman, he sanitized the spectacle of female impersonation, making it more agreeable for the average patron of American vaudeville and later, musical theater. By grounding his stage impersonations of women in their hyper-whiteness, he further reassured audiences that men and women were physically and fundamentally different. Rather than propose radical changes to existing ideologies, these performances allowed Eltinge to bend gender and race within existing norms. Ultimately, then, his transgressions were far less subversive than Tanguay's, who reveled in crossing boundaries and dropping jaws. Rather than mocking women, his performances exalted them, scrutinizing and fetishizing them for all eyes, but most of all, for aspiring white women themselves.

More than sixty years after his death, my central task has been to understand the sometimes contradictory strategies Eltinge employed in an evolving process of self-definition and public presentation and to make sense of how the American public understood such efforts. Such an examination highlights the ways in which the New Woman was a racial phenomenon and the emergence of the black-white binary was gendered. Eltinge both relied on and modified deeply interrelated understandings of race, sexuality, and class-based American gender norms, achieving mainstream acceptance at a time when female impersonation was an increasingly endangered endeavor. As a beloved icon for over fifteen years, Eltinge reassured audiences that, despite the wild and salacious performances they witnessed from women like Tanguay, the elegant Victorian white lady was not yet dead.

Much like Eltinge, biracial male impersonator Lillyn Brown had to carefully navigate contradictory gender, sexual, and racial discourses in rapidly changing times. Yet, as a white man impersonating even whiter women, Eltinge faced an entirely different set of challenges than male impersonators like Brown did. But just as Eltinge brought his gender impersonations to life through race, Brown's career as a male impersonator was dramatically shaped by fluid perceptions of her race.

CHAPTER 3

"SHE IS WHAT SHE AINT"

LILLYN BROWN AND THE MEANING
OF BLACK MALE IMPERSONATION

*I*n 1934, a reporter for *The Baltimore Afro-American* described Lillyn Brown as "a male impersonator who for 26 years has been earning her living by making folks believe she is what she aint."[1] In fact, over a period of sixty years, as a solo performer and member of various ensembles, Brown convincingly portrayed men on stage before black and white audiences. Hailed as both a "good-looking man" and an "exemplary exponent of real femininity," Brown was able to embody both gendered extremes, and, therefore, had much in common with the inimitable white female impersonator Julian Eltinge.[2] Both Eltinge and Brown worked on Broadway and the big-time Keith vaudeville circuits, but their careers differed in important ways. Unlike Eltinge, whom audiences most often knew was a man, Brown was characterized as a "surprise act."[3] Attired in a black and white tuxedo, she used her deep contralto voice to convincingly sing blues, ragtime, and jazz songs, afterwards removing her top hat to reveal long, feminine hair.

Though the racial discrimination she faced kept her from replicating Eltinge or Tanguay's international fame or fortune, her career outlasted theirs by several years. Like the other performers in this study, Brown enjoyed popularity abroad, touring in Spain, Switzerland, France, and England.[4] As the self-proclaimed daughter of an Iroquois father and black French mother, her "exotic extraction" caused some to suggest "her coloring was such that some black friends said they did not realize that she was a Negro until she told them."[5] Though white Americans did not always distinguish between light and dark complexioned African Americans, for black audiences, Brown's racial versatility worked in concert with her gender impersonations, allowing her to finesse alternate perceptions of her as an Indian, a Negro, or an exotic racial hybrid.

Brown performed in the strictly segregated racial milieu created by Jim Crow. During this era, the dividing line between whites and blacks was defined by the inflexible "one drop rule," which deemed any person with even "one drop" of black ancestry "Negro." The same year the Supreme Court declared the constitutionality of "separate but equal" facilities for blacks and whites, in 1896, Brown began her career as a male impersonator at the young age of eleven. Just ahead of the Great Migration, when over half a million African Americans uprooted themselves from the South and moved North to cities, she made her way from Georgia to New York City. In the early twentieth century, New York City had become mecca for assertive "New Negroes," who chose to make the city the headquarters of the newly founded National Association for the Advancement of Colored People (NAACP). Just as importantly, Harlem served as home for black writers, artists, poets, actors, singers, and composers, whose collective creative output produced the Harlem Renaissance. In the era of Prohibition, Harlem was also host to many nightclubs and speakeasies where middle and upper class white audiences came to watch so-called primitive performances of blackness.[6]

Brown often performed black-themed material with all-black casts at venues like the Lafayette and Lincoln theaters, located in the heart of Harlem. For nearly two decades thereafter, she performed as a male impersonator with her husband, William DeMont Evans, touring for several years on the segregated T.O.B.A. circuit (Theatre Owners' Booking Association, sardonically referred to by black performers as "Tough On Black Asses").[7] In the 1920s and 1930s, Brown was part of a small group of cross-over black performers booked on the big-time Radio-Keith-Orpheum (RKO) vaudeville circuit, where managers often hired only one black performer per bill.

As an impersonator, singer, composer, dancer, dramatic actress, comedian, and teacher, she was perhaps the most entrepreneurial performer examined in this study. She ran her own stock company, claimed to own a theater, and declared she was the first person to sing the blues on stage at Chicago's Little Strand theater in 1908.[8] Though this latter claim is difficult to authenticate, in 1921, she became one of the first black women to record the blues on a major record label.[9] Indeed, as leader of "Lillyn

Brown and her Jazzbo Syncopators," she recorded four blues records, sung from both male and female perspectives.[10] Brown's syncopators included such up-and-coming black male instrumentalists as Gavin Bushnell, Ed Cox, and Herb Flemming, who were also members of the all-black bands accompanying more celebrated black female vocalists such as Ethel Waters and Mamie Smith.[11] Of these female blues singers, only Brown made male impersonations a central and enduring part of her repertoire. For this reason alone, she highlights the ways female blues singers transgressed racialized gender boundaries at the turn of the century.

After 1927, Brown adopted the gender neutral performance name "Elbrown," and began performing as a soloist and part of the previously all-male, African American Norman Thomas Quintet.[12] She wrote, produced, and directed at least four plays and musical comedies and black newspapers frequently cited her presence at parties and fundraisers. As an activist and educator, she served as Secretary of the Negro Actors' Guild of America, a racial uplift organization seeking to advance the status of black performers. She also offered aspiring black performers free acting lessons at Harlem's Jarahal School of Music. Though she temporarily retired in the mid-1930s, around age seventy Brown took an unprecedented step by reprising her male impersonations in a series of "one woman shows."

Though the black press hailed her as "the greatest actress of her race" in the field of male impersonation and "the greatest colored contralto of all time," historians know remarkably little about Brown's career and life.[13] Scholars of women's history, African American studies, and musicology have closely examined the contributions of many of Brown's peers, offering intriguing feminist readings of songs recorded by Gertrude "Ma" Rainey, Bessie Smith, and Mamie Smith.[14] Likewise, scholars such as Gillian Rodger and Sharon Ullman have analyzed male impersonators active between 1860 and 1930. With the notable exception of Gladys Bentley, however, few scholars have examined the performances of vaudeville's black male impersonators, nor have they studied the broader significance of race in vaudeville's gender impersonators.[15]

According to David Krasner, for black Americans living in the 1920s, "cultural reality consisted in paradox, and this paradox informed black theater performance."[16] Brown speaks directly to these paradoxes: as a migrant, New Negro, and New Woman, she was also married and deeply religious. As a cross-over performer who inherited minstrelsy's derogatory black stereotypes, she had to accommodate the sensibilities of both black vaudeville audiences in the balconies and white audiences in the orchestra pit.[17] The desire of many Harlem migrants like Brown to assert a new self-determined, modern black identity clashed with the need for financially strapped black productions to appeal to white audiences wanting to see minstrel-inspired, grotesque depictions of African Americans. James Weldon Johnson, himself a former vaudevillian, called the dilemma black artists like Brown faced "the problem of the double audience."[18] One of the key ways in which Brown conquered the double audience was by sending distinct and often contradictory visual and aural messages about race and gender through her costumes and her music. As a biracial gender impersonator, Brown was a double figure herself and she reflected Americans' love/hate relationship with racial and gender ambiguity. Just as Eltinge and Tanguay strove to entice audiences, just short of offending them, Brown did the same.

As a male impersonator active in the late 1920s and 1930s when gender impersonation was taking on fraught new meanings associated with sexual deviance, Brown provides historians with a missing link between the cross-dressers and ethnic impersonators on the vaudeville stage, the "fairies" and the "bulldaggers" who attracted slumming tourists to cabarets, drag balls, and speakeasies, and the innovative and unapologetically sensual black "mothers of the blues." As does Eltinge's, Brown's career illustrates that historians must reexamine how the meaning of gender impersonation was refracted through the lens of race. Her career demonstrates that the experiences of black male impersonators were distinct in several ways from their white counterparts. Though both whites and blacks were concerned with race suicide, unlike white male impersonators, Brown did not use race to neutralize her gender transgressions. She did not suggest male impersonation was something she was compelled to do, nor did she see male impersonations as incompatible with her life as a respectable, feminine, middle-class, married woman. At a time when African Americans were fighting derogatory stereotypes of the primitive black savage, black male impersonators seized an opportunity to perform new visions of modern black manhood. Just when African Americans were deeply concerned with their "racial destiny," black male impersonators such as Brown refashioned black men as cosmopolitan citizens of the world.[19]

LEARNING THE TRICKS OF THE TRADE

Brown told reporters she was the only child of an Iroquois Indian and a black French school teacher.[20] Born in Atlanta, Georgia in 1885, given the Indian birth name Genesee Wanda, those who knew her called her the "Little Girl with the Big Voice." At age nine, Brown dropped out of school and began performing, singing with the musical accompaniment of a nine-piece orchestra made up of "white English girls."[21] This act performed together for two years, earning Brown billing as "The Indian Princess."[22] This stage name indicates that early on, race profoundly shaped Brown's theatrical presence. The juxtaposition of an Indian singer leading nine "white English girls" suggests that the inversion of racial hierarchies was also a key part of her act. While Tanguay suggested that her Indian ancestry explained her primitive nature, for Brown, her Indian background was self-styled as royalty. The contrasting role Indianness played within the same genre and the same historical context suggests that perceptions of race were remarkably fluid.

Brown would later drop this billing and become relatively quiet about her supposed Indian roots, though black critics continued to note her exoticism when reviewing her performances. It is unclear why she eventually omitted her Indian ancestry as a central part of her act. White audiences increasingly classified all Americans as either black or white, and often did not distinguish regional, class, or color differences among African Americans. As a result, it is likely that they did not distinguish between biracial and multiracial black performers.[23] Brown was simply considered a Negro act, albeit a light-skinned one.

At some point early in her career, Genesee Wanda completed her racial transition from "Indian princess" to "colored contralto" by changing her name to Lillyn Brown. This first and last name had racial and sexual linguistic significance. According to *The Language of Homosexuality,* "lily" was a "derogatory term for a male homosexual; a sissy or timid homosexual who is inhibited or morally restrained from overt homosexuality."[24] The *Random House Historical Dictionary of American Slang* assigns "Lily" a similar, but more racially specific meaning: "a black person; a white person; an effeminate boy or homosexual man," while "lily-white" described a fair-complexioned person.[25] Paired together, "Lily" and the color "Brown" created a new identity, which highlighted Brown's own biracial roots and the potentially homosexual subtexts of male impersonations. It is unclear whether or not Brown intentionally invoked these connotations, but the unusual spelling of her first name (i.e. Lillyn vs. Lillian) suggests she consciously associated herself with the many contemporary meanings of the term "lily."

Presumably around the time Brown adopted this new name, she ran away from home, landing in a coal-mining town in Alabama. While singing at a local restaurant, the Queen City Minstrels hired her to sing and dance with the troupe.[26] During one of these minstrel performances Brown saw an opportunity to take on larger acting roles through male impersonation. The interlocutor, who had a role much like the master of ceremonies, "got sick and I cried out—I can do what Mr. Cheerey can, and I begun [sic] to rattle off all the gags and the answers."[27] To the *Pittsburgh Courier,* Brown recalled, "the show was in a panicky state. None of the ballad singers wanted to tackle the part and the end men were utterly helpless."[28] To her delight, the stage manager allowed her to take on the part.

Foreshadowing later costuming decisions, the manager of the Queen City Minstrels determined that Brown should "avoid cutting her beautiful hair."[29] Instead, she curled it and donned a little Lord Fauntleroy outfit, a boy character Tanguay also briefly portrayed as a child.[30] In the show's finale, Brown played a mischievous "picaninny:" "I was Sammy. It was a plantation piece. I did light comedy, teased the old man and he hit me with a stick. I jump and duck and do my specialty. I was dressed in little overalls like a country boy."[31] "I was the hit of the show. They called me 'Little man.' From then on I became the interlocutor and that is how I came to be a male impersonator."[32] Indeed, Brown was such a success that when she "asked for twelve dollars per week (high!)," the troupe agreed.[33] As her early role as a male interlocutor suggests, male impersonation offered women well-compensated employment opportunities. Just as white women used ethnic impersonation to advance their careers, women of all races used gender impersonation to distinguish themselves from chorus girls and step into the spotlight, reciting monologues and performing solos for comparatively hefty paychecks.[34]

Fueled as much by the desire for intimate knowledge of celebrities as by suspicions of deviance, newspapers explored the personal lives of male impersonators, searching for a rationale that could explain their place in this peculiar line of work. Compared to female impersonators like Eltinge, male impersonators were subject to similar—albeit less intense—inquiries. One of Brown's competitors, Alberta "Bert" Whitman also toured on the T.O.B.A. and R.K.O. circuits as a black male impersonator from approximately 1910 to 1930.[35] Whitman performed with her classically trained sisters, Mabel and Essie, but as "the race's" premier male impersonator, she often played a fashionable upper class man known as a fop, dandy, or swell.[36] In 1929 a reporter pointedly asked Whitman "why did you begin impersonating a man?" Whitman explained that seven years earlier, "a boy who sang one of my songs, dropped out." She recalled that "boys were awfully hard to get" so "I rigged up an outfit and filled his place. As a boy I went over big, bigger than in any thing I'd done before. So, a boy I stayed."[37] In both cases, Brown and Whitman volunteered to stand in for unreliable or inept male players. From early on in their careers, audiences responded more enthusiastically to both women as cross-dressers than as female actresses. Yet unlike Eltinge, who constantly expressed regrets about working as an impersonator, both recalled persisting in male impersonations without looking back.

Even more so than Whitman, however, Brown described an early and earnest desire to work as a male impersonator. As a young performer working in Savannah, she recalled doing a rhythm song: "I *wanted* to do Mr. Morgan, *a man's song*. But I wanted to sing it and I did." [38] As the previous chapter demonstrated, Eltinge crafted a narrative which claimed he had been both socially pressured and physically forced to wear women's clothing. Critical to this narrative was Eltinge's self-fashioning as a blue-blooded, cigar-smoking student at Harvard. As a woman, however, Brown used many of the same props of masculinity that Eltinge used off stage to put across her gender impersonations on stage: "I wore white and black trousers, blue serge coat, cigarette—black patent leather pumps, like the collegians were wearing. From then on," she continued, "I was in the biggest vaudeville shows, *but I wanted to wear pants*."[39] Unlike Eltinge, Brown suggested that she acquired male roles only through her own persistence. Though she did not elaborate on why she wanted to wear pants, her matter of fact tone suggests that no explanation was needed. As an enterprising adolescent in the 1890s, Brown may have seen male impersonation as a means to landing better solos and salaries. According to historians Lynn Abbott and Doug Seroff, Florence Hines, another successful black male impersonator, "seems to have *chosen* to perform male impersonation throughout her long career."[40] Both Brown and Hines voluntarily entered cross-dressing for reasons starkly contrasting those articulated by white gender impersonators.

Though she harbored an inclination to wear pants, Brown explained that the realism of her impersonations did not come naturally. In language eerily echoing Eltinge's, Brown explained: "I studied how men move. I followed men and copied their ways. I was the forerunner of the fashion now. 'You are the greatest male impersonator' I was told in Berlin, because with me it was art—*not a natural way of being*. I was feminine as any female ever was." [41] By insisting on her innate femininity and the unnaturalness of her impersonations, Brown demonstrated an awareness of the contemporary belief that gender impersonation was closely linked to inversion and sexual deviance. Although her insistence that it was "not a natural way of being" perhaps betrays some discomfort with this link, she was still proud of the fact that in her realistic performances of manliness, "I really fooled them all."[42]

Even though white critics were more likely to view white performers as artists and black performers as natural entertainers, gender impersonators of all races and sexes confronted the perception that gender impersonation was not art. Katie Barry, an English actress successful in South Africa, Australia, and America, lamented that audiences "wanted me in pants... and I had an artistic soul above pants."[43] Barry's comments reveal her distaste for male impersonation and the belief that such gimmicks were beneath talented white dramatic actresses.[44] Yet Brown never made comments disparaging her profession as Barry did. Despite the discrimination she faced as a black performer, Brown insisted that her impersonations were, in fact, art. And what made them so was the hard work involved in bridging the distance between her "true" feminine self and the realistic illusion of manliness that she presented on stage. Just as *The Baltimore Afro-American* newspaper suggested, Brown claimed that her dress, demeanor, and deep voice fooled audiences into believing "she is what she aint." Though she did so with less urgency than many white gender impersonators and only many years after her vaudeville career was over, Brown separated her own identity from the cross-dressing she did on stage. While Tanguay became rich and famous by convincing audiences she was the irreverent savage white woman she appeared to be on stage, like Eltinge, Brown felt that her success relied on convincing audiences she was *not* what she appeared to be. This contrast between reality and performance made both Eltinge and Brown artists.

THE DISTANCE OF DEVIANCE IN WHITE MALE IMPERSONATION

In her examination of the evolution of male impersonation from 1860 to 1930, Gillian Rodger divides male impersonators into three generations. According to Rodger, critics praised the first, active between 1860 and 1880, for the realism of their male impersonations. For example, Annie Hindle, the first woman to achieve international fame as a male impersonator in the 1870s, "specialized in realistic male impersonations: she shaved regularly to try to effect a shadow of a mustache, and her low voice added to the overall impression of a sexy masculinity."[45] Over the next two decades, male impersonators grew less realistic. By 1900, audiences saw the "third and last generation" of male impersonators in "a fundamentally new way."[46] Instead of praising their realism, at the dawn of the twentieth century, critics emphasized male impersonators' unique personalities and celebrated how unmanly their male impersonations had become.

Most performers from the third-generation of white male impersonators felt compelled to defend their choice of profession. Just as Eltinge told the press he would soon take on male characters, white male impersonator Kathleen Clifford rationalized her work by explaining that her male impersonations were temporary. In 1908, Clifford told reporters, "I'm just a lad for the moment."[47] Six years later, famed British male impersonator Kitty Donner told *The New York Times:* "I have never worn boys' clothes before and I hope I'll never have to wear them again."[48] These sentiments recall the logic behind the ruling issued in 1915 by Yale University administrators who barred actors from impersonating females for more than one consecutive year.[49] If white men impersonating women for more than a year were likely to become womanly off stage, white women impersonating men could do so safely only "for the moment."[50]

Not only did white male impersonators use their exchanges with the press as a way to communicate their disdain for male impersonation, but many third-generation white male impersonators discouraged anything suggesting realism in their performances. Historian Sharon Ullman argues that, though many female impersonators aspired to fool their audience, most male impersonators "were judged on the degree to which 'real men' could *differentiate* themselves from them. That differentiation helped mark critical signs of masculinity in an increasingly public contest over the ownership of male political and social privileges."[51] Whereas white men like Eltinge portrayed sexually mature hyper-white ladies, white male impersonators typically played pre-pubescent boys. In fact, many white male impersonators permitted audiences to laugh at women's deliberately failed attempts to look authentically manly. Yet Eltinge embodied an idealized version of modern womanhood and advised white women how to be better versions of themselves by endorsing the latest fashions, cosmetics, and diets. In the late 1920s, when Eltinge's career began its precipitous decline and discomfort over homosexuality began to heighten, many white gender impersonators felt pressure to make their performances *less* realistic.[52]

At a time when Florenz Ziegfeld's slim, white chorus girls could weigh no more than 125 pounds, opportunities for less than petite white actresses, singers, and dancers were few.[53] It is not surprising, then that white male impersonators were rarely large in stature and that critics celebrated and exaggerated their diminutive size, in part to demonstrate how unmanly they truly were.[54] For instance, *The New York Telegraph* claimed white male impersonator Kitty Donner was only four feet, four inches tall. The reviewer concluded, Donner's "size, or lack of it, is an asset, and not a handicap."[55] Critics affectionately called the petite, white male impersonator Kathleen Clifford a "midget impersonator."[56] Clifford's "boys look and behave real and genuine" but "Miss Clifford does not in the least sacrifice her dainty feminine charm." The more transparently feminine, white male impersonators such as Donner and Clifford appeared to be, the more white American audiences on the big-time vaudeville circuit found them entertaining.[57]

For the third generation of white male impersonators working between 1900 and 1930, "the singers' voices also became an important means of imposing distance between the singer and the song's central character." The majority of male impersonators active in this period were mezzo-sopranos or sopranos; "thus, the moment they began to sing the illusion of masculinity was shattered."[58] Though few male impersonators made records, and even fewer remain extant, Vesta Tilley's recording of "Jolly Good Luck to the Girl Who Loves a Soldier" reveals a relatively high-pitched voice sounding unequivocally female.[59]

White male impersonators also modified their perspectives as narrators, opting to sing in the third-person to discourage audiences from making autobiographical connections between the lyrics and the singer.[60] Whereas the previous generation of male impersonators sang in the first person about specific experiences of love with women, the second generation of male impersonators sang about "the dangers of women" in a general way.[61] When they did sing in the first person, it was often from the perspective of young, sexually inexperienced boys rather than men. In addition to using the third person, after 1900, male impersonators less frequently sang songs also performed by male singers.[62] The strategies these women used to differentiate themselves from inverts and men meant "there was little except their costumes to distinguish male impersonators from other female singers in vaudeville."[63] Indeed, both Tanguay and Sophie Tucker's personae were arguably more manly than that of many white male impersonators.

If audiences interpreted performances as autobiographical, this posed a real risk to male impersonators. One scholar claims that male impersonators "constantly trod a fine line between two different perversions. If they appeared to be too realistically masculine, they were open to charges of lesbianism, but if the male characters were portrayed as too effeminate, they could appear to be homosexual and therefore distasteful for an increasingly middle-class audience that included women."[64] Indeed, experts such as contemporary psychiatrist Krafft-Ebing argued that women who donned men's clothes in theatrical performances were suspect: "Uranism [homosexuality] is nearly always found... in opera singers and actresses who appear in male attire on the stage *by preference*."[65] Further characterizing lesbians and revealing the confused relationship between gender inversion and homosexuality, Krafft-Ebing argued that a woman's desire for masculinity was more important than her sexual desire for other women.[66]

Just as hair texture was an important marker of race, hair length also served as a potent symbol of gender and sexuality. Krafft-Ebing argued, "Uranism may nearly always be suspected in females wearing their hair short, or who dress in the fashion of men, or pursue the sports and pastimes of their male acquaintances."[67] Thus, white male impersonators were extremely careful to keep their hair long and clarify that it was not their preference to wear pants. In so doing, they distanced themselves from the deviance increasingly associated with inverts.

AMBIGUITY AND REALISM IN BLACK MALE IMPERSONATION

In 1931, when Brown performed as a solo male impersonator on the big time vaudeville circuit, one critic suggested that her personal relationship to masculinity ended with the stage. Just as critics highlighted Eltinge's off-stage manliness, George Tyler of *The Baltimore Afro-American* emphasized Brown's femininity off stage. Visiting her at home, Tyler "marveled at the elaborate and charming stage and street clothes of

Figure 13. Brown emphasizing her feminine beauty in a professional photograph taken in 1920 at the Earl-Broady Studios in Schenectady, New York. (International Center of Photography, Gift of Daniel Cowin, 1990).

the star. Her layout gives one the impression of standing in a ladies' garment shop." Referring to Brown by her gender neutral performance name, Tyler argued, "here at home Elbrown devotes her time to sewing, being an ideal wife and hostess, and laying plans to please her audience, while her husband's smile beams upon her and her pet dog lies idly by."[68] Another critic agreed: "In dresses she is neat, petite, comely and vivacious. In fact, she is an exemplary exponent of real femininity that reflects an expressible radiance of beauty unadorned."[69] To highlight the depth of her artistic gender transformation, Brown offered such critics evidence of her "real femininity" when she draped herself in pearls and wore her hair long, posing as a woman for publicity stills (see Figure 13).

Though such photographs aptly captured her feminine side, Brown stands out as a woman who was unapologetic about cross-dressing. In contrast to white gender impersonators of both sexes, she never expressed disdain for her costumes or suggested her impersonations were a temporary stop-gap in her career.[70] Being black at the turn-of-the-century was limiting in many ways, but Brown's marginal racial status seems to have allowed her to more smoothly transgress gender boundaries on the stage. Though *The Baltimore Afro-American* identified her as an "ideal wife and hostess," unlike other white male impersonators, who pointed to their marital status or offered explanations for their single status, Brown did not emphasize her marriage. Although she was married to William DeMont Evans for much of her career, critics never referred to her as Mrs. DeMont or even Mrs. Brown. As a vaudeville duo, their billing as "Brown and DeMont" failed to clarify the sex of either actor, nor did it suggest the two were married. Occasionally, the press suggested their sexes by billing the pair as "Lillyn Brown and William DeMont," but, even then, they were presented as performance partners, rather than husband and wife. The fact that Brown never adopted DeMont's last name, according to American custom, suggests that Brown was unafraid of the prognostications of contemporary sexologists. Instead, she wished to downplay her marital status and deemphasize her husband's role in her career.

Although they married in 1913 when Brown was twenty-eight, like Tanguay, Brown never had any children. In this sense, both women would have been viewed as failing in their duties to reproduce within their respective race. In Krafft-Ebing's theory, though, Brown's lack of children would have handily explained her capacity to "look like a man." Physicians argued that failure to produce children caused women to develop neurasthenia (or nervous exhaustion). Dangerous changes manifested themselves in a barren woman's appearance as well: "No longer reproductive, she would begin to look like a man. Her breasts would shrivel, facial hair develop. Many such women, one highly influential and well-published physician reported, began to wear heavy boots."[71] Again, props like cigars and suits for men and long hair and dresses for women played a key role in negotiating complex understandings of gender. Reversing who wore what had the potential to undermine the entire gender hierarchy. Psychologists' ominous predictions about the masculinization of women who wore pants and failed to have children made it strategic for women like Brown to have pictures of herself taken out of costume, so that audiences could see her lack of facial hair and appropriately gendered props like necklaces, longer hair, and dresses.

Because she was single for much of her career, black male impersonator Alberta "Bert" Whitman was asked about her love life much more often than was Brown. In 1929, *The Baltimore Afro-American* profiled Whitman, seeking to attract readers with the suggestive headline: "Woman, Impersonator of Male Character, Likes Feminine Things, However Won't Confirm Rumor of Impending Marriage."[72] Asked when she would marry, Whitman shook her head left and right "and says, 'Sometime next year—maybe."[73] Perhaps women like Brown and Whitman expressed no disdain for their roles and, in some cases, even encouraged ambiguity about their lives off stage because they were less uncomfortable with their profession than white male impersonators. In particular, Brown and Whitman did not see male impersonations as incompatible with their lives as respectable, feminine black women. One historian suggests that from 1910 to 1930, the protestations of male impersonators grew louder and increasingly sincere because their performances were "distasteful to the performers themselves, the majority of whom shared the same middle-class values or aspirations of their audiences."[74] But Brown and Whitman expressed no distaste for their work and aspired to many of the same middle-class values —respectability, upward mobility through hard work, and, finally, material success.

Though the press often went to great lengths to emphasize the youth, daintiness, and feminine voices of nearly all third-generation white male impersonators, many of the patterns historians have noted in their work did not manifest themselves in Brown's performances. From the young age of fourteen, Brown cultivated a booming contralto singing voice; one newspaper claimed she was famous for her ability to sing in front of large crowds without a microphone.[75] Brown not only shared songs already in the repertoire of contemporary male singers, but she also regularly performed side by side with men, first with her husband and later with four black men in the Norman Thomas Quintet. Both her image and her voice had to sound convincingly masculine to keep up the ruse. Though not as deep or raspy as the voices of Tucker or black male impersonator Gladys Bentley, Brown's voice allowed her to convincingly emulate a male singer. Critics hailed her as "one of the finest male impersonators with her unusual voice" and one of Brown's students, Robert Kya-Hill, described her voice as "deep like a man" and "a tremendous contralto voice."[76] Rather than dispelling the illusion that she was a man, Brown's voice sustained it.

Recorded in 1921, Brown's song "Bad Land Blues" reveals that she popularized at least one song from a sharply different perspective than many of her white counterparts. "Bad Land Blues" is as lyrically explicit as Tucker's bawdy songs, and Brown sang it from a masculine point of view in the first person. Written by Shepard N. Edmonds, "Bad Land Blues" described a man getting drunk and wanting to kill the man who took "his" lover away.[77] Brown declares: "Going to drink all the bad lands booze, That's laying around, And with *my* ammunition band. . . when *I* meet that baby who stole *my lady*, That no-good puppy, There ain't no maybe!, 'Cause he must be found. . . I'm gonna lay his body down, So spread the news." After repeating the chorus, Brown stops singing and asks, "WHAT? You ain't scared of nobody? *Lawd, I* ain't scared of no-body!" Through syncopated rhythms, dialect, and first-person pronouns, Brown told a story about an unfortunate black man and—at least for the duration of the song—she *was* that man.

Brown's habit of singing in the first person and her unwillingness to apologize for her work separated her from white male impersonators. Although religious, married, and dressed in women's clothes off stage, Brown's unapologetic attitude made her relatively radical. Brown was also unique because she wrote, produced, directed, and performed several of her male roles. Indeed, she seems to have had more control over her career as a man than when performing as a woman on Broadway. For example, as a woman, Brown took a part in the Broadway play *Regina*, portraying an Aunt Jemima-esque "compassionate Negro cook" working for an obnoxious, wealthy, white, Alabama family.[78] Such parts were limiting, both because of the subservient roles Brown portrayed and because they were supporting rather than leading roles.

Despite the seemingly transgressive aspects of Brown's male impersonations, she always ended them by removing her top hat to reveal her waist-length hair as evidence of her "real" femininity. Cutting her hair would have eliminated this climactic revelation, making it difficult for Brown to prove that she was really a woman after all.[79] Brown's decision to maintain what critics described as her waist-length hair also suggests

that she never intended to devote herself entirely to male impersonations. Shortly before she retired in 1934, *The Baltimore Afro-American*
claimed Brown's "heavy voice and masculine mannerism helped keep
up the illusion that she was a man until she lifted her top hat and sent
a full suit of long black locks dangling over her shoulders. Lillian [*sic*]
never bobbed her hair. It would ruin her job."[80]

As the boyishly bobbed hairstyle of the flapper became popular in
the 1920s, hair continued to play a key role in negotiating gender and
race roles on stage. In its review of the Irvin Miller production *Harlem
Girl*, the *New York Amsterdam News* noted, in the lead role, Brown
"makes a stunning picture in an evening suit and the audience gasped
and applauded when she removed her top hat and allowed her long hair
to fall over her shoulders."[81] Unlike Tanguay's Sambo Girl or Eltinge's
Sampson Girl, the final reveal of the "real" gender of the Harlem Girl
was the climax of the play. As it was for Harry Houdini, the transformative moment where Brown suddenly escaped her masculine guise and
revealed her long hair suggests that metamorphosis was a critical component of her act. Just as importantly, it also demonstrates that Brown
and her audiences shared the same understandings of the gendered and
sexual implications of hair length as did physicians and psychologists.

Like Brown, many female impersonators often "went in for real impersonation, fooling (or trying to fool) the audience with their wonderful
make-up, clothes, demeanor, voice, and mannerisms." In his memoir,
Vaudeville: The Honky Tonks to the Palace, former vaudevillian Joe
Laurie Jr. recalled that audiences generally did not know the men were
not women until, at the climax of the performance, "'she' would remove
her wig to a big Ahh! from the audience (those who had never seen it
before). He would thank the audience in a deep bass voice, stick out his
chest, and walk off stage real mannish."[82] In addition to magicians like
Houdini, female impersonators who saved the reveal for the end of their
performances may have influenced Brown's big finish. Eltinge rarely, if
ever, removed his wig on stage, but for other female impersonators, these
tricks sometimes sustained the ambiguity over the performer's gender or
race through the finale and even afterward. Laurie recalled that female
impersonator "Ray Monde came on as a woman, at the finish of the act
he removed his wig and showed that he was a man, then for an encore
he removed another wig and showed long beautiful hair like a woman's.
The audience was left guessing."[83] Such acts exposed the performative
nature of gender and made its changeability the crux of the show. Although tan and hyper-white skin were the key ingredients separating

white men from white women for Eltinge, for black women like Brown, hair and clothing played this critical role. In both cases, gender was mutable rather than a predetermined biological reality.

If Brown's impersonations were as convincing as her contemporaries suggest, some audiences might have left her performances believing that, like Monde, she was a man who did a final trick as a woman.[84] Rather than confirming the inherent separateness of the sexes by providing a humorous approximation of grotesque womanhood or transparently feminine boys, such performances confused audiences and temporarily dislocated their sense of reality. They invited them to scrutinize the artificial nature of gender, ultimately suggesting the differences between reality and illusion were unknowable.

In addition to Brown and Whitman, other actresses occasionally performed as black male impersonators between 1900 and 1930, including Teddy Peters, Naomi Price, dancer Ida Forsyne, and Rose Brown.[85] However, with her closely cropped hair, deep voice, and flamboyant style, scholars have afforded Gladys Bentley more critical attention than other black male impersonators. Born in 1910, she was considerably younger than Brown—her junior by twenty-six years. Like Brown, she began her career at a young age, writing her first song at age eight.[86] Both women sang about love from the perspective of both male and female narrators. However, Bentley's reasons for becoming a male impersonator differed sharply from Brown's. Mercilessly teased as a child for being "too masculine," Bentley ran away from home, quickly realizing that she could make money by showcasing her masculinity in New York City. Early in her career, she performed as "Bobbie Minton," and her "growling," "husky" voice, and adept piano playing soon brought her success.[87]

Unlike Brown, Bentley was deeply immersed in New York's gay subculture, but the two had other equally important differences. By the mid-1930s, Bentley had become a much higher paid and more visible icon than Brown and she typically performed in the intimate atmosphere of Prohibition era nightclubs.[88] While Brown portrayed a well-dressed modern black man as a duet or solo act on the ostensibly respectable vaudeville stage, Bentley identified herself as a masculine lesbian, known in contemporary parlance as a "bulldagger." Bentley dropped her masculine moniker, Bobbie Minton, early in her career and *The Chicago Defender* described her as a "curvy male impersonator." It was always clear that she was a woman, though an unusual one at that; she told newspapers that she wore "men's clothes most of the time."[89] By contrast, Brown's performances convinced audiences she was a man and her adoption of the gender-neutral stage name "Elbrown" demonstrated her earnest efforts to disguise her sex.[90] Vaudeville's reputation for respectability and the physical distance it put between the stage and the audience largely prevented vaudevillians like Brown from individually engaging with members of the audience. But the intimate atmosphere of a nightclub allowed Bentley to flirt ostentatiously with female fans. While Brown portrayed herself as an artist, Bentley was a self-made spectacle.

Brown must have been aware that her performances might be viewed as manifestations of Uranism. Just as Eltinge's performances may have appealed to so-called fairies, Brown's performances may have drawn lesbian and gay admirers into her audience as well. Yet, in the 1930s, she began to distance herself from associations with New York's gay subculture and pansy performances, which made a spectacle of effeminate and gay men. When male impersonation began to disappear from the stage in the mid-1930s and vaudeville began to gasp its last long breath, *The Baltimore Afro-American* sharply distinguished Brown from the likes of Bentley, claiming the former "is quite different from the pansie [*sic*] impersonators... because her make believe goes no further than the footlights. Off stage and on, when she desires, she *can* be delightfully feminine, and *prefers* soft, clinging gowns to tailored clothes."[91] Indicating an important shift taking place in the mid-1930s in both Brown's career and the popular perception of black male impersonators, the article declared: "she despises pansies" and at one recent performance "she took off her hat in the middle of her act instead of at the end as per usual when a hoodlum thought she was a 'sweet man' instead of a woman, and started to snicker."[92]

By 1934, New York authorities had already banned male performers from appearing in women's clothing and vaudeville managers increasingly censored material mentioning pansies, at one point, explicitly banning use of the word on stage.[93] Outside the vaudeville theater, the police were also cracking down on New York's gay clubs, stepping up the frequency of raids.[94] It is not entirely surprising, then, that at this point in her career, Brown suggested she was disdainful of pansies. It is impossible to know whether or not Brown actually "despised pansies," or if *The Baltimore Afro-American* was strategically distancing her from the suspect associations audiences increasingly linked to gender impersonation. Whatever the explanation, this was the first time Brown publicly expressed discomfort with her profession and its associations.

While upper class black activists insisted that the future of the race relied upon strict adherence to gender and sexual propriety, until the mid-1930s, women like Brown attempted to provide audiences with a modern vision of successful black manliness.[95] Although Brown bent gender and racial norms far less than did Gladys Bentley, her decision to stand on stage as a gender impersonator and sing the blues from the perspective of a man over a span of sixty years clearly separates her from her white counterparts. Without making excuses for her work, for three decades, she maintained her position as an artist, New Negro, and New Woman.

Brown's career demonstrates that incorporating black male impersonators unalterably changes the history of male impersonation. Thus far, historians have based their conclusions almost exclusively on vaudeville's white male impersonators, obscuring the role of race in negotiating gender and sexual ideologies. But if, as one scholar has argued, men "looked to male impersonators to offer a conceptualized mannequin upon which they could drape their own increasingly fraught gender ideologies," audiences also wrapped their racial ideologies on the backs of black male impersonators. While both white and black male impersonators enjoyed moderate success on different, often segregated, circuits of the vaudeville stage, the visions and sounds of manliness they presented were not carbon copies of one another. Their performances reveal a conversation not only about "codes of masculinity," but about codes of race and sexuality off stage as well as on.[96]

"MANNISH CLOTHING FOR ALL WOMEN"

Though vaudeville audiences and theater critics largely celebrated black and white male impersonators until the 1930s, some critics worried that their transgressions did not stop when they exited the stage. In particular, they feared that rebellious New Women would see these celebrities as role models, taking their fashions to the streets.[97] In 1929, a female reporter for *The Baltimore Afro-American* peppered Alberta "Bert" Whitman with a barrage of questions about her apparent preference for men's clothing off stage: "Why do you go for such mannish styles off stage? Is it that you prefer appearing mannish? Do you think men's styles are more attractive than feminine ones?" Whitman reassured her, "No, I like fluffy things... But of course, I went in for typically mannish styles because it was good for showmanship, and now the public demands me in that type of clothes. I'm not Bert Whitman to them unless I'm as near a man in looks as a girl can be." Like the "ambisextrous" Eltinge and versatile Brown, Whitman embodied both gendered extremes in one body.[98]

As thousands of women flocked to drag balls and cabarets to ogle and flirt with male impersonators, the styles black male impersonators exhibited on stage became increasingly popular on the streets of Harlem in the 1920s and 1930s.[99] In 1933, after Brown had performed in men's suits for over thirty years, *The Baltimore Afro-American* noted the appearance of mannish clothing for all women: "Little shops had on display special three-piece suits for women, mannish hats and broad-toed shoes. Special loose collared shirts of dainty materials, and even underthings of masculine cut" could be found "in the windows of haberdasheries all over Harlem." The newspaper noted that while "male impersonators on the stage have been well known and many have won fame by these characterizations," male attire for women "as an everyday proposition is another thing altogether." The reporter claimed to have overheard one Harlem resident comment, "Don't want no women of mine in pants" adding, "One pair of pants in the family is enough."[100] This article conveyed that what many Harlemites considered suitable on stage was not so on the street.[101] More importantly, the commentary suggested that black women were not only watching male impersonators on the stage, but, to the dismay of black men, choosing to emulate them on the street and "in the family."[102]

Concern over women in pants eventually reached the stage as well. In 1934, Ralph Matthews, a reporter for *The Baltimore Afro-American*, claimed to have "discovered that wearing pants by women is a sin, which means that Lillian [sic] Brown has been a sinner for twenty-six years." Citing a passage from the bible, Matthews quoted Deuteronomy 22:5: "'The woman shall not wear that which pertaineth to a man and neither shall a man put on a woman's garment: for they that do so are an abomination unto the Lord.'" Matthews concluded: "That sounds bad for Lillian [sic] Brown."[103] Though the playful tone of Matthews' article suggests that he did not personally view cross-dressing as a sin, as a pious woman who penned at least two religiously themed plays, Brown must have chafed at Matthews' suggestion. Indeed, it is revealing that within one year of the article's publication, when gender impersonation became increasingly perilous for women wishing to maintain a respectable reputation, Brown retired her male impersonation act.

While Brown's retirement would prove to be only temporary, cross-dressing could still be found on individual women off stage, as well as at drag balls and other organized social events in Harlem. Most major American cities did not explicitly ban cross-dressing until the 1940s or later, but from 1900 to the 1960s, several women were arrested for charges related to cross-dressing. Newspapers sensationalized the transgressions of women, black and white, as young as nineteen and as old as sixty-six, who dressed in men's clothes, arresting them for vagrancy, forgery, larceny, masquerading, and even white slavery. For example, in 1901 *The Washington Post* reported the notorious case of Ellis Glenn Freed, a woman who was arrested in men's clothing and charged with forgery. The article stressed her professional success as a man, noting that for several years she "passed as a man while residing here and performed the work of a man, being a house painter and sign painter, a carpenter, a bricklayer, a butcher, a barber, a teamster, a real estate agent, a horse trainer, a paper hanger, a plumber." And it was specified that she did all well.[104] That same year, *The Atlanta Constitution* reported that a "negro woman of marked size and strength" escaped from prison dressed as a male guard, having stolen the suit of a guard and worn it "under her female garments." She had been serving a two-year sentence for burglary "which she committed while dressed in men's clothes." Emphasizing the connection between clothing and crime, for good measure, the *Constitution* added, "She has committed many crimes masquerading as a man."[105]

In the first two decades of the twentieth century, widespread interest in the illicit behaviors of male impersonators continued. In 1912, *The Morning Oregonian* profiled Nell Pickerell, alias Harry E. Allen, who was "known throughout the Northwest as the most skillful male impersonator that has operated on the Pacific Coast." For the past twelve years, Pickerell wore "trousers," a habit which, over time, became unbreakable. After interrogation by the police, Pickerell confessed: "I can't wear women's clothes. I have worn these so long and walked and talked like a man for so many years it would be impossible for me to make another change of sex." The newspaper concurred, observing that Pickerell's "assimilation of the long stride and basso voice no longer are an effort—they have become natural." Despite censuring violations of gender decorum, the publication of Pickerell's comments seem to suggest that Americans were intrigued by the notion that gender was changeable up until a point. Pickerell claimed she "first tried the impersonation scheme because it was more easy to obtain employment as a man."[106] Her reasons for donning men's clothes parallel those of many theatrical male impersonators, who found that such performances gave them access to better pay and greater visibility.

Impersonators like Pickerell and Freed, though, were particularly offensive because of their unwillingness or inability to reverse their gender transgressions. In fact, when newspapers sensationalized their gender masquerades off stage, they helped create a context that infused the theatrical performances of male impersonators like Brown with illicit charm. By proximity, Brown's loose connection to this criminal behavior was an integral part of the appeal that she offered her audiences. Unlike amateur male impersonators, however, most theatrical male impersonators were not ridiculed as long as they kept their act to the stage. They were generally accepted because their public images as feminine women reassured audiences that their impersonations were temporary and reversible.

While single women were arrested on the street, organized formal affairs encouraged men and women to participate in cross-dressing as a collective activity. Much like Eltinge, Brown must have known about and perhaps took inspiration from the lavish annual drag balls hosted by the Hamilton Lodge at the Rockland Palace and Savoy Ballroom in Harlem.[107] Harlem's infamous drag parties gave thousands of patrons the opportunity to view hundreds of women dressed like "Elbrown." In the words of one observer, such parties offered a "collection of gorgeous creatures" and "a goodly number" of "tuxes on smart women with heavy, throaty voices."[108] Within these balls, historians find "the beginnings of homosexual minority consciousness."[109] However, these balls did not exclude heterosexuals. Just as in vaudeville, spectators who were perceived as properly gendered regularly attended the balls "to see men who out-womened women, and women who out-mened men."[110] In this context, audiences observed attendees disrupt rigid gender, sexual, and racial hierarchies as lesbians, gay men, bisexuals, and heterosexuals of various racial identities all mingled together.

Although most historians have focused on the largest, most notorious balls, several different organizations sponsored smaller costume balls, many of which awarded prizes for the best male and female impersonators.[111] Though white social organizations did not advertise similar events in comparable numbers, advertisements for such events appeared in black newspapers through the 1960s, long after the death of vaudeville and past the period in which historians have argued gender impersonation faded into obscurity due to tightening gender conventions and damaging stigmas.[112] Despite Brown's temporary reprieve from male impersonation, the persistence of formal affairs encouraging attendees to take what they had seen stars like Brown do on the stage into the street and the dance hall suggests that, for black urbanites, gender impersonation did not die as definitive a death in the 1930s as historians have previously supposed. And perhaps black New Yorkers never fully bought into the idea that gender impersonation was necessarily linked to sexuality. Indeed, some black masquerade balls that awarded prizes to the best male and female impersonator also explicitly invited children to attend.[113] Whether on the stages of vaudeville houses, the dance floors of balls, or the streets of Harlem, a variety of impersonators and on-lookers continued to find excitement in places old and new.

DECONSTRUCTING THE MODERN BLACK DANDY

In their search for clues to the past, historians often privilege textual over visual evidence, viewing the statements and written confessions of the subjects they study as direct windows to their lives. Yet male impersonators like Brown demonstrate that photographs, which reveal clothing, complexion, body language, facial expressions, and the relationships between individuals and the objects around them, reveal meaning that complicates the seemingly straightforward messages that some song lyrics conveyed.[114] In particular, clothes were potent cultural texts that conveyed a variety of conflicting messages about the wearer's race, gender, sexuality, class, respectability, and claims to citizenship. Despite being a white female, feathered and furred costumes suggested that Tanguay was a primitive animal. In an age ostensibly obsessed with maintaining boundaries between men and women, blacks and whites, rich and poor, clothing allowed Americans to claim identities across supposedly closed categories. In particular, masculine clothing gave both black and white women access to worlds otherwise denied them, providing the most successful wearers with rewards including wealth, notoriety (sometimes in the form of criminal charges), the admiration of audiences, and even the romantic attention of other women. Outside of popular culture, contemporary psychologists attributed great significance to clothing as the manifestation of women's innermost, often deviant, desires.[115] Though records documenting the performances and personal lives of male impersonators remain scarce, vivid photographs illustrate how they used fashion to reinforce or push against the contours of gender, race, sexuality, and class, even when their songs seemed to convey conservative messages about those same concepts.

As photographs suggest, some women used male impersonation to appeal to a predominantly male audience by revealing the female body through men's fitted clothing.[116] Actresses such as Sarah Bernhardt wore tights when portraying Hamlet and others flaunted their legs as boyish Peter Pans. Former vaudevillian Joe Laurie Jr. recalled, "We had sort of male impersonators in burlesque, if you can call a gal that appeared in a man's jacket and tights a male imp." Laurie believed these impersonators did not fool anyone, claiming, "These parts were usually played by the leading ladies as an excuse to show off their gams, and the majority of them had good excuses!"[117] Although Laurie's comments confirm the erotic subtext some men saw in these performances, men's roles nonetheless allowed women to play leading parts that were previously off-limits.[118] Photographs of Brown contradict Laurie's recollections, showing

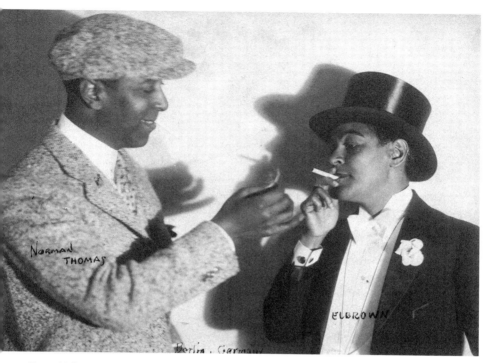

Figure 14. Brown demonstrates her cosmopolitan demeanor, posing in 1928 in a Berlin studio with Norman Thomas, lead singer of the otherwise all male quintet of which she was a member. (Atelier Robertson, Berlin, Germany, International Center of Photography, Gift of Daniel Cowin, 1990).

her adorned in an expensive-looking men's tuxedo, smoking a cigarette while covering her legs, cleavage, curves, and hair (see Figures 14 and 15). She was far less exposed than acrobats, chorus girls, and singing dancers like Eva Tanguay who wore flesh-colored tights, narrow-fitting bodices and heels, or provocateurs like Josephine Baker who bared their breasts.

Through their clothing, we can reconstruct the repertoire of characters played by male impersonators like Brown. Standard characters included the well-dressed dandy, the solider, the sailor, the rural country bumpkin, and the uncoordinated, hapless drunk. However, like Brown, both black and white male impersonators often played dandy or swell characters, well-dressed men of leisure who had money to spend and nowhere important to go.[119] Between 1900 and 1940, black newspapers mentioned several black male impersonators; in addition to Brown, they named Florence Hines, Florence Mills, Aida Overton-Walker, Gladys

Bentley, Alberta Whitman, Baby Cox, Naomi Price, Gladys Ferguson, Laura Livingstone (a.k.a. "Detroit Red"), and Jeanette Seymour. Each woman included a male dandy character in her repertoire and some exclusively performed as dandies.

The dandy's expensive, stylish clothes symbolized modern excess and his songs became vehicles for bragging about his wealth. For successful male impersonators, clothes were perhaps the most important part of the dandy act; they had to be changed several times during each performance to keep the audience thoroughly engaged. In her discussion of the appeal of male impersonators, one scholar concludes that their performances allowed both audiences and performers to simultaneously glorify and lampoon upper class masculinity: "While many of the songs depicting swells denigrate him and could be seen as casting some doubt on his masculinity, they also unabashedly celebrate his excessive lifestyle."[120]

Yet the dandy figure cannot be fully understood without accounting for the ways in which race shaped the meaning of these performances. When portrayed by an African American performer, the significance of the well-dressed dandy shifted dramatically. As dandies, black male impersonators participated in a discourse that was as much about gender as it was about class, modernity, and the future of the race.[121] In the twentieth century, the dandy became the most popular type portrayed by the black male impersonator and existing photographs suggest that Brown portrayed them almost exclusively. Undermining decades of white performers portraying grotesque black buffoons and white female impersonators blacking up to denigrate the unattractive "funny ole gal," in the twentieth century, black women took to the stage to present the black man as a sharp-dressed modern cosmopolitan. At a time when African Americans faced high rates of disease and infant mortality in addition to racially motivated violence, like so-called old-stock Americans, they too were concerned about their future extinction as a race.[122] The modern images of black manliness that male impersonators presented were one means of combatting these anxieties.

Displayed through expensive clothing, wealth was the essential asset of the dandy. In the 1890s, black male impersonator Florence Mills emphasized the dandy's obsession with material things by singing "For I'm the Lad That's Made of Money" and "A Millionaire's Only Son." These songs emphasized the dandy's success and are reminiscent of Brown's hit, "If I was only Pierpont Morgan" and Tanguay's "Oh, You Money!"[123] Appearing in "tops and tails," a formal tuxedo embellished with cufflinks and a boutonnière, Brown's act highlighted the eye-catching accouterments of the dandy lifestyle. When she performed with her husband as two men on the big-time vaudeville circuit, they added white capes, canes and white gloves to the ensemble, creating an image that contrasted sharply with their songs about a rural, pre-industrial Southern past. Working and middle class men must have watched with envy as Brown performed in fashionable, tailored clothes they could ill-afford to

Figure 15. Brown pictured in costume with her husband William Demont Evans. Earl-Broady Studios, c. 1930, (International Center of Photography, Gift of Daniel Cowin, 1990).

purchase. In *Staging Race,* Karen Sotiropoulos argues that black vaudevillians helped forge a respectable black middle class: "Artists' stage success enabled them to purchase some of the first brownstones in Harlem available to African Americans and their organizations' fundraising events, held uptown, became central to the social world of Harlem's new black professional class."[124] Brown was part of this emerging professional class. Instead of offering audiences a mocking send-up of upper class white culture, photographs show her providing a compelling visual blueprint of how to dress for black success (again, see Figures 14 and 15).

When worn by a black performer, the tuxedo with tails, cane, cape, and a top hat countered the image of the ragged, shoeless plantation slave.[125] The dandy also challenged white images of dark-skinned, half-naked Dahomeys on display at the Columbian World's Fair Exposition, where designers of the fair contrasted images of black primitivism with white progress. As visitors walked further away from the white civilized city constructed by white engineers, they encountered the Midway, where exhibits featured transplanted Asians and Africans. Throughout the Midway, Americans considered non-white men (who, they noted, sometimes wore skirts and jewelry) and women indistinguishable.[126] In a period obsessed with the visual dimensions of race, the (over) civilization and effeminacy of white men, and the manliness of women, the dandy's clothes on a light-skinned black woman's body bent and blurred gender, racial, and class distinctions, conveying a complex message about racial modernity and decadence.

THE COLOR OF MODERNITY

Brown's black dandy represented sophistication, mobility and worldliness, which were core elements of a modern black aesthetic adopted by New Negroes. In *Slaves to Fashion,* Monica Miller positions the black dandy as a modern cosmopolitan figure with European, American, and African origins.[127] The black dandy, she contends, became a figure through which black performers, and by extension, black audiences, could resist, even transcend, demeaning minstrel stereotypes of the illiterate, grotesque plantation Negro.[128] So when black vaudevillians like George Walker, Florence Hines, and Brown dressed as the dandy, they did not simply mimic the class-crossing performances of white actors and actresses. Nor were they presenting pansy acts that had homosexual subtexts. Rather, they tapped into a deeply rooted tradition of transgressive black pageantry dating back to Pinkster and Negro Election Day festivals that American slaves celebrated in the eighteenth and nineteenth centuries. Providing a compelling black history of what she calls "crimes of fashion," Miller explains these festivals "featured parades and dances of slaves dressed to the nines in clothing normally reserved for their social and racial betters."[129] Because antebellum customs reveal deep-seated white anxiety over black men and women wearing ostentatious clothing, these were not insignificant sartorial statements. Some whites found the extravagances of black men and women so menacing, they outlawed them. In the mid-eighteenth century, Charleston and New Orleans passed statutes to prevent black "crimes of fashion." And they invented curious punishments for violations of new sumptuary codes: slave owners punished rebellious male slaves by forcing them to wear women's clothing.[130] "Indeed, for whites and blacks, clothing and fashion were a means by which the status of slave and master, whiteness and blackness, masculinity and femininity, Africanness and Americanness was being determined."[131] In the twentieth century, these tensions were still being negotiated on the vaudeville stage where performers like Brown turned such traditions on their head by *choosing* to dress as a man. Through payment and applause, black cross-dressers turned what was previously a punishment into a handsome reward.

Through the black dandy, modern black men and male impersonators committed a series of "crimes of fashion" as well. The problems faced by vaudevillians Bert Williams and George Walker (the latter played a dandy on stage and dressed just as sharply off stage) suggest that, in the twentieth century, Southern whites still considered well-dressed black men an affront to their own manliness. While the pair toured Brown's home state of Georgia, a group of white men, offended by their fancy clothing, forced Williams and Walker to strip, stole their clothes, and left them standing in public naked. Disturbed by the incident, the two swore they would never tour the South again.[132] Although they were all successful black performers, as a male impersonator, Brown was less threatening than men like Walker and Williams. Without challenging white Southern sensibilities, then, she could provide black audiences with a vision of modern black material success. Indeed, in such cases, the black man realized his worldliness and sophistication *through* the black woman's body.

According to Miller, the dandy was a mixed figure: "a product of inter-racial relations, a sliding point on the spectrum of gender and sexuality, a class aspirant and pretender."[133] Brown was a particularly iconic mixed figure because black newspapers so often noted her "exotic extraction." Her fair skin symbolized her racial in-betweeness, a liminal position suiting the black dandy. As a close analysis of Eltinge's career demonstrates, skin tone played a key role in negotiating theatrical representations of white manliness. As fair-skinned women, both Brown and Alberta Whitman were particularly well-suited to portray the black dandy, who rarely assumed the blackface mask.[134] The dandy could be perceived as a vain and overly-materialistic figure, and to white audiences, the lightness of the dandy's skin may have suggested his potential for effeminacy. While this may have been reassuring for white audiences, at the same time, the dandy provided black audiences with a compelling future vision of black material success.

The pervasiveness of skin whitening products, aimed at African American and immigrant women alike, and the popularity of hyper-white female impersonators like Eltinge, attests to the desirability of light skin as a distinctly feminine virtue at the turn of the century.[135] Yet, in overcoming an enslaved past where black mobility and dress were highly restricted, it was more important for black men to establish their worldliness than their dark, strenuous manliness. Indeed, while Africans were showcased at World's Fairs as primitives unfit for citizenship, being too dark or scantily clad could be an obstacle for any African American. Because black men were already portrayed as savage brutes in scientific writings and popular culture, they did not feel the same urgency to live out Theodore Roosevelt's vision of the strenuous life. Instead, they fought back against images of black backwardness by asserting their civilized manliness through their independence and material success.

Though the white press generally classified Brown as a Negro, reporters were often still fascinated—sometimes perplexed—by the fairness of Brown's skin. On the occasion of her death, *Variety* described her as "a mulatto, her father was French, she was light enough to pass as white during her early vaudeville career."[136] At the peak of Brown's career, the *Pittsburgh Courier* described her "most unusual and vivid background," concluding "her extraction naturally gives her analytical magnetism and cunning personality."[137] In a society increasingly conditioned to understand race through visual cues, Brown's race was visually ambiguous; thus occasionally white audiences relied upon contextual clues to determine her race. Even then, the answers were sometimes elusive. Contemporary critic Heywood Broun commented "that the entire cast of *Dixie to Broadway*," a revue in which Brown starred alongside Florence Mills (who played a dandy), were, "according to the American definition, Negroes." However, "there are only a few dark skins among the men and none at all among the women... there is nothing in 'Dixie to Broadway' wholly characteristic of the race from which it draws its performers."[138] Although fair-skinned enough to be perceived by some as white, Brown occasionally relieved any visual indeterminacy about her race by wearing blackface. Scripts of Brown and DeMont's performances have not survived, but reviews and sheet music suggest blackness was a prominent feature of their act. The two billed themselves as "The Black Diamonds of Cardology [sic]," suggesting their financial and cultural value as the male counterparts to contemporary blues-women who called themselves "Black Pearls."[139] The two sang up to twenty songs, which they interspersed with humorous dialogue, a routine involving card-tricks, and complicated dance steps such as the "buck and wing."[140] As with many black performers, one might think white audiences would have been discomfited by Brown's light skin and preferred to see her in blackface, yet only a few publications note her use of blackface.[141]

Though she rarely wore blackface, on many occasions Brown made clear that she was the requisite black act on the bill by performing material white audiences would have understood as specifically black-themed. Shows like *A la Dixie* (1927-1928) featured nostalgic songs about the South, capitulating to derogatory minstrel stereotypes. But like other black performers, Brown and DeMont capitalized on white audiences' narrow expectations, achieving financial stability and fame while claiming a public space for themselves in a rigidly segregated culture.[142] Historian Karen Sotiropoulos argues that many turn-of-the-century black performers self-consciously manipulated racial stereotypes of Jim Dandy, Uncle Tom, and Aunt Jemima, while sending very different messages about respectable artistry that literally went over the heads of white audiences seated in the orchestra pit to reach black audiences in the balconies.[143]

Reviews of Brown seem to bear out this notion. While *The Utica Daily Press* noted she "would present a revue called 'A la Dixie,'" featuring songs that were "characteristic of the old time southern darky,"[144] *The Baltimore Afro-American* called Brown "the greatest colored contralto of all time."[145] The contrast between the visual and aural signifiers of race became especially clear through performances that featured nostalgic songs about slavery in the South sung by a sharp-dressed modern black male impersonator. These mixed messages allowed black and white audiences to each take away their own meanings. Regardless of the lyrical content of their performances and the sensational tone of some cross-dressing acts, even white audiences respected Brown and DeMont as talented performers who presented "Good Clean Comedy."[146] Likewise, it is noteworthy that the black and white press referred to Brown as a "Negro" or "Colored" performer instead of a "coon act."[147] Because she saw her work as artistic and respectable, Brown never described herself as a "coon singer" and existing evidence suggests she did not use the word "coon" in the songs she sang or wrote either.

Brown and DeMont were not alone in being hyper-conscious of their racial reception and cross-racial success. When the Emerson label released Brown's four records in 1921, their catalogue described her as a cross-over artist who was "not only a favorite with her own people, but with white audiences as well. In fact, on the Keith circuit the team of Brown and DeMont always 'gets a big hand.'"[148] In addition, three other record companies released and marketed Brown's recordings under different, apparently ethnically-inspired names. Oriole, Medallion, and Regal record labels released her songs under the names Mildred Fernandez, Maude Jones, and Fannie Baker.[149] Just as she had earlier changed from Genesee Wanda to Lillyn Brown and then Elbrown, she continued to manipulate perceptions of her race by experimenting with her name, projecting different racial images and appealing to different audiences in the process. Black, white, Indian, biracial, migrant or immigrant, male or female, Brown was aptly positioned to conquer these audiences because of her race and gender bending. This versatility allowed different audiences to take away mixed meanings from her performances.

Though some white audiences might have seen her as just another "darky" act, for black audiences, Brown was a crowd-pleasing, modern cosmopolitan whose talents had been tested on both sides of the Atlantic. In September 1930, she used her male impersonations and her newly-minted alter ego as "Elbrown" to replace baritone William Fountaine as the fifth member of the all-male, all-black Norman Thomas Quintet.[150] Brown joined the group just before it left to perform in Geneva, Switzerland.[151] In November of that year, while she toured with the quintet, the *Pittsburgh Courier* touted Brown's international credentials, claiming that she had toured on the R.K.O. circuit since 1915, during which time she played every prominent theatre in the United States and European capitals, adding that "in Paris, where she made her debut, she was a sensation. In Spain, Switzerland, Germany and other places on the continent she maintained her standard of excellence." The *Courier* also claimed Brown and the quintet "just returned from a creditable European engagement, where they were featured in England, France, Germany and Russia."[152]

Again, the black press emphasized Brown's worldliness, publicizing her supposed friendships with "Lord Beaumont, of English nobility, Princess Murad and many other international celebrities."[153] Brown also claimed to be personally acquainted with English aristocrats and, with her singing, entertained Nancy Cunard, wealthy heir to the Cunard shipping lines and a prominent white patron of Harlem's black artists.[154]

Furthermore, she claimed her song "Oh Lord, Send me a Man" was an "international hit" on Gold Seal Records. Black newspapers kept their readers informed of her transatlantic travels, noting that on April 2, 1930, Brown would "sail for Paris" with S.H. Dudley Jr., a well-respected black producer and actor.[155] These reports symbolized more than Brown's own boasting or a slow news day for black newspapers; they offered black readers regular updates on accessible icons of cosmopolitan urbanity.[156] Instead of bragging about her salary, as reports of Tanguay and Eltinge often did, both the black press and Brown herself emphasized her transatlantic travels. Whereas Tanguay exploited insecurities about the declining masculinity of white men by transgressing racialized boundaries of femininity, as a woman, Brown, used vaudeville as a venue to reshape visions of sophisticated, modern black manhood.

While favored urbanites like Brown were spared the most scathing criticism, less established male impersonators from rural areas were not. For example, in 1916, the *Chicago Defender* published a letter in an advice column expressing disdain for aspiring male impersonators. A Tennessee woman, identifying herself as Birdie Brass, a "male impersonator with a low range," asked, "Would you advise me to come to Chicago?" The editor unequivocally replied: "For the [love] of Mike, do not come to Chicago! This town is simply overrun with male impersonators." Implying that Brass would lack the cosmopolitan appeal of urban black male impersonators, the *Defender* suggested "a country impersonator wouldn't stand much [chance] with these city birds."[157] To this reporter, male impersonators were fundamentally sophisticated urban figures.

As a native of Georgia, Brown was once in a position similar to that of Birdie Brass. But for those who did travel to northern cities, migration was a formative experience, unifying New Negroes in cities like New York, Chicago, Philadelphia, and Detroit. While much of the music Brown wrote and performed reproduced nostalgia for the Southern plantation, it also revealed the significance of the migration experience for migrants themselves. The lyrics to "Back Home Again," a song Brown and DeMont wrote and probably performed in *Roll On* (1926) or *A la Dixie* (1927–1928), conveyed a distinct sense of displacement. Similarly, in "Dixie Days," Brown sang directly to a Southern audience when she reminisced about her childhood. Again, such songs carried multiple meanings to different audiences: they tapped into white nostalgia for a pre-industrial, rural Southern lifestyle where contented slaves lived on plantations, yet they also reflected the real life experiences of both Brown and DeMont. Likewise, they resonated with 500,000 black migrants who, beginning in 1915, relocated to Northern cities during the Great Migration.[158]

In a period when taking a train across the Mason-Dixon line was a life-changing experience, traveling back and forth across the Atlantic Ocean was even more deeply transformative. African American men like Paul Robeson, Cab Calloway, Duke Ellington, and William Warfield along with black intellectuals like Langston Hughes, James Weldon Johnson, and W.E.B. Dubois (by one account, both well-dressed dandies themselves), exercised their right to move.[159] As modern black men, they had the resources, talent and desire to travel abroad, speaking, dancing, singing, and writing at the request of paying international audiences. As a dandified male impersonator, Brown enjoyed many of the same privileges. As Brown proudly recalled in 1960, "'You are the greatest male impersonator' I was told in Berlin."[160] For black performers and those who envied them, travel abroad symbolized success, wealth, culture, and sophistication. Indeed, crossing geographic boundaries and leaving behind a violent racial past and present was an especially important mark of modernity during the nadir of American race relations. Performers like Brown, who used the dandy to move between the sexes and segregated worlds of black and white America, achieved profound psychic and physical freedom.

CONCLUSION

In the 1950s, black male impersonator Gladys Bentley started her life all over again, this time as a married, dress-wearing, heterosexual-identified, pious member of the Temple of Love in Christ.[161] In 1952, she published an article in *Ebony* magazine, boldly entitled "I Am a Woman Again," in which she expressed the horrors of her former lifestyle and explained how she discovered her femininity by undergoing hormonal therapy.[162] Instead of fading into obscurity, the most notorious modern black male impersonator publicly documented the deep regret she felt about her former career, suggesting that, like other "lost souls," she regretted "inhabit[ing] that half-shadow no-man's land which exists between the boundaries of the two sexes."[163] To complement her autobiographical essay, Bentley invited photographers into her home to provide visual evidence of her gender transformation: she mugged while "taste-testing dinner" and "turning back [the] cover of [the] bed" in order "to make homecoming husband comfortable."[164]

As the loudest, biggest, most visible icon of black male impersonators, Bentley's repentant voice provides a sad coda to male impersonation as an alternative path for performing black women. For good reason, historians have difficulty making sense of Bentley's refutation of her former life as a lesbian and male impersonator, arguing that her "ultimate capitulation to social norms... should not be allowed to overshadow her immense accomplishments."[165] Given the lack of primary resources and critical scholarship on black male impersonators, it is tempting to imagine that Bentley spoke for other black male impersonators. But the life and career of Brown tell us a very different story.

As Bentley traded in her white tuxedos for matronly dresses, Brown dusted off her dandy wardrobe. Despite retiring in 1934, she maintained her presence in New York City's black public sphere. She not only stayed active in show business in the 1940s and 1950s, taking female roles in Broadway plays, but also became Secretary of the Negro Actors' Guild of America and taught singing, dancing, and acting for such up and comers as Sugar Ray Robinson, who was once an aspiring dancer.[166] After the death of her first husband in 1940, Brown married again, reprising her impersonations in her seventies.[167] Well-preserved with white hair, her voice as deep as ever, Brown continued to perform, write plays, and sing the blues, this time mostly for church and theater groups. Five years after Bentley's death in 1960, Brown wrote and performed a new song, "I'm Blue and Rockin.'" Later that year, at the age of 75, Brown allegedly recorded the song on Victoria Spivey's label, Spivey Records.[168] Hardly a "lost soul," Brown's decision to reprise her male impersonations made clear that she *chose* to work as a male impersonator and did not regret having made that choice. Unlike Bentley, Brown's actions illustrate that, even in the repressive atmosphere of the Cold War, she did not find performative cross-dressing irreconcilable with church-going, marriage, old age, and feminine respectability.

By the 1950s, the world around Brown had changed drastically. Though new visual codes emerged which marked different signs of gender and sexual deviance, it was no longer deeply transgressive or deviant for women to wear pants on the street or stand on the stage.[169] At the end of her life, Brown's audience was younger and smaller in size, but her legacy remained the same: as a biracial cross-dresser, she not only represented the ambivalent "no-man's land," which lacked clear boundaries between manhood and womanhood and blackness and whiteness, but she also continued to perplex and dramatize the twentieth-century "problem of the color line."[170]

From 1890 through the first half of the twentieth century, thousands paid to see women like Brown do on stage what authorities policed on the street and newspapers sensationalized in the press. After 1930, the line between good-humored and illicit activity became increasingly narrow, but that line was less impermeable for black performers than for white.

Those who did not restrict their impersonations to the stage, and especially those romantically linked to other women, were given the least latitude and subjected to the closest scrutiny. Like Bentley, some women started entirely new lives. But for audiences wishing to celebrate a new cosmopolitan vision of black modernity, women like Brown continued to give them the chance to do so.

Like many vaudevillians, Brown represented a rupture between old and new ways of life. She balanced the traditions she inherited from nineteenth-century American minstrel players who derogated black Americans with the modern, urbane cosmopolitan New Negro. In an era obsessed with racial, sexual, and gender difference, on stage Brown lived both within and above such classifications. The next chapter turns to one of Brown's more successful, but equally complex contemporaries, "Red Hot Mama" Sophie Tucker. Though not a gender impersonator, as a performer who embodied blackness, Jewishness, whiteness, manliness, and female rebellion, Tucker's race and gender bending performances symbolized many of the same tensions permeating vaudeville and American culture.

CHAPTER 4

"THE JEWISH GIRL WITH A COLORED VOICE"

SOPHIE TUCKER AND THE SOUND
AND SHAPE OF TRANSGRESSION

─────────────── • ◆ • ───────────────

*M*any remember Sophie Tucker as a portly woman with a raspy voice who, in her eighth decade, made guest appearances on television shows in sparkling dresses and outlandish hats. They recall a plucky woman with a larger-than-life personality who sang bawdy ragtime, jazz, and blues songs. Yet from 1907 to 1909, Tucker perfected her signature style under a blackface mask and she continued sporadically to "black up" in her performances through 1926. As she transitioned out of blackface, she purposefully continued to employ dialect and Southern-based themes, pairing them with her newly whitened face. As her complexion appeared to change, Tucker's singing, clothing, and performance style also evolved. She began to copy the performance styles of black singers, offering audiences a dynamic, seemingly transracial sound in which her voice did not seem to match her body.[1]

Tucker has long been a figure of fascination for scholars. Her willingness to openly discuss women as sexual creatures with desires not unlike those of men has prompted some historians to categorize her as a prophet of feminism.[2] Scholars of Jewish history have also examined Tucker at the zenith of her career, portraying her as an intrepid cultural icon and reformer, a woman unafraid of bringing sex to the stage and screen.[3] However, such interpretations obscure the ways in which Tucker built her career by appropriating and modifying fluid and interrelated perceptions of both gender and race on the vaudeville stage.

Recently, Lori Harrison-Kahan has made a more nuanced argument that Tucker was able to sustain multiple performances of race. Focusing on how "fictional interracial encounters" were imagined in literary texts between black and Jewish women from 1920 and WWII, Harrison-Kahan perceptively argues that Tucker used "blackness and Jewishness to fashion a pluralistic, rather than purely white, American identity, while simultaneously asserting her sexual independence in defiance of traditional gender roles."[4] However, by situating Tucker largely outside of vaudeville, and by primarily emphasizing Tucker's autobiography, Harrison-Kahan stresses Tucker's sense of self over the responses of her audiences and critics.

Conversely, this chapter explores white and black audiences' perception of Tucker's race and gender bending performances, focusing on the role sight and sound played in shaping these perceptions. It contributes a new perspective to existing work on Tucker by focusing on her early career, using digitized collections of many of her first phonograph recordings juxtaposed with reviews of her performances published in both black and white newspapers.[5] This chapter argues that Tucker structured her performances around the clashing incongruities between visual and aural understandings of gender and race. Borrowing from American minstrel performers working in the generation before her and the black blues queens with whom she competed, Tucker offered audiences multiple contradictory performances of the sights and sounds of gender and race. In the first two decades of her career, she strategically played with audience perceptions of gender and racial ideologies by experimenting with her image, environment, and sound, portraying herself at different moments as white, Jewish, black, manly, and womanly. More remarkably, she managed to convince audiences that these identities could coexist within one body.

Ultimately, a close analysis of Tucker's performances within the framework of vaudeville reveals that, just as Julian Eltinge's performances demonstrated that whiteness was often synonymous with femininity at the turn of the century, for white audiences, perceptions of manliness were often coupled with blackness. Eltinge used preexisting racialized understandings of femininity to assert his rugged outdoor manliness off stage and temper his gender bending on stage. Just as Tanguay's performances offered audiences a racialized masculine female, Tucker used fluid understandings of race to undermine prevailing gender norms. Like those examined in previous chapters, Tucker's performances provide a case study of the halting and uneven process that split a nation of immigrants and natives into blacks and whites, and brought together the supposedly separate spheres organizing men and women in Victorian America.

"THE GIRL WHO CAN SING COON SONGS"

In 1886, Sonia Kalish (later Sophie Abuza, then Sophie Tuck, and finally, Tucker) was born in Russia. She arrived in the United States with her family as an infant, spending her early childhood in Boston.[6] She spent the rest of her youth in Hartford, Connecticut, washing dishes, serving food and occasionally singing to customers in her parents' kosher restaurant. Abuza's family restaurant was a popular destination for Jewish vaudeville performers traveling through the area. While stereotypical depictions of Jews were not uncommon in popular culture at this time, Jewish performers and songwriters were starting to find success, particularly in small-time, neighborhood theaters. Though most had Americanized their birth names, in the first decade of the twentieth century, Irving Berlin, Al Jolson, Fanny Brice, and Eddie Cantor emerged as rising national stars.[7]

As Eric Goldstein has recently argued, Jewish Americans had an "uneasy relationship to whiteness" between the late nineteenth century and World War II.[8] Like New Women and New Negroes, the increased immigration of Jews to the United States in the late nineteenth century encouraged "old-stock" Americans to associate them with change and instability.[9] Because of their somewhat troubled position in the black/white racial binary, in the early twentieth century Jewish immigrants and their children developed a particularly complex relationship with African Americans. As racial identities continued to solidify in the 1910s and 1920s, Jewish Americans and African Americans were both perceived as racial outsiders who had identifiably particular traits. Though Jews were perceived as Others in uneven ways and their foreignness was always secondary to that of African Americans and Native Americans, nonetheless, Jews were more empathetic to the plight of African Americans than many other groups.[10] This context would frame Tucker's career as a young performer who cultivated a black sound early on.

Tucker's biographer, Armond Fields, claims that her career began when she auditioned at an amateur night at Poli's Wonderland Theater in Hartford.[11] Though Tucker's audition went well, she remained a discontented teenager in Connecticut. In search of a way to rebel against her orthodox Jewish parents, on May 14, 1903, Tucker abruptly married local mechanic Louis Tuck, who, as Tucker recalled in her autobiography, promised to help get her "out of the kitchen and have some fun."[12]

Two years later, Tucker gave birth to a boy named Albert, but found herself still living with her parents and working at their restaurant. She was determined to escape the life of drudgery that was her mother's fate and resented Tuck for failing to free her from it.

Perceptions of Tucker's socio-economic upbringing played an important role in shaping views of her authenticity and racial Otherness. Unlike Eltinge, who cultivated the myth of an upper class pedigree in order to present refined, high-class art, Tucker ingratiated herself with her audiences by loudly lamenting her childhood as the daughter of an impoverished working-class immigrant family. She openly discussed her meager beginnings on stage. Without irony, she explained in her autobiography: "I'd worked so hard. My hands were smooth and white now. No one would suspect them of long association with the dishpan and scrub pail." She added that nature had given her "my smooth, fine skin, that was pleasingly white now, since I had learned how to care for it."[13] Like Eltinge's advertisements for whitening products, Tucker suggested that whiteness was not biological, but a gendered, class-based status to be earned and maintained. Racial transformation was possible and, as the "Jewish girl with a colored voice" would demonstrate later in her career, moving between racial categories was a distinct possibility.[14]

After becoming estranged from her husband, at the age of nineteen, Tucker ran away from home to begin a stage career in New York City. Her actions foreshadowed her willingness to reject Victorian norms of white femininity, which bound women to their roles as obedient daughters, nurturing mothers, and deferential wives. From the first moment she stepped on stage, Tucker's loud, abrasive sound shaped a musical genre called "coon shouting," which demanded a particular kind of emotional intensity, energy, and earsplitting volume from its practitioners. Writing in 1930, John T. Niles, described coon shouting as an "ancient" art transplanted to America in the twentieth century, where it was dominated by female performers.[15] Probably adapted from stereotypes of the shiftless urban free black known as "Zip Coon," the title of coon shouter was most often (though not exclusively) applied to white performers who, like nineteenth century minstrels, spoke in "Negro dialect" and claimed to emulate antebellum black Southerners.

Contemporary reviews credited Tucker with being one of the first coon shouters, having "originated that method of singing songs."[16] Although her biographer asserts that Tucker "picked up her distinctive coon-shouting style on her frequent visits to the vaudeville theater where she could observe and later practice such renditions," Tucker told the press that her talent for coon shouting was instinctive: "Between you and me, I couldn't help going out on the stage and doing the work. Call it natural, if you wish. Maybe it was."[17] The key to coon shouting was sounding impassioned and unrestrained in the way diverse working and middle class, immigrant and native, white and near-white vaudeville audiences expected black performers to sound. Though Eltinge and Brown both claimed to have studied the opposite sex in order offer artistic and realistic impersonations, Tucker claimed her singing style was natural. Despite the fact that she was performing white perceptions of a racial underclass, Tucker claimed only to represent herself on stage just as Tanguay did. As one reviewer noted, Miss Tucker "strikes the low notes and the high notes, she can flat and sharp in a way representative of the colored singer."[18]

Tucker took an active role in playing up the racial dimensions of her supposed natural talent by emphasizing her lack of formal training. She asked reporters, "Did you know that although I train my bands I can't read a note of music?"[19] Such claims had racial implications. Accomplished black composer Eubie Blake, who got his big break in 1915 when Tucker included one of his songs in her act, underscored the pressure African American performers felt to project an image of natural, untrained talent. When he created *Shuffle Along* with Noble Sissle, the pit band "was told to memorize the entire score and not use sheet music. We did that because it was expected of us." He added that "white people didn't believe that black people could read music."[20] Whether or not Tucker was musically illiterate, as she claimed to have been, she must have known that white audiences expected black performers to lack formal training. Unlike the most successful gender impersonators, in the eyes of critics, her lack of training made her a natural entertainer, but not an artist.

In 1912, Tucker told the press, "I'm so glad I'm alive,'" and "my ability to coon shout is the best gift I've had bestowed on me" adding, "I do love to coon shout."[21] While white gender impersonators claimed to despise their laborious line of work, Tucker suggested coon shouting was a passion, rather than a profession. "Another thing that keeps my mouth spread into a smile," she continued, "is that my folks are all alive and happy. I work for them."[22] Connecting her sonic and racial transgressions with her gender bending, Tucker explained that she functioned as the patriarch of her family, buying her parents a new house and "seeing my brother admitted to the bar, after four years' work which I had paid for with my coon shouting."[23]

Critics agreed that Tucker's talent was natural and that her voice was so loud and unpolished that it sounded almost inhuman. In his

review of her first full-length play, Julian Johnson said Tucker's raw voice
sounded terrible in ensembles or with orchestral accompaniment, "but
when viewed and heard alone, in all its undimensionable immensity, the
dynamite explosion which the Lord gave Miss Tucker instead of a voice...
has nothing human about it."[24] Volume and endurance were particularly important characteristics of a successful coon shouter. Impressed
with her energy, critics proclaimed that Tucker had "iron lungs," and
boasted that "her chanting is of the same volume" whether "she has her
face or her back turned to the audience."[25] Still others noted her 1,000-
song repertoire, and her ability to sing 100 songs a night.[26] Much like
Tanguay's claim to superhuman strength tapped into enduring myths
about the supposed superior strength of animals and racially-Other
women, Tucker's powerful voice appeared to have racially-Other origins as well. Though May Irwin and Anna Held were also fair-skinned
coon shouters active on the vaudeville stage, until the commercial successes of black blues singers in the 1920s, Tucker's voice stood out from
most female singers for its ability to project across huge theaters without
the benefit of a microphone.[27] While the nasal, "babyish, flapper voice"
emphasized exact elocution and stressed the civilized white, diminutive
femininity, and middle-class origins of other female performers, critics
remarked that Tucker's voice was stronger than any man or woman of
any race: "As for Sophie—no white, black, saffron or red hopes have yet
arisen to take away her ragtime championship in the fortissimo class."[28]

DENYING AND REVEALING RACE AND GENDER

In 1908, Tucker secured an audition with Chris Brown, manager of a
small amateur music hall in New York City. While exiting the stage she
claimed to hear Brown remark: "This one's so big and ugly the crowd out
front will razz her. Better get some cork and black her up."[29] As Tucker
recounted in her autobiography, this comment reverberated in her mind
throughout her career. She continually asked herself: "If he was right,
what chance had I, now or ever?"[30] Supposedly relegated to blackface
performance because she did not conform to racial or gender conventions of white womanhood, Tucker claimed Brown's assistant took her
to the dressing room and blacked her up, fashioning her into a Mammy
character: "He got some ordinary corks from liquor bottles, lit a match,
burned the corks, and smeared my face, ears and neck. I was in street
clothes—a tailored suit. He gave me a pair of black cotton gloves, tied a
red bandanna over my hair; with lipstick he painted me a grotesque grin-
ning mouth."[31] After her first blackface performance on amateur night,

Tucker convinced a booking agent to schedule her on the small-time circuit, but only after she agreed to use the burnt cork mask. "Let me leave off the black," she begged. "Try me out the way I am and see if I don't go over." But it was to no avail.[32] By her own account, in this way Tucker reluctantly launched her career as a blackface singer, headlining as "the Ginger Girl, Refined Coon Singer" and the "Manipulator of Coon Melodies" between 1907 and 1912.[33] From this point on, Tucker sought to augment her performances not just by sounding loud, but by cultivating a specifically black sound through both aural and aesthetic avenues.

Though Tucker claimed she loved to coon shout, she framed her use of blackface much in the same way Eltinge did his impersonations of women. Both claimed external forces compelled them to adopt a guise with which they were uncomfortable. While Tucker did this in retrospect through her autobiography published in 1945, Eltinge offered these explanations directly to the press more urgently and continuously throughout his career. Such framing excused elements of their race and gender bending performances that were unsavory to them. While Eltinge expressed his discomfort in the 1910s and 1920s when gender impersonation was increasingly linked to homosexuality, Tucker expressed her uneasiness with blackface in the 1940s, when cracks in the Jim Crow system were starting to appear and changing racial sensibilities no longer embraced blackface performances. It is not surprising, then, that she would reiterate her discomfort with the blackface mask in interviews with the black press and conversations with her great-grandniece in the 1950s, when the Civil Rights Movement gained national visibility with the Montgomery bus boycott and the Supreme Court ruling on school desegregation.

As it was for gender impersonators, the climactic reveal at the end of each of Tucker's blackface performances was the apex of the show. Just as Brown removed her top hat to reveal her long locks and dispel the illusion of manliness during the finale of each performance, Tucker teasingly removed one of her black cotton gloves to reveal a white hand and demonstrate that she was, in fact, a white female. Like gender impersonators, Tucker insisted she always fooled her audiences, who believed she was a real Negro: "My greatest difficulty was convincing the audience I was a white girl, My Southern accent had got to be as thick and smooth as molasses."[34] Like Brown singing "Dixie Days," Tucker further emphasized her supposed Southerness by singing songs that romanticized a Southern past like "Pick Me up and Lay Me Down in Dear Old Dixieland."

Contemporary reviews of Tucker's early performances seem to confirm her claim that her audience was hard-pressed to believe she was not black. Tucker claimed this stunt rarely failed to shock audiences, who struggled to make sense of the incongruity before them. The review of one critic confirms this claim, suggesting, "the audiences have been considerably fooled as to Miss Tucker's color."[35] Yet the fooling "was all relieved Tuesday night when she removed her gloves and her wig and showed that she was as white as any white girl."[36] Another critic confidently reported, "she is a white woman." The critic added, "So completely does she deceive her audiences that not until the end when she removes her black gloves and fluffy wig do they realize she is not a negress."[37] This reveal emphasized the sight of whiteness and the sound of blackness, in this case, subordinating the particularity of Tucker's tenuously white Jewishness.

Like Tucker, African American singer Ethel Waters described her own race bending performances, which paralleled Tucker's early blackface performances. Waters starred in the blackface comedy "Hello, 1919!," portraying a Jane Crow character. Just as audiences thought Tucker was black, Waters claimed "the white audience thought I was white, my features being what they are, and at every performance I'd have to take off my gloves to prove I was a spade."[38] In both cases, the audible evidence of race proved difficult to reconcile with its visible signifiers. Both women exposed the elasticity of race and eroticized the racial reveal, borrowing from the slow stripteases of burlesque dancers. This perplexing climax and ensuing confusion made both performances more titillating. The suspense of acts like Tucker's early blackface performance lay in the question of authenticity: Was this singer black or white? Just as convincing cross-dressers like Eltinge and Brown left audiences initially confused and then amazed at the performer's deft manipulation of gender, Tucker and Waters momentarily suspended audiences' assumptions about race.

Each of the performers addressed in this study relied on racial subtexts to carry out their acts. But like Eltinge, Tucker's early performances required her to do so explicitly by wearing a physical mask.[39] Early in her career she felt bitter about being forced to perform in blackface. "Why did I have to appear in blackface? Why couldn't I have my chance as myself, as the other girls in the company had theirs?"[40] According to her great-grandniece, Tucker later explained, "I was unsure of myself, young and determined to get work." She continued, "If I resented the blackface, it was because it prevented me from appearing as myself, like the prettier girls. Blackface denied my femaleness."[41] Fair-skinned women like Tucker felt that darkening their complexion destroyed their femininity. Though she embraced the sounds of blackness by describing her love of coon shouting, Tucker balked at visually representing blackness on stage.

Other white vaudeville women who wore blackface shared Tucker's sense that blackface (and blackness generally) denied them the femininity that was their natural birthright. Audience responses to the performances of Southern-born Lulu and Mabel Nichols, who performed as a sister act the same year Tucker began her career in blackface, seem to validate Tucker's fears. According to M. Alison Kibler, "rather than receiving marriage proposals from fans, the Nichols sisters regularly faced accusations that they were men, largely because they borrowed the conventions of the traditional, male-dominated minstrel show. "At every performance," the sisters recalled, "we can hear someone in the front say: 'Oh that one's a man. They can't fool me; I've seen too many minstrel shows.'"[42] The sisters' failure to exhibit their own pale skin coupled with the pervasiveness of cross-dressing in American vaudeville caused audiences to assume they were being tricked. Because the Nichols sisters performed alongside gender and racial impersonators, audiences expected that cross-dressing was just another part of their act.

STRENUOUS ACTS, MANLY MAMAS

While Tucker used the blackface mask to suspend assumptions about her race, her frequent manipulation of gender themes in her songs confirms modern American audiences' continued fascination with gender bending as well. Though she did not wear men's clothing or bill herself as a gender impersonator, Tucker sometimes switched the sex of her song's narrator, to the delight of her audiences. For example, she sang two different versions of the same song, "I'll Be the Meanest Man in Town" and "I'll Be the Meanest Girl in Town." In hits such as "Phoebe Jane," "Does She Love Me? Positively-Absolutely," "Don't Put a Tax on the Beautiful Girls," "Please Don't Take My Harem Away" and "High Brown Blues," Tucker sang from the perspective of a smitten or scorned man.[43] Yet she also continued to sing many songs in dialect from the perspective of a woman as well.

What is unique about Tucker then, as the two versions of "I'll be the Meanest Man" and "I'll be the Meanest Girl" suggest, is that through the voice of blackness, she was able to sing from both a female and male perspective. Contemporary white Americans believed "savage (that is, nonwhite) men and women were believed to be almost identical, but men and women of the civilized races had evolved pronounced sexual differences."[44] Thus, Tucker's syncopated rhythms, dialect, and deep voice suggested blackness, but because white audiences perceived black men and women to be so similar, her voice could represent both black women and black men. Likewise, Brown's recordings reveal that she did not change the register of her singing voice in shifting from black male to black female roles.[45] Tucker wanted audiences to believe she was an authentic source of blackness, and that meant possessing gender versatility as well.

Tucker was not the first fair-skinned female performer whose coon shouting style, large body, and jovial personality evoked blackness. In the 1890s, May Irwin's "fat body was linked to her good humor, a trait that was also associated with the easy-going mammy and with maternity."[46] Yet the press tempered this on stage image by describing a more feminine off stage persona. Just as *The Baltimore Afro-American* attempted to neutralize Brown's gender transgressions by describing her as an "ideal wife and hostess," writers belabored descriptions of Irwin's domesticity, proclaiming, too, she was a "model housewife."[47] In several of her vaudeville songs, Irwin visually reinforced this maternal image by singing about children as they surrounded her on stage.

By contrast, Tucker never performed with children and was rarely described as maternal. In her hit song, "My Yiddishe Mama," she directly invoked her Jewishness while extolling the virtues of motherhood, yet she rarely publicly acknowledged being a mother herself. Having left her infant son, Albert, in the care of her thirteen-year old sister Anna, Tucker only occasionally saw him throughout her career and the press rarely mentioned him either.[48]

Rather, the press focused on Tucker's off-stage behavior that was more manly than maternal. She developed a reputation for making songs popular and then allowing other singers to use them. Though she never wrote her music, she told the press that she sacrificed several songs for the sake of other performers, because "Sophie Tucker is *big* and *strong* and a hard worker."[49] Just as Eltinge explained his single status by suggesting it would be selfish of him to marry, like a proper patriarch, Tucker suggested that she provided for her family and even her competitors.

Instead of highlighting her life as a wife, homemaker, or mother, newspapers chronicled Tucker's physical displays of fearless heroism. During a trip to London, American newspapers reported that Tucker also "became mixed up in a free for all fight" leaving "the fray with a black eye. As she left the theater" she was "mobbed by women autograph hunters." While separating two women fighting for her autograph, she "was hit in the eye."[50] It is even more revealing that newspapers on both sides of the Atlantic reported that while in England, Tucker "saved a child today from being run down on the main street. Miss Tucker jerked the child uninjured from the path of an automobile, but was herself struck by one of the car's headlights. One of her legs was slightly bruised but she went straight on with her work."[51]

Just as tales about Tanguay's unnatural strength had racial implications for turn-of-the-twentieth-century audiences, Tucker's ability to acquire only a "slight bruise" and head straight back to work after being hit by a car evoked enduring beliefs that non-white women were immune to pain and possessed superhuman strength. While Tanguay's persona, costumes, music, and off stage antics suggested a generic animalistic Otherness, Tucker's coon shouting, use of the blackface mask, and dialect suggested a particular kind of Otherness—blackness. As Jennifer Morgan and Laura Briggs have convincingly argued, doctors and laymen alike perceived black women in particular as being categorically different from white women.[52]

Both Tucker and Tanguay offered audiences fair-skinned versions of turn-of-the-century "female masculinity," where women claimed the authority, physical power, sexual prowess, wealth, and courage associated with white men. The ways in which reporters described the highly physical nature of Tucker's off-stage life echo the many physical conflicts they also attributed to Tanguay during the same two decades. On several occasions, writers described both Tanguay and Tucker in the midst of violence, but Tanguay was always the instigator and Tucker the defender. While "Egotistical Eva" Tanguay was eerily strong, Tucker was tough and courageous. In this way, Tucker lived up to Theodore Roosevelt's axiom that "greatness is the fruit of toil and sacrifice and high courage."[53] Nonetheless, both women lived lives far more strenuous than white women were supposed to, as they refused to remain still, and to make marriage, homemaking, and child-rearing their priorities. Hoping to shore up his manly image, Eltinge must have been jealous of Tucker's publicity, because he could not have invented press that more effectively conveyed an admirable brand of modern American manliness. Yet instead of labeling Tucker an invert who was perversely strong and interested in manly pursuits, the press embraced Tucker's chivalrous behavior, understanding it through the lens of race.

Tucker offered audiences an opportunity to understand her gender bending in terms of race through the lyrical content of her songs. Unsentimental songs such as "No Man Is Ever Going to Worry Me," "I Don't Want to Get Thin," and "I Ain't Takin Orders from No One" also suggested the kind of irreverent attitude that Tanguay conveyed through her signature song "I Don't Care." For neurologists like George Beard, the sentiments expressed in these songs highlighted the barbarism and savagery of the singers. According to Beard, worry was one of the primary causes of nervous exhaustion in modern America. "Much of the exhaustion connected with civilization is the direct product of the fore-thought and foreworry that makes civilization possible," Beard wrote. "This forecasting, this forethinking," was "the very essence of civiliza-tion as distinguished from barbarism."[54] In this light, even if Tucker had not sung in dialect, she would have bent prevailing racial norms of nervous, civilized white women. Although neither Tanguay nor Tucker wrote their own songs, as fair-skinned females who behaved as white New Women should not, both offered audiences something they sought after. In making both Tucker and Tanguay two of the most popular acts in the history of vaudeville, audiences demonstrated their enduring de-sire to see and hear race and gender bending performances.

In his widely read treatise, George Beard also argued that savage races released emotions spontaneously, whereas modern white Americans had become preoccupied with propriety and were overly constrained by inhibition. They had difficulty laughing or crying, whereas "the savage and the child laugh or cry when they feel like it."[55] By this logic, fair-skinned singers like Tucker could also invoke the sound of blackness by combining linguistic experimentation with seemingly uncontrolled expressions of emotion and joy.

As Beard would have predicted, audiences equated Tucker's large physical presence and joyful, uninhibited personality with racial Others. Managers billed her as the "Singer of Joy Songs" and the press quipped, "Sophie Tucker Spells Joy."[56] One newspaper published a poem in dialect about Tucker making explicit the perceived connection between her size, buoyant personality, and the archetypal contented slave: "Pretty in a nice, big way. Happy all the livelong day. Imprisoned sunshine in her smile. Everybody loves 'dat chile'—Sophie Tucker, Everybody is her pal. Really she's a dandy 'gal.'"[57] The writer concluded: "Sophie is a peck of sun-shine. To be absolutely correct, Sophie is about 14 bushels of sunshine." Here, the image of the well-fed, contented plantation Negro appeared in the form of a deep-voiced, fair-skinned Jewish immigrant woman. It was intended to be a pleasant and happy image for Northern audiences.[58]

VIRILE VOICES AND BIG UGLY BODIES

In contrast to white female performers who invoked blackness like Tucker, other female vaudevillians such as Lillian Russell and Anna Held began their careers as chorus girls in the Ziegfeld Follies.[59] Once they achieved fame as glamorous iconic white beauties, like Eltinge, they supplemented their ample income by endorsing beauty products.

By 1919, Florenz Ziegfeld had established rigid and complex criteria for selecting his chorus girls, including "six chief points of beauty," eventually expanded to include the following requirements: pale white skin, large brown or blue eyes, straight and proportional teeth and nose, slim ankles, size five feet, a buoyant walk, five feet five inches tall, weighing not more than one hundred twenty five pounds. Uniform beauty standards helped recruiters streamline the process of filtering out women they considered unsuitable.[60] Such a narrow description of white femininity would have immediately excluded Tucker, who tipped the scales near two hundred pounds.

From the first time she stepped out on the stage, critics linked Tucker's weight to her deep voice, suggesting that both signaled a lack of femininity and whiteness. Belaboring the point that her voice was unnaturally low and loud for a woman, one critic noted Tucker's "short stumpy figure," "pudgy hand," and "big booming voice."[61] They described both her voice and body in terms evoking, if not, corporeal manliness, something far different from the vogue for lithe, pale, glamorous Ziegfeld girls. In addition to sharing songs with other male performers, something even white male impersonators were reticent to do, Tucker cultivated a sound similar to black male impersonators like Brown. Both Brown and Tucker sang blues and jazz numbers, using their deep voices to adopt the personae of men, misused and abused by wandering women.

At a time when understandings of American manliness were being threatened and dramatically reconstructed, critic Ashton Stevens juxtaposed female impersonator Eltinge with Tucker, simultaneously suggesting the impotence of Eltinge's voice and the virility of Tucker's. "Speaking of elephants," Stevens began, "she has a voice" that "well, if Julian Eltinge's was as virile as Miss Tucker's, he would be executing a long overdue male impersonation."[62] Tucker probably outweighed Eltinge, and with her thundering voice, easily out-sang a man more famous for his small waist than his voice. The comparison suggested that both performers sonically transgressed gender boundaries, and that sound was just as important to understandings of gender as was sight.

Though later in her career, Tucker insisted she was forced to perform in blackface because vaudeville managers thought she was too "big and ugly," her size became a trademark feature, matching her booming, coon shouting voice and making her all the more memorable.[63] Suggesting her Tanguay-esque masculinity and supernatural strength, one critic quipped, "Miss Tucker can move an audience and a piano with equal address."[64] Published descriptions of Tucker also dramatized her size by juxtaposing her with smaller white men. In December 1929, after news leaked of Tucker's third marriage, the press described her husband, Abe Lackerman, as a merchant who "barely came up to her bosom."[65] Describing her first encounter with formidable vaudeville manager Tony Pastor, even Tucker's first biographer, Michael Freedland, used similar terms, claiming Pastor was "as small as Sophie was large."[66] Describing Tucker's success in gendered terms in 1978, Freedland described her as "a red rag to a bull," adding: "(changing the metaphor to the feminine gender wouldn't be fair to Sophie)."[67]

Tucker's body and costuming evolved throughout her career; she continuously reinvented her image as she changed her sound. After being described as "elephantine" for ten years, in 1917, critics noted Tucker adopted a new look: she has "a Lillian Russell figure" and wears "a flock of Kitty Gordon gowns and a pair of pantalettes." Nonetheless, the critics said, "Sophie to the old-timers doesn't look natural."[68] Since very early in her career when Tucker claimed her talent for coon shouting was natural, the illusion of authenticity was central to her public image. Yet again, the concept of naturalness and authenticity revealed racial and gendered meanings. When Tucker adopted conventions of white femininity by reducing her size and emulating fair-skinned beauties like Lillian Russell, critics felt betrayed and disappointed. Looking too feminine felt fake. She no longer seemed as authentic as when she appeared on stage weighing two hundred pounds. This failure to look natural meant that critics felt looking white and womanly did not suit someone like Tucker.

Perhaps picking up on cues from her critics, in the 1920s, Tucker returned to her former weight, appearing to glory in the size that distinguished her from the bevy of beautiful, long-legged white chorus girls with whom she competed early in her career. Of her first film, *Honky Tonk* (1929), critics surmised that the "Good-natured, jovial" Tucker was singing "of being quite satisfied with her weight. During one sequence one anticipates that there is going to be a scene or so devoted to Miss Tucker doing her reducing exercises before the radio, but this stage entertainer forgoes the idea, permitting an amusing dog to obey the unseen owner of the voice by bending down and rolling over."[69] Critics perceived Tucker's character as a direct representation of her own satisfaction with her weight and her ability to playfully invert power dynamics. Indeed, this conflation with the personal and professional was deliberate; in the film, she portrayed a hard-working night club singer named Sophie.

Tucker's large figure also helped her talk about sex in ways her white female contemporaries often deemed too explicit. In her autobiography, she perceptively noted that it would have been more difficult for a thin woman whose appearance matched the white standard of ideal beauty to address sexually charged topics in her performances. Tucker reasoned: "Take a pretty, sexy-looking girl and let her pull something of [this] sort and it's offensive right away. It's smutty without being funny."[70] However, Tucker felt she could perform such songs "because I was big and gawky, and entirely lacking in what the fashion writer nowadays call 'allure,' I made a song such as that funny but not salacious."[71] Tucker's repertoire of so-called hot songs included "Nobody Loves a Fat Girl but Oh How a Fat Girl Can Love" and "You've Got to See Mama Ev'ry Night." Although she stressed the significance of her weight, it would have been viewed as equally improper for a woman with fair skin to sing about sex in such an unapologetic way. Here again, Tucker took refuge in her connection to blackness. Singing in dialect allowed her to summon enduring stereotypes about oversexed black women, and that helped her to be "funny" without being "smutty" just as much as her weight did.

Applying lessons from her tour of the burlesque circuit in 1909, Tucker continued to infuse her performances with sexual innuendo, again approximating perceptions of oversexed blackness by calling herself a "Red Hot Mama," a name which gained currency in 1924 after the production of *Red Hot Mama*, an all-black musical.[72] Unlike Bessie Smith and Ma Rainey, who mixed the double entendre with explicit references to sex, death, domestic violence, and alcoholism, Tucker sang more playfully about sex in veiled terms. She used the double entendre to convey suggestive messages about sex because it allowed her to evade the most scathing moral criticisms, helping her maintain some semblance of white feminine purity even as she approximated erotic blackness. The double entendre also let her suggest that if audiences read sex into her songs, it was not her fault. For instance, while performing with The Gay Masqueraders in Chicago, Tucker playfully warned her audience that she might "sing songs that could be 'taken another way,' to which the audience responded 'sing'em.'"[73] Just as she selectively played up her whiteness, Jewishness, and approximations of blackness, in different contexts, Tucker also emphasized or downplayed the risqué side of her songs through calculated inflection, pauses, laughter, winking, and dancing.

In November 1910, Tucker's penchant for singing hot songs landed her in the national spotlight after she was abruptly dropped from a bill when a city official objected to her "immoral" act.[74] Given the controversy, even Tucker felt the need to justify her use of hot songs.[75] In the face of criticism, she asserted: "I've never sung a single song in my whole life on purpose to shock anyone. My 'hot numbers,'" are all written "around something that is real in the lives of millions of people." She concluded,

"I insist, it's not dirty. My hot numbers...are all moral." Emphasizing a critical distinction, Tucker asserted, "They have to do with sex, but *not* with vice."[76] Although she insisted on this difference, Tucker never claimed her work was art, as Eltinge and Brown both did. By singing hot songs in dialect and calling herself a "red hot mama," Tucker transformed herself from the respectable white young lady to the oversexed, black woman. While Eltinge also relied on the perception that he was an artist, Tucker, Brown, Tanguay and Eltinge's gender bending could be excused and made more comprehensible through the lens of race.

Just as costumes were critical components in the visual negotiation of gender, race, class, and sexuality for all vaudevillians, as Tucker's career continued to pick up steam and she moved further into the Jazz Age, she continued to change her costumes. Published in 1908, one of the known first reviews of Tucker's blackface performances described Tucker as "wearing a gown typical of the dressed-up colored woman, which perhaps it might be better, in these times of 'swell' dressing, to

Figure 16. Sophie Tucker in hat and fur, c. 1920. (Billy Rose Theatre Division; New York Public Library for the Performing Arts; Astor, Lenox, and Tilden Foundations, Digital ID: nypl_the_4107).

improve."[77] Although she continued to speak in dialect even after she stopped performing in blackface, Tucker eventually made noticeable changes to her wardrobe; clothes and costumes helped established her wealth and decadence. Critics observed, "there is no woman in vaudeville who wears better clothes. Her evening gowns, luxurious fur wraps and exquisite jewels, appeal to the eye as her songs appeal to the ear."[78] Starting in the early 1920s, Tucker generously adorned herself in furs and jewels on and off stage, and her ostentatious collection caught the attention of on-lookers everywhere she went (see Figure 16).

In a lengthy review of Tucker's 1926 performance at London's popular "Harlemesque" Kit Kat Club, Pierre Van Paassen observed that she was "seen everywhere around London, always wearing the most amazing gowns with a barbaric display of jewels."[79] Van Passen's use of the word barbaric was not incidental; it suggested Tucker's violation of feminine modesty and transgression of civilized standards of dress. Tucker's costumes evoked comparisons with Ma Rainey, a fellow OKeh artist and a large bodied, deep-voiced, unapologetically sexual, blues-singing black woman. Ma "Goldneck" Rainey acquired her nickname from the large gold necklace she sported, from which five, ten, and twenty dollar gold pieces dangled around her neck. As a large black woman, Ma Rainey's glamorous costumes also challenged the image of the unattractive, masculine Mammy. As women who came from working-class backgrounds, the immodest styles Tucker and Rainey wore insisted on their visibility and their ability to indulge in such luxuries signified their financial independence. Just as Tanguay wore her penny dress, Tucker, and Rainey literally wore their disdain for white middle-class feminine modesty.

ENDING BLACKFACE, SELLING BLACKNESS

Though Tucker was one of a few white women who painted her face black on stage, from minstrelsy through vaudeville and musical comedies, many black and white men regularly wore the mask to visually signal the performance of blackness to their audiences. However, this trend did not last forever. Historians disagree in dating the demise of blackface performance, but most place its decline in the 1930s. But, as Tucker's career demonstrates, blackface performance practices and styles were not abandoned, but slowly integrated into other types of stage performance, namely vaudeville, burlesque, and in films such as *The Jazz Singer* (1927).[80] We can, nonetheless, identify moments when it became clear that many Americans, particularly black Americans, were no longer interested in coon shouting and blackface acts. Just as big-time vaudeville managers excluded performers using the word "pansy" in their acts, they also began to exclude coon shouters from their bills, demanding performers omit terms such as "chocolate" and "coon."[81]

Though never praised for having a beautiful white complexion, Tucker did eventually "leave off the black," and, at least in her mind, her departure from blackface marked a critical juncture in her career. She recalled that in 1912 (though others suggest it was closer to 1909), her career in blackface ended abruptly, when her costume trunk failed to arrive on time for a matinee performance, forcing her to perform without any makeup in her own clothing.[2] Tucker remembered, "I had never yet walked out on stage without some sort of disguise." Although she claimed to hate performing in blackface, she later recalled, "it was the hardest thing in the world for me to step out of the wings" of the stage "with no covering on my blonde hair, and no make-up." She added, being "in tights and a G-string I wouldn't have felt more stripped."[83] Because the audience expected a blackface performer, Tucker made an impromptu announcement, which began in dialect and quickly transformed into standard English: "You-all can see I'm a white girl. Well, I'll tell you something more: I'm not Southern" she said, continuing, "I'm a Jewish girl, and I just learned this Southern accent doing a blackface act for two years."[84] Instead of omitting her use of dialect for the remainder of her performance, Tucker kept the rest of her act the same and achieved more success than ever. Although her figure and face would never be considered conventionally beautiful, Tucker demonstrated to theater managers that she could please an audience without wearing the burnt cork mask. From that point on, she claimed she was subsequently allowed to perform as herself.[85]

Tucker faced the problem of getting audiences accustomed to hearing the same sound from a newly whitened face. At her first performance in Chicago, she claimed to involve the audience in this transition by asking them "if they wanted her to appear in blackface, and they shouted for her to 'stay white.'" Tucker then "launched into the rage 'Naughty Eyes' while the audience cheered and stamped their feet in approval. When she sang 'I Want Someone to Call Me Dearie,' each pause, each exaggerated phrase brought whistles and appreciative groans."[86] If blackface denied her femininity, Tucker likely felt buoyed by this new mandate to "stay white." Although she probably felt it affirmed her femininity, her audiences' preference suggests that Tucker's appeal increasingly resulted from her ability to provide a sensationally incongruous blend of white face and black sound.

In the performances following Tucker's first appearance without blackface, critics continued to pick up on the racial implications of her style. "She is up there among the firsts telling the story of the black, black wench who couldn't help lovin' that yaller coon, and telling it to that ever lovin' moke, just a pleadin' an' a beggin,' so that the picture is there, and you are seeing and hearing the whole business." Again, describing her sound in explicitly racial terms, critics applauded her ability to sing with "Ethiopian volume."[87] Critics continued to respond to her work in this way, even as they recognized the change in Tucker's stage appearance: "Miss Tucker has taken her wench out of the black Darktown Conservatory, and slapped her on the boards just as she belongs."[88] These responses indicated to Tucker that she was wise not just to parody blackness, like other blackface performers, but to sound black while remaining visibly white. To the surprise of vaudeville managers like Chris Brown and Tony Pastor, the favorable response to Tucker's new hybridized character, who sounded black, but looked white, revealed that Tucker was more appealing out of blackface. Instead of creating an instant metamorphosis from black to white, as Tucker had done when she removed her black glove at the end of a performance, her act now focused on the continuously clashing incompatibility of her voice and complexion.

For Tucker, no newfound scruples about the racially demeaning aspects of her act stopped her from performing in blackface and calling herself a coon shouter. Reflecting on the first decade of her career, Tucker told the press, "The first thing I dropped was coon shouting" adding, "everybody imitated it and killed it. My departure from that method was sheerly good business. I used it until it was no longer distinctively Sophie Tucker's."[89] In reality, Tucker's transition from coon shouter to jazz singer and blackface to bareface performer was much less definitive. Even after the incident when her trunk failed to arrive ten years earlier, supposedly ending her career as a blackface performer, Tucker continued to perform in both black and white, alternating acts between evening and matinee performances. In the same day, she played a white woman in a scripted musical comedy and appeared in blackface in intermediate acts, allowing stagehands to change the curtained set behind her.[90]

After supposedly having "gotten away from it," in 1917 Tucker sang "The Darktown Strutters' Ball," written by black composer Shelton Brooks. Despite the fact that she had not recently performed in blackface and claimed no longer to be a coon shouter, but a rag timer, critic Walter Anthony of the *San Francisco Chronicle* wrote: "The popularity of Sophie Tucker is perennial. It follows her like dialect follows the 'coon shouter,' nor do the years seem to affect the hold she has on her audiences." Anthony continued, "Her manipulation of her lyrical material is graced as ever with an equal amount of energy involved in digging a sewer, into which most of her verse might be consigned." But audiences liked Tucker "and her Jazz band's antics—descendants straight from the hysteria of a Georgia camp meeting in Darktown—remain a gigantic hit."[91]

At this time, Tucker had begun performing with five young white male musicians she called her "Five Kings of Syncopation" (see Figure 17). Although her "Kings of Syncopation" were white unlike Brown's "Jazzbo Syncopators," this critic's description of the performers as "hysteric" "descendants" of "Darktown" makes clear the racial reception of the group's performance style.

Responding to the newfound popularity of jazz, in 1919, Tucker began marketing herself as a jazz singer, but told the press "I've been doing this sort of thing for 14 years but it's only the last two years that people got so crazy about it." She concluded, "Jazz is just the old darkey [sic] folk songs sung a little faster. They used to have jazz on the plantations before there was such a thing as a cabaret in America and before that they sang jazz in Africa."[92] Tucker credited black musicians as stylistic innovators of jazz, yet saw herself as the natural vehicle for black expression. Even out of blackface, she offered white audiences the same joyful, cathartic experience they felt while laughing at the blackface minstrel burlesquing the travails of Uncle Tom and Mammy. Both Tucker and minstrel players provided the familiar "darkey" sound audiences enjoyed.

After 1919, Tucker continued to modify her musical style to anticipate new trends, changing her billing with each adaptation. She opened "The Sophie Tucker Room" in Reisenweber's New York City cabaret and once again reinvented herself, demonstrating her power by firing all five "kings of syncopation." To replace the all-male, white musicians, she hired a new "jazz band—comprising a pianist, clarinetist, coronetist, drummer and violinist." In an even more decisive move, Tucker "hired three young Negro women to back her on a number of songs and perform several dance routines of their own." While Tucker sang "Ev'rybody Shimmies Now," these women performed the sexually suggestive dance.[93] To publicize Tucker's new act, Reisenweber's advertisements called her the "Queen of Jazz." Not coincidentally, during the Harlem Renaissance, Tucker chose black women's bodies and voices to infuse new life and sensuality into her career.[94] In the mid-1920s, Tucker

Figure 17. "Ev'rybody Shimmies Now" Sheet Music. Sophie Tucker pictured with her Five Kings of Syncopation, 1918. (Author's Personal Collection).

made this transition complete when she began performing with an all-black band. While black newspapers reported that she performed to standing room only audiences in Manchester, Glasgow, Dublin, and Belfast, a "12-piece band composed of Race musicians" accompanied her.[95] Now a recognizable name and face, returning permanently to blackface would only have provided an outdated parody of blackness. In the 1920s, she needed to compete with white audiences' fascination with black "Empresses," "Mothers," and "Queens" of the blues, who sold thousands of phonograph records and garnered extensive publicity from both the white and black press.

If Tucker feared displacement by black female singers, her anxiety was not unfounded. In 1920, less than one year before Lillyn Brown recorded four songs for the Emerson label, blues innovator, songwriter, and music entrepreneur, Perry Bradford, first introduced OKeh Records to African American blues singer Mamie Smith. Bradford succeeded in convincing OKeh records of the profits black singers could generate, suggesting that Smith replace Tucker in a recording session.[96] Three years after the unprecedented success of Smith's hit "Crazy Blues," OKeh records apprised its distributors of "the growing tendency on the part of white people to hear their favorite 'blues' sung or played by famous colored 'blues' artists."[97] In the "Negro Vogue" of the Harlem Renaissance, managers, storeowners, and white artists like Tucker realized that white listeners preferred the patented black experience and black listeners were eager to patronize "race artists."

The warning OKeh issued its distributors in 1923 was not ignored. One year after Tucker's record label advised sellers about the increasing importance of the color of sound, she expanded her cadre of young black dancers from three to eleven.[98] Later that spring, Tucker included "a Negro dancer negotiating recent jazz numbers."[99] Interestingly, she introduced "My Yiddishe Mama" while performing with these new dancers, illustrating her penchant for blending multiple, seemingly incongruent, identities within one performance.

HEARING RACE AND GENDER

Despite Tucker's eventual casting off of the blackface mask and the decline of coon shouting, she continued to suggest her blackness by employing the Southern dialect she had polished during the first two years of her career. This affected accent had a particular kind of appeal. According to Robert Dawidoff, to a white working-class audience, "black speech seemed scary and strange and funny to whites, even during the twenties, like immigrant speech, like city speech, exotic."[100] "The singing of black music, using black intonation and wording," he continued, "was a matter of inflection, like learning a foreign language, or, better, learning a new style, putting on company manners."[101] Because Tucker's appeal lay in the incongruity between her appearance and her black sound, Tucker's career depended upon her ability to put on this black speech, a phenomenon Susan Gubar calls "racial ventriloquism."[102]

Because 90 percent of black Americans lived in the South until 1915, "even on its own, the southern drawl, performed with a relaxed larynx and a predominance of lazily articulated consonants and elongated vowel sounds, sometimes functioned as a marker for blackness."[103] To the white Northern ear, Tucker apparently mastered this definitively black Southern sound. Tucker was not alone in her attempt to put on black speech. Fanny Brice, another Jewish singer/comedienne who started her career as a coon shouter, even claimed that her residency in Harlem helped her nail down "proper" black speech.[104] Other Jewish performers like Al Jolson also conspicuously integrated the two most obvious characteristics of Negro dialect into their speech: dropping the "final-G" (as in "goin' to town) and the deliberate substitution of "aren't" with "ain't."[105] In reviews of Tucker's work, critics rarely failed to pick up on these racially-coded linguistic aspects of her performances. One noted, "There is little better in vaudeville than Sophie Tucker's broad A's and silent R's" while another critic suggested that Tucker sang in "reverse English."[106]

It is not incidental that Tucker, Brice, and Jolson were all Jewish. In the 1920s and 1930s, as Jewish Americans increasingly began to see the world in terms of black and white and their own whiteness depended on their willingness to adapt to existing racial norms, they began to differentiate themselves further from African Americans.[107] Nonetheless, Tucker continued to cultivate a black sound and hope audiences mistook her for black at the same time that other Jews became increasingly uncomfortable with any associations of blackness. Some even began to rely on scientific scholarship to insist there was no "link between Africa and the Semitic past."[108] For example, in 1911, a Jewish American archeologist "stormed out of the Universal Races Congress in London when he learned that the Jews were to be grouped with the African and Asiatic races in the congress's ceremonies."[109] Yet, at this time, Tucker drew more deeply than ever on her connection to blackness on the stage.[110]

Tucker was not the only fair-skinned female performer in the Jazz Age who audiences believed genuinely sounded black. Connie, Helvetia, and Martha Boswell were also widely perceived as sounding black.[111] Because artists like the Boswell sisters and Tucker were products of a culture deeply invested in an audible sense of race, they, too, "understood their own music in terms of racialized sound and sonic difference, if not always buying into the concept."[112] As both black and white female Southern blues singers became popular in the 1920s, more Northern white audiences heard authentic Southern accents in popular music. Though early race records were initially marketed towards black consumers, months after Mamie Smith released "Crazy Blues" in 1920, phonograph companies began marketing them directly to white audiences. In 1921, an OKeh advertisement published by *Talking Machine World* claimed that sales of recordings made by an African American group called the Norfolk Jazz Quartette far exceeded expectations and "it isn't the colored race which is responsible for this jump in record sales. The big demand comes from the white people."[113]

Unlike the svelte, Southern Boswell sisters, Tucker's performances borrowed more heavily from the traditions of white male minstrels, who incorporated humorous female impersonations done in blackface in their performances. Tucker also differed from the Boswells in that she attempted to court black and white audiences, something reviews published by critics in black newspapers reveal. Her ownership of whiteness, Jewishness, and blackness lay in her own stylistic ambiguity. Tucker's manipulation of perceptions of her race allowed her to transition almost seamlessly into other genres when coon songs became outdated in the early twenties. She maintained her popularity and relevance when nearly all other coon singers fell by the wayside by moving from coon shouting and ragtime, to blues and jazz race records. Tucker blended these multiple identities in a way that distinguished her from her peers and predecessors, ultimately refusing to restrict herself to any single stylistic or racial category. As Laurie Stras has argued about the Boswell sisters, with Tucker "it was almost impossible to tell where whiteness ended and blackness began."[114]

After she stopped using the burnt cork mask during her live performances, the phonograph and the radio enabled Tucker to reach larger audiences. However, these technological innovations produced a new "visual indeterminacy" about her race at the same time the black/white racial divide became increasingly color-oriented.[115] As Matthew Guterl, David Roediger, Matthew Frye Jacobson, and others have explained, based on visual cues, Americans began to assign everyone to one of two racial categories—black or white.[116] Though once foreign interlopers, Southern and Eastern European immigrants—including Jewish immigrants like Tucker—became white, while those with even "one drop" of so-called black blood stayed black. But as the growth of race records indicates, there was clearly an intersecting aural dimension to understandings of race, which was further intersected by gender as well.

Tucker both benefited from and consciously capitalized on aural confusion about her race and gender. Her partnership with OKeh records, a leading producer of race records, and the company that released Mamie Smith's surprisingly popular "Crazy Blues," enhanced her ability to create music that seemed both black and white. But for some listeners, Tucker's race could be a source of genuine confusion. Technological innovations took away what were thought to be reliable visual signifiers of gender and race, such as complexion, clothing, and hair, leaving listeners to discern them solely by sound. Phonograph periodicals and advertisements from the 1920s generally helped audiences identify the race of artists by segregating music into the hillbilly music of white artists and the race records of black artists. However, on occasion, black newspapers advertised Tucker's music as race records, alongside that of well-known black artists Alberta Hunter, Bessie Smith, Charlie Jackson, and Ethel Waters. Thus, written advertisements for phonograph records could also be misleading indicators of Tucker's race, further contributing to racial confusion.[117] When label executives chose to market Tucker's music as race records, they consciously contributed to confusion over her race at the same time most Americans were grasping for a consistent, coherent way of understanding race.

Though they enjoyed the sponsorship of white benefactors during the Harlem Renaissance in the 1920s, with the onset of the Great Depression, black singers, artists, writers, and actors lost access to record contracts, publishing firms, and Broadway roles. Yet, even in the 1930s, the importance of sounding black for Tucker endured. In her autobiography, Tucker boasted of an instance of collective racial and gender confusion caused by the incongruity between her sound and sight. For her first performance in Holland around 1934, she expected Dutch audiences would not understand her or be familiar with her music because, "outside of a very few people who may have seen me in London, and those who know my phonograph records, nobody in Holland knows who I am or what I can do." When she received a standing ovation, however, Tucker asked the manager for an explanation. The manager responded: "If you could understand Dutch, you would have heard the words the entire audience let out in one gasp at your entrance: 'My God! She's a white woman!'" Tucker identified her ambiguously raced and gendered voice as the cause of confusion, concluding: "the Dutch thought from my phonograph records and my syncopation and deep voice that I was a colored star." She further claimed that Dutch shopkeepers advertised her as an "American Negro Singer."[118]

By her own recollection, Tucker suggested Dutch audiences would not have found her performances worthy of a standing ovation if she had, as expected, turned out to be Negro. Without the addition of her first name, they might also have been surprised that she was a woman because her voice was so deep. Rather than her performance per se, their shock over the incongruence between her sound and sight prompted them to applaud her enthusiastically. The same shock and incongruence awaited Eltinge in Germany and Brown in Berlin when both allegedly fooled theatergoers unfamiliar with their fame into believing they were the gender they impersonated.[119]

This kind of confusion was not accidental and it is revealing that Tucker boasted of it in her autobiography, which, like her vaudeville routines, also contained its own performative, self-promoting elements. Whether or not this incident ever really happened, by including it in her autobiography, Tucker wanted to assure her ability to be remembered for inciting racial confusion of international proportions.

Further evidence suggests that some phonograph and radio listeners genuinely believed Tucker was black even in the late 1930s. In 1937, after Tucker had made dozens of phonograph recordings, *The Chicago Defender* published an article entitled, "I Thought you Were a Negro; Luise Rainer to Sophie Tucker." Rainer, a Viennese screen and stage star "created a flurry" when introduced to Tucker because she remarked, "I've heard you on the phonograph, but I thought you were a Negro." As if to explain the confusion, *The Defender* subsequently described Tucker as a "well-known blues artist who is a friend to the actual profession and has appeared on many benefits side by side with race artists." *The Defender* noted that Tucker "took the remark as more or less a joke."[120]

Tucker's light-hearted reaction and *The Defender's* observation that she was not insulted by the racial mix-up suggested that, if made to the wrong kind of fair-skinned woman, Rainer's comment would have caused much more than a "flurry." Luckily for Rainer, Tucker had no anxiety about her aural racial ambiguity. Most likely, she took the comment as a compliment and boon to her career, for she had long tried to "sound black." *The Defender* believed that, unlike most white women, Tucker did not consider being mistaken for black insulting and her friendly response probably encouraged the paper to represent Tucker favorably in the future.[121]

While aural confusion over her race led audiences to assume Tucker's voice belonged to a black body, at other moments in her career the sound of her voice led to confusion over her gender. Tucker's deep voice became such a central part of her public persona that, when Jews were largely absorbed in the white half of the black/white racial binary late in her career, in 1957, she burlesqued perceptions about her own manliness when she appeared on the popular television show, *What's My Line?* Tucker starred as a mystery celebrity guest whom blindfolded panelists attempted to identify by her voice, taking turns asking her "Yes" or "No" questions. Tucker answered the first question, bellowing "NOOOO" in her trademark deep voice, leading the next panelist to confidently ask if she "would be considered a leading man?" At this question, the knowing audience burst into laughter. When another panelist finally asked "are we certain that you are male?" Tucker again used her husky voice to answer "NOOOO," causing the next blindfolded contestant to exclaim, "This is the most robust female we've ever had on the show!" to which Tucker enthusiastically nodded her head in response. To the question, "Are you a singer?" Tucker bellowed, "YES" and the contestant responded "A bass!" In disbelief, yet another skeptical panelist asked: "Now wait a minute—is somebody answering for our guest?" When told no, the panelist suggested that one female could not have such a powerful voice, asking, "Are you a group?" After the audience stifled its laughter and Tucker again answered "NO," the panelist objected, "You can't tell me that's a girl."

Tucker's appearance on *What's My Line?* suggests that, even late in her career, she cultivated a manly sound, deliberately lowering her voice when answering the contestants' questions. This was the same deep sound that had long been associated with blackness. When the white female panelist protested, "You can't tell me that's a girl," what she implied was "You can't tell me that's a *white* girl." The elated response of surprised Dutch audiences, Luise Rainer's confusion over Tucker's race, and Tucker's appearance on *What's My Line?* each represents critical moments of gender and racial confusion in Tucker's career. These three incidents replayed an old scenario for Tucker, one which recreated the distance—mediated by the costume, blackface mask, and the stage—between the audience and the performer. Such incidents demonstrate that Tucker used sound to confuse and disrupt visually-based racial and gender binaries. Like many vaudevillians who kept audiences guessing about their identities, the confusion she created was the pivot around which her performances turned.

BENDING AND BORROWING BLACKNESS

As her career progressed, Tucker continued to rely on the same prominent black male songwriters and musicians employed by black female blues singers. In fact, she used the very same songwriters as Alberta Hunter, Mamie Smith, Bessie Smith, and Ethel Waters. Black audiences knew this because black newspapers prominently publicized the mainstream successes of black lyricists and composers. For example, Jo Jordon, Noble Sissle (co-creator of *Shuffle Along*), Shelton Brooks, Maceo Pinkard, and Andy Razaf received coverage in the black press for writing songs used by Tucker. *The Baltimore Afro-American* went so far as to refer to Tucker as one of Razaf's "pupils."[122]

In 1916, Tucker called attention to the talents of these songwriters and insisted on "giving credit where credit is due."[123] This fairness distinguished Tucker from less modest performers like Tanguay and drew attention to the fact that she sang the songs of several young black and Jewish songwriters, such as Shelton Brooks and Irving Berlin. Although she billed herself as a coon shouter, *The Chicago Defender* advertised Tucker's performances because she provided advertisement revenue and excellent exposure for Chicago's black composers and lyricists. Tucker had every reason to use black songwriters because her patronage unwhitened her music for black audiences wishing to support black artists. Simultaneously, it exoticized her music for white audiences preferring the so-called authentic sound of black artists.

As Tucker's fame grew, the color of her lyrics became an issue of great importance to black listeners and readers. In 1934, *The Chicago Defender* printed a reader's question about who wrote Tucker's most famous song: "'I saw in a white newspaper that 'Some of These Days' was written by a white man. Is this true?'"[124] The question highlighted the importance of the color of Tucker's music. The *Defender's* answer both distanced Tucker from the song's creation and allied her with its unprecedented success.[125] While it was important for the black press to give credit where it was due, Tucker relied on her associations with black composers to cultivate a convincingly black sound.

Emphasizing the way in which she bent gender norms for Jewish women, Mark Slobin has argued that because she "closely followed the path of male Jewish colleagues" Tucker had "few female counterparts."[126] Yet in many ways, Tucker's career had more in common with black female performers like Ethel Waters and Alberta Hunter than with other Jewish performers or white women. Although Hunter, one of Tucker's most prominent Jazz Age contemporaries, began her career in the 1920s and 1930s, their careers followed eerily similar trajectories: both signed and recorded race records with the OKeh label (Tucker in 1922 and Hunter three years later) and both sang many of the same songs written by the same black composers, each interspersing these songs with idiosyncratic conversational interludes. Both were darlings of the city of Chicago who also took their careers abroad, performing simultaneously in England in 1936. Hunter and Tucker were also among the first to break the taboo of mixing black and white men and women on stage; Tucker employed black male musicians to back her on stage, while Hunter claimed to be the first black woman backed by white male musicians.

Given evidence that Tucker tried to take singing lessons from Hunter, the similarities between their careers and vocal stylings seem like more than coincidence. In 1978, Hunter told the *New Amsterdam News*, "Sophie wanted me to teach her some blues, but I wasn't about to teach her *anything*."[127] As a savvy businesswoman, Hunter must have been well aware that Tucker had been cultivating a black sound for years and was her competition in an environment prizing authenticity and originality. Although it likely pleased Tucker, it must have been all the more irksome to Hunter, then, when *The Chicago Defender* called Hunter "The Harlem Sophie Tucker."[128] In her autobiography, published in 1951, Ethel Waters made claims similar to Hunter, recalling that in 1918, Tucker "came several times to catch my act" and that Tucker even "paid me a little money to come to her hotel suite and sing there for her privately. She explained that she wanted to study my style of delivery."[129]

Tucker's early protestations that her work was natural and she had no musical training belie the fact that she clearly worked hard to perfect her performances of blackness, developing a Southern accent, taking voice lessons from black women, and gaining weight when critics bemoaned her supposedly unnatural look. Though she behaved like an artist, going through significant work to prepare for her performances, her approximations of blackness depended on her hiding the work she put into making them seem real. If she was perceived as an artist, Tucker would not have been able to claim her performances were natural manifestations of her own inner blackness. By insisting that she was *not* an artist, then, Tucker was highly distinct from gender impersonators who argued their work was not natural at all.

Tucker's maid, a black woman named Mollie Elkins, provided her with an entrée into the community of black artists. Tucker called Elkins one of her closest friends and most trusted allies and, as Lori Harrison-Kahan has recently noted, Elkins played a prominent role in Tucker's career, providing her with a direct connection to other black artists.[130]

Tucker admitted that, through Elkins's intervention, she discovered the song "Some of These Days," which later propelled her into international fame. Written by then unknown black songwriter Shelton Brooks, "Some of These Days" came to Tucker's attention at the insistence of Elkins. Tucker recalled Elkins chastising her: "Since when are you so important you can't hear a song by a colored writer?" *The Baltimore Afro-American* even provided an "Afro artist's illustrated conception of the scene," depicting the moment when Tucker, whom the paper referred to as the "Jewish girl with a colored voice," agreed to listen to Shelton Brooks perform his song.[131]

In the three years after Tucker published her autobiography, black periodicals such as *The Baltimore Afro-American*, *The New Journal and Guide*, and *Negro Digest* printed stories attributing Tucker's fame to Elkins's professional and personal guidance.[132] Although such anecdotes position Elkins as Tucker's very own selfless "Mammy," at other times Tucker stressed her own blackness by portraying Elkins as her girlish peer and sister. For example, when Tucker landed a shot to perform at a benefit show, she borrowed "a dress which Mollie had worn for years, her purple slippers, her silk hose. Even her make-up kit, plus a new box of white powder."[133] In 1948, Tucker told *The Baltimore Afro-American* that Mollie was "'a handsome woman,' as light as [Tucker] was and the two of them, she a Jewish girl and Mollie a colored girl, could have passed as... two sisters."[134] Even at this late stage in her career, Tucker continued to confound optical understandings of race by suggesting there were no visual distinctions in complexion between her and Elkins. This conflicted with the impulse many Jews increasingly felt to physically distinguish themselves from African Americans.

Tucker claimed she repaid Elkins's kindness by providing for her once she achieved financial success. Tucker told black newspapers that her maid was like her mother, sister, grandmother, and friend.[135] But Elkins provided more than just friendship; she kept Tucker well-connected with other black artists, offering her access to the backstage rooms of skeptical black stars like Alberta Hunter and the catchy compositions of black composers like Shelton Brooks. This relationship gave Tucker a liaison between the often segregated worlds of white and black artists and helped her make an enduring claim on black kinship.[136]

In different contexts, both black and white critics discussed Tucker in terms of race, and again, the incongruity between her sound and image was key. White papers varied as to whether or not they mentioned her Jewishness, and black-owned papers did so more rarely. One review published in the black press offers particular insight into popular reception of Tucker's race, suggesting her supposed blackness overshadowed her Jewishness. In 1929, the *New York Amsterdam News* published an article comparing Tucker's appearance and so-called primitive vocal style to Nora Holt, a woman of alluring "Creole femininity."

> Mrs. Nora Holt, a blond Creole... has a presence and a manner similar in many ways to those of Sophie Tucker. She has the same mop of curly golden hair, the same perky, good-humored lift of the head, the same appealing, crumpled smile. But her voice is even more astonishing. It can produce sounds not comparable with orthodox singing at all, or indeed any human utterance. They range from the deepest bass to the shrillest piping, and are often unaccompanied by words. This... absolute rhythm, which bursts from Miss Holt's mouth with a primitive ferocity, is singularly effective.[137]

Just as *The Baltimore Afro-American* described Tucker and her black maid as girls who looked like sisters, both the *New York Amsterdam News* and *The London Times* (where the article originally appeared), compared Tucker to "race artist" Nora Holt in both appearance and performance style. Three years before *The Baltimore Afro-American* linked Holt to Tucker, contemporary writers such as Lothrop Stoddard provided support for this comparison arguing that both Negroes and Jews shared "frizzy or wooly hair, thick lips, and prognathous jaws."[138] One physician suggested that Jews had "swarthy" complexions, which signaled their connection to African Americans.[139] Such comparisons would have alarmed most Jews at a time when many sought to distinguish themselves from African Americans. As "creole" figures of purportedly mixed racial heritage, Tucker and Holt's voices and bodies appeared to be—in the words of Issac Goldberg—the product of "musical miscegenation."[140] Likewise, Tucker's manly acts and deep voice mixed incongruously with her glamorous dresses to produce a mixed gender bending figure as well.

Unlike Tucker, who expressed no objection to being identified as a coon shouter or race artist, Anna Held, who was known as the "ivory white," "Ziegfeld girl," chafed at the classification. In 1900, Held told the press: "[coon-singing] is a style of entertainment that is very much misunderstood because it often misleads public opinion as to the true character of the singer."[141] Held's comment demonstrates that audiences made direct connections between the performances they saw on stage and the performers. In addition to the supposed likeness between Tucker and Nora Holt, Held's statement also suggests that audiences understood Tucker as being culturally "Negro" or "Creole." Here, Tucker followed in the footsteps of Tanguay, encouraging interpretations of her racial Otherness despite being a fair-skinned woman.

Although her performances often reinforced black stereotypes, Tucker's stage characters challenged the black-white binary, resisting the association of race with skin color, while emphasizing sound, size, and sexuality as racial and gender determinants. Though she sometimes sang in Yiddish and occasionally referred to herself as "a Jewish girl," Tucker drew attention away from her Jewishness when she felt inclined to do so, while emphasizing it at advantageous moments. Adept at self-marketing, Tucker knew how to offer audiences a performer they could relate to. While she sometimes told the press she was born in Russia, when speaking with *The Boston Daily Globe*, she allegedly claimed to have been born in Boston.[142] She began singing "My Yiddish Momma" in 1925 and did it when she anticipated a large Jewish constituency in her audience. Tucker claimed to study her audience before each performance, helping her determine when it was most advantageous to sing a song in Yiddish or dialect, or the style of blues or jazz. Such actions ingratiated her with her audience and helped her remain a racially flexible performer.[143]

Several scholars have discussed the implications of immigrant performers—particularly Jews—coon shouting, blacking up, and speaking in dialect. Pamela Brown Lavitt has argued that "coon songs and cakewalking were Anna Held's beauty secrets." According to Lavitt, "subtending references to blackness did not stain her complexion nor taint her celebrity; rather, undeclared 'black' images prettied and anglicized both."[144] Likewise, Lavitt claims Tucker's "mix of racial disguise and dialect humor" confirmed her "'bonafide' whiteness" and "laid bare her *white* Jewishness."[145] In *Blackface, White Noise* Michael Rogin makes a similar argument about male Jewish performers like Al Jolson and Eddie Cantor becoming white men off stage by applying the blackface mask on stage.[146] Rogin also acknowledges an aural dimension to this process, but he argues that through song, Jews became white and "music was the melting pot's instrument."[147]

Yet a close analysis of Tucker's career demonstrates that blackface and dialect did not provide an unambiguous passage to white femininity. Tucker used blackface in the first decade of the twentieth century when Jews were more comfortably considered white and she had less reason to insist on her whiteness. It was not until the 1920s and 1930s, when Tucker dropped the blackface mask and continued to cultivate a black sound, that American Jews' hold on whiteness seemed to loosen.[148] In the aftermath of the Red Scare following World War I, the association many Americans made between Jews and communism, and the Ku Klux Klan's new focus on Jews and Catholics, Jewish identity became increasingly contested.[149]

Tucker's performances, then, did not simply mask her Jewish Otherness by poking fun at the more marginal black Other. Rather, the aural elements of her performances positioned her as a figure simultaneously exuding blackness, Jewishness, manliness, and femininity. Though she was not entirely comfortable with visually representing blackness, because authenticity was often synonymous with blackness in the Jazz Age, Tucker continuously sought to augment perceptions of her authenticity through black sound early and often. Just as it did for Tanguay, Tucker's commercial success gave her access to many of the privileges of white manhood, including impressive financial resources and a powerful public voice. However, coon songs, dialect, jazz, and blues music did not make Tucker white, just as embodying a manly persona did not make her appear more feminine. Rather, they fashioned her into a creole figure. Tucker became a unique emblem of gender and racial hybridity—the "Jewish girl with a colored voice."[150]

CONCLUSION

By the early 1930s, when vaudeville was all but dead, Tucker had made only a few feature length films, and she was performing live in front of smaller and smaller audiences in nightclubs and cabarets. The phonograph and radio proved important instruments in sustaining her career, allowing listeners to imagine the disembodied voice they heard belonging to a black body. Though she was one of the most successful, Tucker was not the only woman whom fans found difficult to categorize within the hardening racial binary. On the radio, Mildred Bailey, another fair-skinned blues singer whose mother was Native American, was mistaken for a black woman, as were the three white Boswell sisters from New Orleans.[151] Conversely, black male impersonator Brown, who incorporated syncopation and dialect in her songs and thus "sang black," could supposedly pass for a white woman in person. Like many vaudevillians that kept audiences guessing about their true identities, the confusion such performers created lay at the heart of their appeal.

When teased apart, visual and aural performances of gender and race complicate the standard narrative of the cultural work performed in blackface and dialect. These performances did not always clearly separate the vehicle of blackness (in this case, Tucker) from the lingering idea of racial Otherness. Unlike her male Jewish contemporaries, such as Eddie Cantor and Al Jolson, Tucker did not abandon blackness when she dropped the burnt cork mask. Instead, she surrounded herself with black musicians, dancers, singers, composers, and lyricists in an effort to complicate and camouflage her own whiteness. She continued to embrace confusion over her gender and race, as her deep voice and big body simultaneously linked her to blackness and manliness. Like Tanguay, her performances provided audiences with a small space in which to resist the rules dictating how fair-skinned women should sound, look, and act in the new century.

EPILOGUE

"Ever since a certain sad day in 1932, when the dusty, faded curtain of the Palace was rung down for the last time, a refrain has gone across the land from the fabled corner of Forty-seventh Street and Broadway: 'Vaudeville is dead.'"

—Karl Schriftgiesser, *The New York Times Magazine,* Apr 19, 1942

In the late 1920s, vaudeville performers struggled to continue engaging their audiences and failed to maintain their exorbitant salaries. Their decline was a precipitous and unpleasant one. By 1928, Eva Tanguay was earning just 15 percent of the salary she earned in 1911.[1] The rise of the motion picture industry contributed enormously to the demise of the vaudeville theater and the performers who gained their fame and fortune before its footlights. Beginning in the mid-1920s, many vaudeville houses began shortening their performance bills, which had previously included between six and ten separate acts, reducing them slowly and even replacing them with short films.[2] Eventually, many of these houses closed for renovations and reopened as movie theaters. By 1929, the Great Depression depleted the disposable income of most working- and middle-class Americans, as well as the fortunes of many of its performers, helping to seal the fate of vaudeville.

Other, less tangible, changes affected the careers of race and gender benders like Tanguay, Eltinge, Brown, and Tucker. Historians George Chauncey and Carroll Smith-Rosenberg have convincingly argued that in the 1930s, a rigidly defined hetero-social culture solidified, which precluded women from forming intimate relationships with other women and men with other men. Chauncey, in particular, argues that this revulsion against "gay life" and its "excesses" was a response to new gender crises linked to the Great Depression, and later, World War II.[3] By then, the strenuous life and sedentary life were no longer a convincing way to distinguish gender. Instead, men and women would increasingly define themselves as normal based on their sexual desire and conquest of the opposite sex. These gendered and sexual crises manifested themselves in the careers of vaudeville's race and gender benders in the mid-1930s, when Brown temporarily retired, after being harassed into revealing her "true" gender early in her act. They peaked by 1940, when new laws against transvestism forbade Eltinge from wearing dresses. Though Brown reprised her male impersonations in the 1950s, Eltinge descended into alcoholic oblivion and died in 1941, clearly a victim of the revulsion against gender transgression. As Sharon Ullman puts it, "the popular joys of 1912 had become the criminal perversions of 1940."[4]

The intense craze over primitivism also ended in the 1930s. Many cabarets closed and, with the end of the Harlem Renaissance, black performers and writers were once again shut out from mainstream media. Once a wealthy wild girl, Tanguay lost her fortune in the stock market crash of 1929. Her luck reversed itself so fully that in the 1940s she wrote to automobile magnate Henry Ford begging him to give her a car she could not afford to buy herself.[5] She had to rely on her formal rival, Tucker, to pay for the surgery she needed to remove the cataracts that had rendered her blind.[6] With no more pennies to throw away, she died in 1947, destitute and alone, impoverished and infirm. In the 1950s and 1960s, Brown continued performing on Broadway and in neighborhood theatrical productions, while Tucker performed in cabarets and made guest appearances on television shows. By 1970, all four performers were dead.

Of these four figures, today the American public has largely forgotten all but Tucker. Though scholars still write about Tanguay and Eltinge, they do so with an eye aimed almost exclusively at gender, at the exclusion of more complex understandings of the interdependency of gender and race. This study has attempted to recover and unpack these histories, recuperating them from previous analyses that have focused on a single dimension of their performances. In doing so, it sheds light on the inseparability and instability of gender and racial constructs.

As Karl Schriftgiesser explained in 1942 in *The New York Times Magazine*, "There was no radio in the heyday of vaudeville and no motion picture house on the corner. These two upstarts 'killed' vaudeville but it did not kill the spirit."[7] Indeed, as Tanguay predicted in her song "One Hundred Years from Now," vaudeville's race and gender benders have kept us talking, though the conversation has changed. The appeal they held and the spirit they embodied endure. Perhaps the most obvious evidence of their persistence lies in platinum-selling, Grammy-winning, American pop singer, songwriter, and fashionista Lady Gaga. Since her arrival on the national stage of American popular culture in 2008, rumors have persisted that Lady Gaga is, in fact, not a lady at all. In 2010, Gaga engaged these rumors directly, including references to her supposed transgenderism in her music videos.[8] She has also posed for photographers as her male alter ego, Jo Calderone. It is not incidental that, in posing as Calderone, Gaga signifies her manliness with an oversized cigarette and short black hair, in addition to a men's suit. These were, after all, the same cues that performers like Brown used to put across her male impersonations, and they are part of the same strategy Eltinge used to convince audiences he was manly out of his corsets off stage. Although critics never suspected any of the performers in this study were transgender, there are striking parallels between Lady Gaga and Tanguay, in particular. Much like the forty-pound penny dress Tanguay wore in 1909, a century later, Gaga appeared on stage in equally flamboyant and outrageous costumes, most notably appearing at the 2010 MTV Video Music Awards in a dress made of raw meat. Her ensembles often lack pants and, at times, look more like works of architecture than clothing. They strive to inspire in onlookers a mix of disgust and desire.

Her first record-breaking album was entitled *The Fame Monster* and in many ways, Gaga tries neither to be man nor woman, nor even human. Her penchant for posing with her face snarled and her hands twisted into claws, suggests that, like Tanguay, she purposely elicits comparisons to wild animals, speaking directly to the enduring American fascination with other-worldly spectacle. In many ways, like Gaga, some of the most successful and memorable pop culture icons of the late twentieth and early twenty-first century resemble vaudeville's turn-of-the-century race and gender benders. Like the performers examined in this study, more modern icons like David Bowie, Michael Jackson, Grace Jones, Boy George, Madonna, Marilyn Manson, and Prince have built their careers upon their flashy defiance of gender and race-based norms. Like many successful vaudevillians, their performances raise questions about where whiteness and blackness, manliness and femininity, straight and gay, animal and human, begin and end.

Present-day performers reflect the tensions of a post-modern society, where sexuality has perhaps become that most central component of our identities but interest in the fluidity of race and gender has only grown. Of course, current performers wear less clothing and have bigger budgets than their vaudeville predecessors. Their stages are now television sets, websites, and Twitter feeds. Their interactions with audiences are less intimate than those of their vaudeville predecessors, for whom live performance, spontaneity, and physicality were critical. Nonetheless, it is clear that performers like Lady Gaga and Tanguay—even Michael Jackson and Eltinge—suggest striking continuities in the ways American performers appealed to audiences over the last century.

Modern interest in individuals who push at gender and race-based norms has not been limited to singers and dancers. In April of 2015, 20 million Americans watched as the Olympic champion formerly known as Bruce Jenner self-identified as a transgender woman in an exclusive television interview. Roughly two months later, Jenner appeared as a woman on the cover of *Vanity Fair*, donning a corset in a feature story titled, "Call me Caitlyn."[9] Just a few days after Jenner's cover story was published, every major news outlet in the nation began churning out stories about Rachel Dolezal, then President of the Spokane, Washington chapter of the NAACP.[10] Dolezal became newsworthy after her parents publicly alleged that she had altered her appearance to pass as a black woman for nearly a decade. Media outlets have continually displayed "before and after" images documenting the physical transformations of both Jenner and Dolezal. Though the two figures emerged in different contexts and have elicited very different responses, they have captured the nation's attention by appearing to bend and blur the fundamental ways in which many Americans understand identity.[11] Their stories have revitalized heated discussions about identity, authenticity, and the extent to which race and gender are perceived as malleable constructions in the 21st century.

This study has demonstrated the ways in which vaudeville's race and gender benders reflected the specific concerns of turn-of-the-century Americans. These vaudevillians revealed the daily instabilities and contradictions of modern American life. In the face of the tremendous social changes unfolding between 1900 and 1930, racial and gender dichotomies became more fixed. While cultural authorities like Theodore Roosevelt, G. Stanley Hall, Lothrop Stoddard, and Richard von Krafft-Ebing attempted to study and stabilize these hierarchies, vaudevillians sensationalized their fluidity.

Eva Tanguay, Julian Eltinge, Lillyn Brown, and Sophie Tucker enticed millions of Americans because they captured their infatuation with the contradictions, paradoxes, and incongruities that flavored "the modern temper."[12] As Jane and Jim Crow renegotiated access to public space along the color line, women entered the public sphere, prominent sexologists redefined deviance to include close same sex relationships and cultural pundits criticized the emergence of the mannish New Woman and the effeminate man. Vaudeville performers disrupted—in some cases resisted, in others, accelerated—these processes. Women like Tanguay suggested that white women were more primitive and savage than their male counterparts; Tucker demonstrated that one could be both a Jewish girl and possess a "colored voice." Eltinge and Brown illustrated that gender, rather than a fixed essence, was a provocative game available to anyone with a desire to play, and the outcome of that game was largely dependent on perceptions of race. These performers engaged Americans because they represented the incongruity and dissonance they felt daily; they confounded definitions of black and white, man and woman, us and them. Ultimately, they allowed audiences to suspend their assumptions about gender and race, unmooring prevailing systems of logic by creating new gender and racial hybrids.

NOTES

ABBREVIATIONS

BRTC: Billy Rose Theatre Collection (NYPL)
ETP: Eva Tanguay Papers, Benson Ford Research Center (BFRC),
   The Henry Ford (THF), Dearborn, Michigan
HTC: Harvard Theatre Collection, Houghton Library (HL), Harvard University
ICP: International Center of Photography, New York, New York
IJS: Institute of Jazz Studies, Dana Library, Rutgers University, Newark,
   New Jersey
JRDD: Jerome Robbins Dance Division (NYPL)
NYPL: New York Public Library for the Performing Arts, Lincoln Center
RLC: Robinson Locke Collection (NYPL)
STC: Sophie Tucker Collection (NYPL)
TWC: Townshend Walsh Collection (NYPL)

INTRODUCTION

1. Caroline Caffin, *Vaudeville: The Book* (New York: Mitchell Kennerley, 1914), 15, 18.
2. Gillian Rodger, "Male Impersonation on the North American Variety and Vaudeville Stage, 1868–1930." (PhD diss, University of Pittsburgh, 1998), 15.
3. Karen Sotiropoulos notes that only one black act was typically allowed on each evening's bill. Karen Sotiropoulos, *Staging Race: Black Performers in Turn of the Century America* (Cambridge, Mass.: Harvard University Press, 2006), 44.
4. Ann Douglas suggests that at Keith theaters, audiences "were instructed by printed cards and signs to 'avoid the stamping of the feet;' 'the clapping of the hands' was the correct response. 'Talking during the acts' was prohibited, as were smoking, drinking, or 'laughing too loudly.'" In a departure from the policies of minstrel and burlesque houses, at vaudeville shows, women suspected of prostitution were not granted admission. Ann Douglas, *Terrible Honesty: Mongrel Manhattan in the 1920s* (New York: Farrar, Straus and Giroux, 1995), 379.
5. Karl Schriftgiesser, "Rebirth of Vaudeville" *New York Times Magazine*, Apr 19, 1942, 18.
6. Eric Lott, *Love and Theft: Blackface Minstrelsy and the American Working Class* (New York: Oxford University Press, 1993), 18.
7. Many of these houses operated under a centralized booking system, owned and run by the Keith syndicate. For further explanation of the Keith circuit and the distinctions between the "big time" and "small time" circuit, see

M. Alison Kibler, *Rank Ladies: Gender and Cultural Hierarchy in American Vaudeville* (Chapel Hill: University of North Carolina Press: 1999), 18–20 and Sotiropoulos, *Staging Race*, 44.

8. Sophie Tucker, *Some of These Days: The Autobiography of Sophie Tucker* (New York: 1945), 46.

9. For working-class women living in New York City, "theater-going was among the most popular of all amusements, rated the favorite by nearly one-quarter of the women interviewed." Susan A. Glenn, *Female Spectacle: The Theatrical Roots of Modern Feminism* (Cambridge, Mass.: Harvard University Press, 2000), 14. Ann Douglas suggests "educated guesses made at the time as to the proportion of women in the average theater audience ranged from a cautious 50 percent to an excited 80 percent." Both these figures seem high compared with the findings of a contemporary survey, "The Exploitation of Pleasure," which argued that women constituted one-third of the typical vaudeville audience. This study also claimed that 60 percent of vaudeville audiences were working class and 36 percent were clerical workers. Michael Marks Davis, "Exploitation of Pleasure: A Study of Commercial Regions in New York City," (New York: Department of Child Hygiene of the Russell Sage Foundation, 1911).

10. Douglas, *Terrible Honesty*, 380.

11. In the tradition of Gayle Rubin, I understand gender to be a social construction that ascribes value, appearance, and behaviors to biological sex in order to organize and distinguish human bodies. I use the term gender (instead of sex) in this book to reflect the language contemporaries most often used in the early twentieth century. "The Traffic in Women: Notes on the Political Economy of Sex," *Toward an Anthropology of Women,* Rayna Reiter, Ed. (New York: Monthly Review Press, 1975).

12. Sharon R. Ullman, *Sex Seen: The Emergence of Modern Sexuality in America* (Berkeley: University of California Press, 1997), 49.

13. See chap. 5, "The Corking Girls," of Kibler in *Rank Ladies* and chap. 4, "Racialized, Glorified American Girls" of Linda Mizejewski's, *Ziegfeld Girl: Image and Icon in Culture and Cinema* (Durham: Duke University Press, 1999).

14. Douglas, *Terrible Honesty,* 35.

15. Jeffrey Melnick, *A Right to Sing the Blues: African Americans, Jews and American Popular Song* (Cambridge, Mass.: Harvard College, 1999), 180; Barbara Grossman, *Funny Woman: The Life and Times of Fanny Brice (A Midland Book)* (Indianapolis: Indiana University Press, 1992), 115; "Castle Square Will Present a Maggie Mitchell Success This Week," *Boston Sunday Journal,* Jul 19, 1903, 10. For an excellent discussion of vaudeville's female athletes, see chap. 6, "The Upside Down Lady" in Kibler, *Rank Ladies.*

16. John F. Kasson, *Houdini, Tarzan, and the Perfect Man: The White Male Body and the Challenge of Modernity in America* (New York: Hill and Wang, 2001), 11.

17. See chap. 11, "Skyscrapers and Airmindedness," Douglass, *Terrible Honesty.* For more on the cultural changes wrought by the 1920s, see Lynn Dumenil, *The Modern Temper: American Culture and Society in the 1920s* (New York: Hill and Wang, 1995).

18. Melissa Weinbrenner, "Movies, Model-T's and Morality: The Impact of Technology on Standards of Behavior in the Early Twentieth Century," *Journal of American Culture* 44, no. 3 (Jun 2011): 647–659.

19. For more information on the education of New Women in the Progressive Era, see Lynn D. Gordon, *Gender and Higher Education in the Progressive Era* (New Haven: Yale University Press, 1990).

20. Peter G. Filene, *Him/Her/Self: Gender Identities in Modern America* (Baltimore: The Johns Hopkins University Press, 1998), 11.

21. Martha H. Patterson, *Beyond the Gibson Girl: Reimagining the American New Woman, 1895–1915* (Urbana: University of Illinois Press, 2005), 6. See also Hendrik Hartog, *Man and Wife in America: A History* (Cambridge, Mass.: Harvard University Press, 2000), especially chap. 3 on divorce.

22. George Chauncey, "From Sexual Inversion to Homosexuality: The Changing Medical Conceptualization of Female 'Deviance,'" Kathy Peiss and Christina Simmons with Robert A. Padgug, Eds. *Passion and Power: Sexuality in History (A Radical History Review Book)* (Philadelphia: Temple University Press, 1989), 87.

23. George Chauncey, *Gay New York: Gender, Urban Culture, and the Making of the Gay Male World, 1890–1940* (New York: Basic Books, 1994), 48.

24. Most argued that sexual inversion was much broader than homosexuality; being homosexual meant sexually desiring the same sex, while sexual inversion meant adopting the behaviors, personality and clothing of the opposite sex. Chauncey, "From Sexual Inversion to Homosexuality," *Passion and Power*, 90.

25. Chauncey, *Gay New York*, 297–298.

26. For a discussion of the relationship between public fascination with gender impersonators like Eltinge and the persecution of men who cross-dressed off stage, see Ullman, *Sex Seen*, 60–71.

27. Marjorie Garber, *Vested Interests: Cross-dressing and Cultural Anxiety* (New York: Routledge, 1992), 27.

28. Carroll Smith-Rosenberg, "Discourses of Sexuality and Subjectivity: The New Woman," Martin Baumi Duberman, Martha Vicinus, and George Chauncey, Eds., *Hidden From History: Reclaiming the Gay and Lesbian Past* (New York: Penguin, 1990), 269.

29. Garber, *Vested Interests*, 35.

30. See chap. 2, "Anglo-Saxons and Others, 1840–1924" in Matthew Frye Jacobson, *Whiteness of a Different Color: European Immigrants and the Alchemy of Race* (Cambridge, Mass.: Harvard University Press, 1998), especially 82–85.

31. See Brook Thomas, Ed., *Plessy v. Ferguson: A Brief History with Documents* (Boston: Bedford Books, 1997).

32. Victoria W. Wolcott, *Race, Riots, and Rollercoasters: The Struggle over Segregated Recreation in America* (Philadelphia: University of Pennsylvania, 2012), 25–26.

33. For more information on the Great Migration, see Joe William Trotter Jr., *The Great Migration in Historical Perspective: New Dimensions of Race, Class, and Gender (Blacks in the Diaspora)* (Bloomington: Indiana University Press, 1991); James R. Grossman, *Land of Hope: Chicago, Black Southerners, and the Great Migration* (Chicago: University of Chicago

Press, 1989); Davarian Baldwin, *Chicago's New Negroes* (Chapel Hill: University of North Carolina Press, 2007). On black migration to Harlem, see Gilbert Osofsky, *Harlem: The Making of a Ghetto: Negro New York 1890–1930* (New York: Harper and Row, 1971), and chap. 8, "Taking Harlem" of Douglas, *Terrible Honesty.*

34. Mizejewski, *Ziegfeld Girl*, 6.
35. See David R. Roediger, *The Wages of Whiteness: Race and the Making of the Working Class (Haymarket Series)* (London: Verso, 1991); Noel Ignatiev, *How the Irish Became White* (New York: Routledge, 1995); Jacobson, *Whiteness of a Different Color* (Cambridge, Mass.: Harvard University Press, 1998); Matthew Pratt Guterl, *The Color of Race in America, 1900–1940* (Cambridge, Mass.: Harvard University Press, 2001); Thomas A. Guglielmo, *White on Arrival: Italians, Race, Color, and Power in Chicago, 1890–1945* (New York: Oxford University Press, 2003); Eric L. Goldstein, *The Price of Whiteness: Jews, Race, and American Identity* (Princeton: Princeton University Press, 2008).
36. On evolving legal quantifications of race in terms of "blood" and other characteristics, see Peggy Pascoe, "Miscegenation Law, Court Cases and Ideologies of 'Race' in Twentieth-Century America," *The Journal of American History* 83, no. 1 (Jun 1996): 44–69.
37. Kibler, *Rank Ladies*, 150.
38. Andrea Stulman, Dennett, *Weird and Wonderful: The Dime Museum in America* (New York: New York University Press, 1997).
39. On intersectionality, see "A Black Feminist Statement: The Combahee River Collective," *All the Women Are White, All the Blacks Are Men, But Some of Us Are Brave*, Gloria T. Hull, Patricia Bell Scott, and Barbara Smith, Eds. (Old Westbury, NY: The Feminist Press, 1982), 13–22; Kimberly Crenshaw, "Mapping the Margins: Intersectionality, Identity Politics, and Violence Against Women of Color," *Stanford Law Review*, 43, no. 6 (1991): 1241–99; Iris Berger, Elsa Barkley Brown, and Nancy A. Hewitt, "Intersections and Collision Courses: Women, Blacks, and Workers Confront Gender, Race and Class," *Feminist Studies*, 18, no. 2 (Summer 1992): 283–294; Evelyn Brooks Higginbotham, "African American Women's History and the Metalanguage of Race," *Signs*, 17, no. 2 (Winter 1992): 251–274.
40. Judith Butler, *Gender Trouble: Feminism and the Subversion of Identity* (New York: Routledge, 2006), xv.
41. Butler, *Gender Trouble*, xxxi. Building on this notion of gender performance, Halberstam's concept of "female masculinity" has also urged me to look for manifestations of masculinity outside the male body. Judith Halberstam, *Female Masculinity* (Durham: Duke University Press, 1998). My understanding of cross-dressing has been influenced by Marjorie Garber, who has argued transvestites have stood at the crossroads of gender hierarchies, often frustrating simple binaries and creating "a space of possibility structuring and confounding culture." Garber, *Vested Interests*, 17.
42. Butler, *Gender Trouble*, xviii.
43. For recent examples, see E. Patrick Johnson and Mae G. Henderson, Eds., *Black Queer Studies: A Critical Anthology* (Durham: Duke University

Press, 2005); Julian B. Carter, *The Heart of Whiteness: Normal Sexuality and Race in America, 1880-1940* (Durham: Duke University Press, 2007); Chad Heap, *Slumming: Sexual and Racial Encounters in American Nightlife, 1885-1940 (Historical Studies in Urban America)* (Chicago: University of Chicago, 2009).

44. Siobhan B. Somerville, *Queering the Color Line: Race and the Invention of Homosexuality in American Culture (Series Q)* (Durham: Duke University Press, 2000), 4.

45. See Laura Browder, *Slippery Characters: Ethnic Impersonators and American Identities (Cultural Studies of the United States)* (Chapel Hill: University of North Carolina Press, 2000); Michael Rogin, *Blackface, White Noise: Jewish Immigrants in the Hollywood Melting Pot* (Berkeley: University of California Press, 1996); Pamela Lavitt, "First of the Red Hot Mamas: 'Coon Shouting' and the Jewish Ziegfeld Girl," *American Jewish History* 87, no. 4 (1999): 253–290.

46. Lott, *Love and Theft*, 20. For another recent example of the multiple natures of racial performances see, Lori Harrison-Kahan, *The White Negress: Literature, Minstrelsy, and the Black-Jewish Imaginary (The American Literature Initiative)* (New Brunswick: Rutgers University Press, Rutgers, 2011).

47. See Kibler, *Rank Ladies*; Glenn, *Female Spectacle*; Sotiropoulos, *Staging Race*; Kasson, *Houdini, Tarzan, and the Perfect Man*; Andrew L. Erdman, *Blue Vaudeville: Sex, Morals and the Mass Marketing of Amusement, 1895–1915* (Jefferson, NC: McFarland and Company, 2004).

48. See bibliography for a full list of archival and manuscript collections consulted.

49. In searching for newspaper articles published between 1890 and 1950, I used four different sources: *ProQuest Historical African American Newspapers*, a database that includes several prominent nationally-distributed black newspapers, *ProQuest Historical Newspapers*, which includes the largest nationally-distributed papers; the *Early American Newspaper Database*, featuring smaller, regionally-based newspapers; and a private database that includes over twelve million pages of New York state regional papers. (Available at http://www.fultonhistory.com/Fulton.html). See bibliography for a complete list of newspapers and periodicals consulted.

50. Joe Laurie Jr., *Vaudeville: From the Honky Tonks to the Palace* (New York: Henry Holt and Company, 1953); Ethel Waters with Charles Samuels, *His Eye is on the Sparrow* (Garden City: Double Day and Company, 1951); Charles Stein, Ed. *American Vaudeville as Seen by its Contemporaries* (New York: Alfred A. Knopf, 1984).

CHAPTER 1

1. Rennold Wolf, "The Highest Salaried Actress in America," *Green Book Magazine* 8 (Jul 1912): 776.

2. Jane Westerfield, "An Investigation of the Lifestyles and Performance of Three-Singer Comediennes of American Vaudeville" (PhD, diss. Ball State University, 1987), 26.

3. Douglas, *Terrible Honesty*, 52.

4. "Champagne Bath for Hair," *The Bellingham Herald*, Dec 1, 1906, 24. Six years after her death in 1947, an obscure biopic called *The I Don't Care Girl* (directed by Lloyd Bacon, Twentieth Century Fox Film Corporation, 1953) brought Tanguay briefly back into the spotlight.

5. Laurence Senelick describes a man named B. Scarpie who worked as an Eva Tanguay impersonator and sometimes stripped during his act. Laurence Senelick, *The Changing Room: Sex, Drag, and Theatre (Gender in Performance)* (New York: Routledge, 2000), 379, 403, n113; "Eva Tanguay's Bonnet," *Washington Post*, Sep 26, 1909, SM2.

6. Andrew L. Erdman, *Queen of Vaudeville: The Story of Eva Tanguay* (Ithaca: Cornell University Press, 2012), 5, 19. On the web, see Jody Rosen's article, "Vanishing Act: in Search of Eva Tanguay," *Slate*, The Slate Group, LLC, *Washington Post* Company, Dec 1, 2009, Accessed Aug 1, 2013.

7. In *Blue Vaudeville* and more recently, *Queen of Vaudeville*, Erdman notes the scant attention paid to Tanguay and builds upon previous work with his own substantial research using the Eva Tanguay Papers. Though his discussion is primarily biographical and generally avoids analysis of the racial implications of Tanguay's work, curiously, Erdman persists in using language and metaphors describing her in terms of her 'wildness,' just as contemporary observers did. For instance, he compares Tanguay in her feature film, *The Wild Girl*, to "a lion taken from the plains of Africa and forced to saunter back and forth in a cage" (199). While Tanguay appears on the cover of two major works examining the role of women in American vaudeville, Kibler's *Rank Ladies* and Glenn's *Female Spectacle*, she is not a primary figure in either text and Kibler only mentions Tanguay three times. Several other scholars discuss Tanguay briefly, including Charles and Louise Samuels, *Once Upon a Stage* (Dodd, Mead and Company, 1974); Robert W. Snyder, *The Voice of the City: Vaudeville and Popular Culture in New York* (New York: Oxford University Press, 1989); Trav S. D., *No Applause, Just Throw Money: The Book that Made Vaudeville Famous* (New York: Faber and Faber, 2005); Robert C. Allen, *Horrible Prettiness: Burlesque and American Culture (Cultural Studies and the United States)* (Durham: University of North Carolina Press, 1991); and Robert C. Toll, *On With the Show: The First Century of Show Business in America* (New York: Oxford University Press, 1976). For a brief biographical profile of Tanguay, see Frank Cullen, *Vaudeville Old and New: An Encyclopedia of Variety Performers in America*, 2 volumes (New York: Routledge, 2006).

8. Glenn, *Female Spectacle*, 2-3.

9. Marianna Torgovnick, *Gone Primitive: Savage Intellects, Modern Lives* (Chicago: University of Chicago Press, 1990), 8.

10. Andrea Stulman Dennett, *Weird and Wonderful: The Dime Museum in America* (New York: New York University Press, 1997), 19.

11. Laura Briggs, "The Race of Hysteria: 'Overcivilization' and the 'Savage' Woman in Late Nineteenth-Century Obstetrics and Gynecology," *American Quarterly* 52, no. 2 (June 2000): 246.

12. In her muckraking pamphlets, *Southern Horrors* and *A Red Record*, Ida B. Wells wrote a widely-distributed, scathing rebuke of the ways in which

white men vilified black men as beast-like rapists who lusted after chaste white women. Ida B. Wells, *Southern Horrors and Other Writings: The Anti-Lynching Campaign of Ida B. Wells, 1892–1900 (Bedford Cultural Editions Series)*, Jacqueline Jones Royster, Ed. (Bedford/St. Martin's, 1996).

13. Gail Bederman, *Manliness and Civilization: A Cultural History of Gender and Race in the United States, 1880–1917 (Women in Culture and Society)* (Chicago: University of Chicago Press: 1996), 25. For more on freak shows and savagery in popular culture in the nineteenth century, see Linda Frost, *Never One Nation: Freaks, Savages, and Whiteness in U.S. Popular Culture, 1850-1877* (Minneapolis: University of Minnesota Press, 2005).

14. *The Birth of a Nation*, Directed by D. W. Griffith, Produced by Harry Aitken (Epoch Producing Co, 1915).

15. For an excellent discussion of the role of Burroughs's fiction in shaping gender roles in American popular culture, see chap. 3 of Kasson, *Houdini, Tarzan, and the Perfect Man* and the conclusion of Bederman, *Manliness and Civilization*.

16. Chauncey, *Gay New York*, 48–49.

17. Bederman, *Manliness and Civilization*, 184.

18. Kristin Hoganson, *Fighting for American Manhood: How Gender Politics Provoked the Spanish-American and Philippine-American Wars (Yale Historical Publications Series)* (New Haven: Yale University Press, 1998), 139.

19. Bederman, *Manliness and Civilization*, 184.

20. Theodore Roosevelt, "The Duties of a Great Nation," *Campaigns and Controversies* (1898), 291; Cited in Hoganson, *Fighting for American Manhood*, 144, 244 n18.

21. Roosevelt, "Grant," *American Ideals*, (1900), 430–41; Cited in Hoganson, *Fighting for American Manhood*, 145, 245, n32.

22. Zachary Ross, Ed., *Women on the Verge: The Culture of Neurasthenia in Nineteenth-century America* (Stanford, Calif.: The Iris and B. Gerald Cantor for Visual Arts, 2004), 11.

23. Ross, *Women on the Verge*, 11–13.

24. S. Weir Mitchell, *Fat and Blood: An Essay on the Treatment of Neurasthenia and Hysteria* (London: J.B. Lippincott & Co., 1891), 24; Ross, *Women on the Verge*, 11–13.

25. Ross, *Women on the Verge*, 13.

26. Roosevelt, "The Strenuous Life," *American Ideals*; Cited in Hoganson, 153, 257, n55.

27. "When Teddy is a Partner of Mine," Music by George J. Trinkaus, Lyrics by George L. Albig, Box 7, ETP, BFRC, THF.

28. "Something About Eva," *Indianapolis News*, Oct 8, 1904; Westerfield, "An Investigation," 13.

29. Richard Henry Little, "Little Quips and Quirks," *The Chicago Daily Tribune*, Feb 15, 1912, 10.

30. Richard Henry Little, "Mr. S. Pepys, Jr, Observeth Mistress Eva Tanguay," *Chicago Examiner*, n.d., Promotional Materials, Newspapers Clippings, 1911–1915, Box 9, ETP, BFRC, THF.

31. Eva Tanguay, "Success," *Variety*, Dec 12, 1908, 34. (Underlining as in original); Promotional Materials, Newspaper Clippings, Undated, Box 9, ETP, BFRC, THF. Also quoted in Westerfield, "An Investigation," 165–167.

32. Eva Tanguay, "Success."
33. Filene, *Him/Her/Self*, 7.
34. Newspaper article, n.p., n.d., Clippings 14, HTC, HL, Harvard.
35. Wolf, "The Highest Salaried Actress in America," 783.
36. Kasson, *Houdini, Tarzan and the Perfect Man*, 11.
37. Ibid.
38. George Beard, *Sexual Neurasthenia [Nervous Exhaustion]* (New York: E. B. Treat, 1884), 36.
39. Newspaper article, n.p., Mar 12, 1913, Clippings 14, HTC, HL, Harvard.
40. "Eva Tanguay: The Evangelist of Joy," *Variety*, Apr 30, 1915; Westerfield, "An Investigation," 21, n47.
41. "Eva Tanguay, 68, Dies on Coast: Vaudeville's 'I Don't Care' Girl," *New York Herald Tribune*, Jan 11, 1947, 59; Westerfield, "An Investigation," 27, n61.
42. "'The Sambo Girl' Failed to Get Here," *The State*, Mar 17, 1905, 2.
43. Wolf, "The Highest Salaried Actress in America," 783.
44. "The Cyclonic Eva Tanguay," *Washington Post*, Apr 10, 1910, S2.
45. Caffin, *Vaudeville*, 37.
46. "[Tanguay] Quit the 'Sun Dodgers,'" n.p., Oct. 24, 1912, Clippings 14, HTC, HL, Harvard.
47. Sarah Bernhardt, *My Double Life* (London: William Heinemann, 1907), 81. Cited in Harrison-Kahan, *The White Negress*, 22.
48. Performers who portrayed the Circassian Beauty allegedly achieved this look by aggressively teasing their hair after soaking it in beer. For more on the Circassian beauty, see chap. 3 of Frost, *Never One Nation* 81; Michele Mitchell, *Righteous Propagation: African Americans and the Politics of Racial Destiny after Reconstruction* (Chapel Hill: University of North Carolina Press, 2004), 213.
49. "Nothing Bothers Me—Music and Lyrics," Words and Music by C. Florian Zittel, 1907, Musical Scores, Box 6, ETP, BFRC, THF.
50. "I Don't Care," Extra Verses, Lyrics by Jean Lenox, Music by Harry O. Sutton (Shapiro Remick and Company, 1905), TCS 92, Sheet Music-Prod, (Sambo Girl), HTC, HL, Harvard.
51. Glenn, *Female Spectacle*, 41.
52. For a first-person description of Tanguay's dancing, see Caffin, *Vaudeville*, 37–38. See also Robert M. Lewis, Ed., *From Traveling Show to Vaudeville: Theatrical Spectacle in America, 1930-1910* (Baltimore: Johns Hopkins Press, 2003), 319.
53. "Tanguay Victorious; Eva's Rebellion Not in Vain," *Evening American*, n.d., Folder 1913, Promotional Materials, Newspapers Clippings, 1911–1915, ETP, BFRC, THF.
54. Westerfield, "An Investigation," 11.
55. Ibid.
56. "Food That Makes Giants," *Washington Post*, Mar 31, 1911, 6.
57. "Eva Tanguay and Anna Held," *Philadelphia Inquirer*, Jan 22, 1910, 8.
58. See chap. 1, "Some Could Suckle Over Their Shoulder," Jennifer Morgan, *Laboring Women: Reproduction and Gender in New World Slavery* (Philadelphia: University of Pennsylvania Press, 2004).

59. Briggs, "The Race of Hysteria," 262.

60. Erdman, *Queen*, 93–4.

61. "Nothing Bothers Me," Musical Scores, Box 6, ETP, BFRC, THF.

62. Westerfield, "An Investigation," 10.

63. Ibid.

64. Samuels, *Once Upon a Stage*, 61; Westerfield, "An Investigation," 46.

65. "Eva Tanguay Arrested," *New York Times*, Mar 2, 1910, 18.

66. Douglas Gilbert, *American Vaudeville: Its Life and Times* (New York: Dover Publications Inc., 1963), 329; Westerfield, "An Investigation," 46.

67. "Famous Impersonators on the Stage of Each Other's Sex About to Marry," *The Evening World*, n.d., Folder 1906–1910, Newspaper Clippings, 1900–1905, Box 8, ETP, BFRC, THF; "At the Theaters, Eva Tanguay," *Dayton Journal*, Oct 4, 1906, Newspaper Clippings, 1900–1905, Box 8, ETP, BFRC, THF.

68. Halberstam, *Female Masculinity*, 2.

69. Though Tanguay's love life is outside the scope of this study, Andrew Erdman details Tanguay's various romantic relationships with men, including her three marriages in chap. 8 and 9 of his book, *Queen of Vaudeville*.

70. Bederman, *Manliness and Civilization*, 8.

71. Ibid.

72. Eva Tanguay, "I Don't Care, *The American Weekly, New York American Journal*, Jan 26, 1947, 7.

73. Jane Westerfield argues "Eva's salary didn't matter to anyone but her, actually, but the rumors of her extraordinary salary just showed that Eva must be something really special in order to earn it." Westerfield, "An Investigation," 5.

74. Wolf, "The Highest Salaried Actress in America," 779.

75. "Eva Tanguay in the Keith Bill," *Boston Daily Globe*, Jan 10 1911, 11.

76. Stanley (illegible) to Eva Tanguay, Dec 14, 1910; J. Hilton Thomas to Eva Tanguay, Dec 15, 1910, Professional, Fan Letters, 1910–1938, ETP, BFRC, THF.

77. Wolf, "The Highest Salaried Actress in America," 776.

78. Ibid., 782.

79. Samuels, *Once Upon a Stage*, 55.

80. Newspapers Clippings, 1911–1915, Promotional Materials, Folder 1913, Box 9, ETP, BFRC, THF.

81. "Wedding Bells Will Ring Soon for Eva Tanguay," *Atlanta Constitution*, Jan 21, 1927, 1.

82. "Eva Tanguay Says No," *Grand Forks Daily Herald*, Sep 3, 1908, 7.

83. "Eccentric Comedienne Back at Keith's With Some New Gowns and New Songs," *Boston Daily Globe*, Sep 14, 1915, 3.

84. "'Marriage Grand'—Eva Tanguay," *Chicago Herald*, Dec 20 1917, Promotional Materials, Newspaper Clippings 1916–1930, Box 9, ETP, BFRC, THF.

85. Bederman, *Manliness and Civilization*, 8.

86. Ibid.

87. Glenn, *Female Spectacle*, 63; "I Don't Care," Sheet Music-Prod, Sambo Girl, HTC, HL, Harvard. Tanguay claimed this song was first written for the 1903 musical *The Chaperones*, in which she had a small role. The

song was so popular that another production called *The Sambo Girl* was written to showcase Tanguay's rising popularity, prominently featuring "I Don't Care!" Most likely, since Tanguay was not then a star, she used the lyrics after they were written to create her stage persona, presenting her life autobiographically through her music, a perspective that endeared her to audiences. Tanguay consciously maintained this ostensibly autobiographical approach throughout her career, using interludes between songs to discuss her personal life and what newspapers had recently printed about her.

88. "Eva Tanguay Arrested," *New York Times*, Mar 2, 1910, 18.
89. Gilbert, *American Vaudeville*, 329; Westerfield, "An Investigation," 46.
90. Bederman, *Manliness and Civilization*, 8.
91. Westerfield, "An Investigation," 30.
92. "Eva Tanguay was Arrested," *Kansas City Star*, published as *Kansas City Times*, Jul 5, 1909, 3.
93. Musical Scores, Box 4–7, ETP, BFRC, THF.
94. "Shows How Salome Did It," *Los Angeles Times*, Aug 4, 1908, II8.
95. Filene, *Him/Her/Self*, 8.
96. Briggs, "The Race of Hysteria," 249.
97. Ibid., 255.
98. Briggs, "The Race of Hysteria," 250; Mitchell, *Righteous Propagation*, 82, 90–91. In an attempt to challenge these assumptions and refrain from offending the sensibilities of segregated audiences, black female performers like Aida Overton Walker wore more modest costumes than their white counterparts and were rarely featured in romantic plotlines. See Glenn's discussion of black female portrayals of Salomé in *Female Spectacle*, 108–118. On modern black female performers generally, see also Sotiropoulos, *Staging Race* and David Krasner, *Resistance, Parody, and Double Consciousness in African American Theatre, 1895–1910* (New York: St. Martin's Press, 1997) and David Krasner, *A Beautiful Pageant: African American Theatre, Drama, and Performance in the Harlem Renaissance* (New York: Palgrave Macmillan, 2002).
99. Glenn, *Female Spectacle*, 79.
100. Wolf, "The Highest Salaried Actress in America," 781.
101. "A Scene Behind the Scenes," n.p., n.d., Promotional Materials, Newspaper Clippings, 1931–1947, ETP, BFRC, THF.
102. Kasson, *Houdini, Tarzan, and the Perfect Man*, 35.
103. I have borrowed this phrase from Ken Burns' documentary on Johnson, *Unforgivable Blackness: The Rise and Fall of Jack Johnson* (Hollywood, California: PBS Home Video, 2004).
104. Westerfield, "An Investigation," 33.
105. Glenn, *Female Spectacle*, 98.
106. Ibid.
107. Ibid., 96.
108. Samuels, *Once Upon a Stage*, 63.
109. Tanguay's explanation of using a "Negro boy" may, in fact, literally suggest that she chose a young black actor in order to get around such rules, or to temper the potentially explosive nature of this altered narrative. Yet,

she may also have simply used the term "boy" because it was a common pejorative practice of many whites that denied the manhood of African Americans by calling black men—regardless of age—"boys."

110. Samuels, *Once Upon a Stage,* 64; Westerfield, "An Investigation," 36, n84.

111. Westerfield, "An Investigation," 35, 53.

112. Samuels, *Once Upon a Stage,* 64.

113. Westerfield, "An Investigation," 34. In reality, though, critics noted that Tanguay's performance was more modest than that of many other Salomé performers. "Tanguay Won Them All," *Kansas City Times,* Jun 9, 1913, Promotional Materials, Newspapers Clippings, 1911–1915, Box 9, ETP, BFRC, THF.

114. Mizejewski, *Ziegfeld Girl,* 6.

115. Wolf, "The Highest Salaried Actress in America," 776.

116. Samuels, *Once Upon a Stage,* 67.

117. Sotiropoulos, *Staging Race,* 186; Glenn, *Female Spectacle,* 108–10; Erdman, *Queen,* 114–16.

118. Though these strategies were more common for male performers, they were not unheard of and Sophie Tucker used all three in her early career. See chap. 5 of Kibler, "The Corking Girls," especially 119–123, 137–140 in *Rank Ladies.*

119. One early exception includes the song "My Sambo" from *The Sambo Girl.* "My Sambo," Musical Scores, Box 6, ETP, BFRC, THF.

120. Erdman, *Blue Vaudeville,* 135.

121. Westerfield, "An Investigation," 23.

122. Erdman, *Queen,* 104–5.

123. "When the Doc Makes a Monkey Out of Me," Words and Music by Edwin Weber, Musical Scores, Box 7, ETP, BFRC, THF. Also cited in Erdman, *Queen,* 104–5.

124. Briggs, "The Race of Hysteria," 257–58.

125. Mizejewski, *Ziegfeld Girl,* 127.

126. Wolf, "The Highest Salaried Actress in America," 780.

127. Tanguay was not the first actress to inspire comparisons to animals. Though critics did not directly compare Sarah Bernhardt, a French actress who toured American between 1880 and 1918, to animals, she was "repeatedly linked to animals, wild and otherwise" and "by 1885, she had begun to collect a private menagerie of parrots, monkeys, cheetahs, lion and tiger cubs, exotic birds, and wolfhounds. She took her animals wherever she went, and a profusion of animal skins—tiger, jaguar, beaver, bear, buffalo, crocodile—lay heaped on floors and divans in her sumptuous living quarters in Paris." Douglas, *Terrible Honesty,* 45, 52.

128. Even Westerfield asserts that Tanguay was born "in the wilderness of Marbelton, Canada." Westerfield, "An Investigation," 5.

129. Wolf, "The Highest Salaried Actress in America," 777.

130. "Chats with Player Folks and Stories of the Stage," *Boston Daily Globe,* Mar 25, 1912, 11.

131. Beard, *American Nervousness,* 92.

132. Ibid., 184.

133. Ibid., 185.

134. Ibid.
135. Ibid., 129.
136. *The Sambo Girl*, Script, Professional, Scripts, Box 1, ETP, BFRC, THF.
137. Promotional Materials, Newspaper Clippings, 1906–1910, Box 8, ETP, BFRC, THF. Also quoted in Erdman, *Queen*, 73.
138. Beard, *American Nervousness*, 120.
139. Caffin, *Vaudeville*, 38.
140. *The Wild Girl*, Directed by Howard Estabrook (Eva Tanguay Film Corporation, 1917).
141. Erdman, *Blue Vaudeville*, 136.
142. Ibid.
143. Ibid.
144. Advertisement for *The Wild Girl, Moving Picture World*, vol. 34, Oct 1917 (New York: Chalmers Publishing Company), 188. Internet Archive, Museum of Modern Art Library.
145. *Variety*, Jul 25, 1908; Westerfield, "An Investigation," 36, n85. Emphasis mine.
146. Douglas, *Terrible Honesty*, 52.
147. Caffin, *Vaudeville*, 42.
148. Glenn, *Female Spectacle*, 3.
149. Ibid., 66.
150. Critics disagree as to whether or not Tanguay met standards of feminine beauty, which, as Lois Banner has demonstrated, were in flux throughout Tanguay's nearly three decades in show business. The slim boyish figure of the flapper would not become the standard ideal of feminine beauty until the 1920s. Nonetheless, in *Horrible Prettiness*, Robert Allen argues that "Tanguay was never regarded as physically attractive—indeed, for most of her twenty-five year career she was considerably overweight" (273). Though photographs suggest that Tanguay's weight fluctuated throughout her career, several reviewers' comments about her shapeliness suggest Allen's does not reflect the views of Tanguay's audience.
151. Allen, *Horrible Prettiness*, 272–274.
152. "Eva Tanguay is Fussy, but She Doesn't Care," *Chicago Daily Tribune*, Oct 17, 1909, B3.
153. "Eva Tanguay in Keith's Vaudeville," *Boston Daily Globe*, Nov 10, 1914, 6.
154. Ibid.
155. "Tanguay Packs the House," *Daily News*, Promotional Materials, Chicago, May 18–31, 1913, Box 9, ETP, BFRC, THF.

CHAPTER 2

1. Philip R. Kellar, "Making a Woman of Himself," *Green Book Magazine*, Dec 1909, 8–9, vol. 182, Reel 15, RLC, NYPL.
2. Garber, *Vested Interests*, 69.
3. Untitled, *New York Mirror*, Sep 20, 1911. RLC, vol. 182, Reel 15, 98, NYPL.
4. "The Prettiest Girl on the Stage is a Man," *The Julian Eltinge Magazine*, c. 1911, 22, TWC, NYPL.
5. For an example of popular interest in Eltinge see "The Julian Eltinge Project" at www.thejulianeltingeproject.com. For an example of scholarship

that considers Eltinge, see Daniel Hurewitz, *Bohemian Los Angeles and the Making of Modern Politics* (Berkeley: University of California Press, 2007). Other brief discussions of Eltinge are included in Kasson, *Houdini, Tarzan and The Perfect Man* (New York: Hill and Wang, 2001), Senelick, *The Changing Room* (New York: Routledge, 2000), and Ullman, *Sex Seen*.

6. Eltinge distributed his magazine at his performances and sold them through the mail for ten cents per issue, the same price as popular magazines such as McClure's. The other newspapers and magazines I consulted rarely, if ever, mentioned his magazine. This may be in part due to the magazine's presumed short tenure; I was able to locate only three extant issues available at the Townshend Walsh Collection at the New York Public Library. I have estimated that these issues were published between 1911 and 1912. In *Sex Seen*, Ullman argues they were published between 1912 and 1913, 54.

7. Eltinge's father, Michael Joseph Dalton, was the son of Irish immigrants and his mother, Julia Edna, was "of English extraction." The press never mentioned Eltinge's ethnicity. Information about his ancestry comes from Joan Vale's discovery of his death certificate. Joan Vale, "Tintype Ambitions: Three Vaudevillians in Search of Hollywood Fame" (M.A. Thesis, University of San Diego, 1985), 46, n20.

8. "Eltinge in England," *New York Dramatic News*, n.d., RLC, vol. 182, Reel 15, NYPL.

9. "World's Foremost Imitator of Women," n.p., n.d., RLC, vol. 182, Reel 15, NYPL; "College Boy as Chorus Girl," written by fashion writer Helen Follet Stevans under the pseudonym "Mme Qui Vive," n.p., Jul 7, 1907, RLC, vol. 182, Reel 15, NYPL.

10. Rennold Wolf, "The Sort of Fellow Julian Eltinge Really Is," *Green Book Magazine*, Nov 1913, 794, ser. 3, vol. 432, RLC, BRTC, NYPL.

11. Archie Bell, "Jack Dalton's Big Brother," *Cleveland Plain-Dealer*, Jan 1911. RLC, vol. 182, Reel 15, NYPL.

12. "College Boy as Chorus Girl," NYPL. In other versions of the story, Eltinge first performed at the age of fourteen with the First Corps of Cadets in Boston. "Julian Eltinge Started Characterizations Early," *Washington Post*, Oct 16, 1927, F1. For information on the Hasty Pudding Club as the oldest Ivy League university to regularly feature male drag shows, see Garber, *Vested Interests*, 60.

13. "College Boy as Chorus Girl," NYPL.

14. Joan Vale claims that Eltinge's only affiliation with Harvard "took place in 1903 when Eltinge engaged a group of Harvard students to appear in a summer stock company." "Tintype Ambitions," 46, n16.

15. Several articles claimed he was a member of the Harvard class of 1902. "World's Foremost Imitator of Women," n.p., n.d., RLC, vol. 182, Reel 15, NYPL, 13; "Julian Eltinge Isn't Effeminate When He Gets His Corsets Off." n.p., c. 1904, RLC, NYPL; Mme Qui Vive, "College Boy as Chorus Girl," n.p., Jul 7, 1907, RLC, vol. 182, Reel 15, 14, NYPL; *Quinquennial Catalogue of the Officers and Graduates, 1636–1930*, Harvard University (Cambridge, Mass.: The University, 1930).

16. "Food That Makes Giants," *Washington Post*, Mar 31, 1911, 6.

17. "College Boy as Chorus Girl," NYPL.

18. "All these are Pictures of the Same Person," n.p., 1904, RLC, vol. 182, Reel 15, NYPL.

19. Ibid.

20. "Would Let Woman Choose Own Way," *Boston Daily Globe,* May 13, 1912, 11.

21. "All these are Pictures of the Same Person," n.p., 1904, RLC, vol. 182, Reel 15, NYPL.

22. Bederman, *Manliness and Civilization,* 25.

23. F. Michael Moore, *Drag! Male and Female Impersonators on Stage, Screen and Television* (Jefferson, N.C.: McFarland and Co. Inc, 1994), 109. The *Washington Post* even reported that Eltinge accidentally set a record for eating the most expensive dinner, paying $1,800 for his meal. "Star Buys $1,800 Dinner," Oct 18, 1914, SM2.

24. An essay, "Who Would You Rather Be?" made this comparison explicit: "A.H. Woods pays Julian Eltinge $1,625 a week as Star in 'The Fascinating Widow' for forty weeks. The United States pays William H. Taft $1,442.12 a week as President for fifty-two weeks." "Who Would You Rather Be?" Feb 21, 1912, Julian Eltinge Clippings, RLC, NYPL.

25. *Variety,* Jul 27, 1912, Julian Eltinge Clippings, RLC, NYPL.

26. Laura F. Edwards, *Gendered Strife and Confusion: The Political Culture of Reconstruction (Women in American History)* (Chicago: University of Illinois Press, 1997), 125.

27. Montgomery Phister, "People of the Stage," n.p., Jan 15, 1911, RLC, vol. 182, Reel 15, NYPL.

28. "Wearies of Corsets," *Los Angeles Times,* May 4, 1917, III3.

29. "How Julian Eltinge as 'The Fascinating Widow' Dons His Costumes in Jig Style," *Julian Eltinge Magazine,* c. 1912, 11, TWC, NYPL.

30. Julian Eltinge, "Fads and Hobbies," *The Julian Eltinge Magazine,* c. 1911, 14, TWC, NYPL.

31. "World's Foremost Imitator of Women," n.p., n.d., RLC, vol. 182, Reel 15, NYPL.

32. "College Athletes Act Best in Skirts," *New York Times,* Dec 12, 1915, Section II, 16, col. 1. Cited in Garber, *Vested Interests,* 63.

33. "Eva Tanguay 5c cigars," Professional, Product Endorsements, 1913, Box 1, ETP, BFRC, THF.

34. "Plays and Players," RLC, ser. 3, vol. 432, 101, NYPL.

35. "Julian Eltinge in the Role of Prince Charming," *New York Star,* Dec 26, 1917, RLC, NYPL.

36. Filene, *Him/Her/Self,* 74.

37. "Successful Sex Faking Accomplished By Few," *Los Angeles Times,* Nov 24, 1912, III1.

38. Garber, *Vested Interests,* 69.

39. "Amusements, Majestic," *Little Rock,* Jan 15. c. 1920, RLC, NYPL; "College Boy as a Chorus Girl," NYPL.

40. Eltinge and his manager opened the Forty-Second Street Eltinge Theatre in New York City. The building still stands today as an AMC movie theater in Times Square.

41. A. Bell, "The Julian Eltinge of China," *Theatre*, Jan 1917, 25: 36, 58. As cited in *Bulletin of Bibliography and Dramatic Index*, 9, no. 6, 156, n189.
42. Montgomery Phister, "People of the Stage," n.p., Jan 15, 1911, RLC, vol. 182, Reel 15, 54, NYPL.
43. "Julian Eltinge," *Variety*, Apr 23, 1910, RLC, vol. 182, Reel 15, 54, NYPL.
44. "Eltinge Packs the Orpheum," n.p., c. 1910, RLC, vol. 182, Reel 15, 54, NYPL.
45. "Popular Julian," *The Julian Eltinge Magazine*, 54. TWC, NYPL. Emphasis mine.
46. "Comments From the Highways and Byways on Julian Eltinge in the 'The Fascinating Widow,'" *Julian Eltinge Magazine*, 58, c. 1911, TWC, NYPL.
47. "Julian Eltinge," *Vanity Fair*, Jun 4, 1909, RLC, vol. 182, Reel 15, 45, NYPL. Emphasis mine.
48. "Eltinge Will Quit Feminine Roles to Play 'Shylock,'" n.p., Jan 8, 1911, RLC, vol. 182, Reel 15, NYPL.
49. Untitled, n.p., n.d., RLC, vol. 182, Reel 15, NYPL.
50. Garber, *Vested Interests*, 63.
51. *The New York Times* criticized the formulaic nature of Eltinge's storylines: "The recipe for such an entertainment must be fairly simple. Take a plot concerning the fortunes of a rough-spoken, devil-may-care fellow and puzzle your brains till you have devised some situation wherein he must don feminine finery as a disguise. Add one suggestion that his cheek is incongruously rough and another that he must not be left alone with the girls lest they tell him things he ought not to hear. Flavor from time to time with guarded drinks, smokes, curses, and fist clenchings, just to indicate that all this is not at all to his liking. Stir briskly and serve in a hurry." "Julian Eltinge in Klein's Last Play," *New York Times*, Aug 28, 1915, 7.
52. Moore, *Drag!* 104.
53. *Julian Eltinge Magazine*, TWC, NYPL.
54. "'The Fascinating Widow' at the Liberty Theatre," n.p., Sep 28, 1911, RLC, NYPL.
55. Moore, *Drag!* 102. Emphasis mine.
56. Untitled newspaper clipping, *Toledo Times*, Feb 24, 1912, ser. 3, vol. 431, 4, RLC, NYPL.
57. Indeed, in 1893, a *New York Times* reporter described the Dahoman exhibition at the Columbian Exposition, suggesting that the "savages' sexual difference was so indistinct that the Dahomans might have a larger 'assortment' of sexes than the usual two." Bederman, *Manliness and Civilization*, 36.
58. Toll, *On With The Show*, 249.
59. "A Disgrace to Vaudeville," *The Standard and Vanity Fair*, Sep 1904, RLC, vol. 182, Reel 15, NYPL.
60. Ibid.
61. Chauncey, *Gay New York*, 290.
62. "College Boy as Chorus Girl," NYPL.
63. "His Own Designer," *The Julian Eltinge Magazine*, c. 1911, 26, TWC, NYPL.

64. Otheman Stevens, "Eltinge a 'Real' Woman Impersonator as a Widow He Becomes Fascinating," *Los Angeles* _____ *(illegible)*, RLC, NYPL.
65. "Charming Julian Eltinge Captivates Clemmen Crowds," Dec 31, 1917; "A Disgrace to Vaudeville," Jun 10, 1905, RLC, NYPL.
66. "Julien [*sic*] Eltinge," n.p., n.d., RLC, NYPL.
67. Ullman, *Sex Seen*, 51. For more information on Browne, see his entry in Frank Cullen's *Vaudeville Old and New*, vol. 1, 150-151.
68. Ullman, *Sex Seen*, 58.
69. Moore, *Drag!* 99.
70. "Julian Eltinge's Latest," *New York Mirror*, Aug 7, 1909, RLC, vol. 182, Reel 15, NYPL.
71. Eltinge's cobra dance was modeled after Ruth St. Denis's. Untitled, n.p., n.d., RLC, vol. 182, Reel 15, 52, NYPL.
72. Walter Anthony, "Eltinge's Show is Great Vaudeville," *Post-Intelligencer*, Jun 30, 1919, RLC, NYPL.
73. Julian Eltinge, "The Troubles of a Man Who Wears Skirts," *Green Book Magazine* 13 (May 1915): 816.
74. "Julian Eltinge," *Variety*, Dec 12, 1908, RLC, vol. 182, Reel 15, 35, NYPL.
75. "New Vaudeville Acts," *Dramatic Mirror*, May 1, 1909, RLC, vol. 182, Reel 15, NYPL.
76. "Majestic. Julian Eltinge." n.p., c. 1919, RLC, NYPL.
77. Other contemporary female impersonators include the teams of Stealing and Hutton and "Love and Haight," a man calling himself "Mary Elizabeth," Francis Yates, and British star Malcolm Scott. For more information, see Ullman, *Sex Seen*, 52.
78. Untitled newspaper clipping, n.p., c. 1904. RLC, vol. 182, Reel 15, 3. NYPL; "All These Are of the Same Person," n.p., n.d., RLC, vol. 182. Reel 15, NYPL.
79. "An Odd Picture of an Odd Star," *Stage Pictorial*, n.d., 20, RLC, NYPL.
80. Chauncey, *Gay New York*, 292.
81. Ibid.
82. Ibid., 297.
83. Julian Eltinge, "The Troubles of a Man Who Wears Skirts," *Green Book Magazine* 13 (May 1915): 814.
84. Chauncey, *Gay New York*, 293.
85. An incident in which Eltinge punched a man in a New Orleans nightclub for calling him a "fairy" confirms that Eltinge wanted (at least publicly) to distance himself from the fairy identity. Vale, "Tintype Ambitions," 55, n76.
86. In 1917, the *Detroit Journal* reported that on the set of his film, *The Countess Charming*, Eltinge refused to leave his dressing room: "When Mr. Crisp [the director] called to him to come out, Mr. Eltinge stuck a carefully coiffed head out of the dressing room window, removed a pipe from his mouth and said: 'Not on your life. I wouldn't walk across that place in this get-up for a million dollars." "Eltinge Objects to Ball Gown in Street," *Detroit Journal*, c. Jan 1917, RLC, NYPL.
87. Glenn, *Female Spectacle*, 112. In *Sex Seen*, Ullman quotes Amy Leslie, of the *Detroit News*, citing Eltinge for "brawling and stampeding out his fury half the time because these creatures who always flock together are

crazy about him." Leslie described an incident when "pariahs" sneaked behind stage to meet Eltinge: "'Eltinge stepped out, caught sight of their fanciful ensemble, and let a roar out of him that shook the scenery. His pretty wig was off, his black jet sleeves rolled up to fight, and he looked like a stricken bull in the arena. The prim gentles fled. One of them yelled, 'Somebody throw her a fish; she's a sea lion.'" *Detroit News,* Sep 10, 1913, RLC, NYPL; Cited in Ullman, *Sex Seen,* 60, 153, n66.

88. Chauncey, *Gay New York,* 51.

89. Ibid., 48.

90. Lewis Erenberg, *Steppin' Out: New York Nightlife and the Transformation of American Culture* (Chicago: University of Chicago Press, 1981), 18.

91. Julian Eltinge, "The Troubles of a Man Who Wears Skirts," *Green Book Magazine* 13 (May 1915): 814–15.

92. "English's—Cohan's Minstrel," *Indianapolis News,* Sep 30, 1908, RLC, vol. 182, Reel 15, NYPL; Moore, *Drag!* 99.

93. "Cohan's and Harris' Minstrels," Dec 1909, RLC, NYPL; Moore, *Drag!* 98. For original sheet music to "The Belle of the Barber's Ball" by George M. Cohan (1908) see the digital collection of The Library of Congress.

94. "Julian Eltinge," *New York Dramatic News,* Aug 24, 1907, RLC, vol. 182, Reel 15, NYPL.

95. English's—Cohan's Minstrel," *Indianapolis News,* Sep 30, 1908, RLC, vol. 182, Reel 15, NYPL.

96. Moore, *Drag!* 99.

97. Ibid.

98. For example, *Amos n' Andy,* an enormously popular radio show on air through the 1930s, was voiced by white actors who spoke in dialect and wore blackface in publicity stills.

99. Mizejewski, *Ziegfeld Girl,* 127.

100. Untitled, *Variety,* Apr 24, 1909, RLC, vol. 182, Reel 15, NYPL.

101. "Cousin Lucy by Charles Klein. At the Detroit Opera House, Oct, 30," *Detroit News,* RLC, ser. 3, vol. 432, 114, NYPL.

102. Archie Bell, "Jack Dalton's Big Brother," *Cleveland Plain-Dealer,* Jan 1911. RLC, vol. 182, Reel 15, NYPL.

103. One writer used Eltinge as the centerpiece of an essay discussing notorious female criminals such as Ethel LeNeve and Miss Jean Barclay Thurnherr. "Successful Sex Faking Accomplished by Few," *Los Angeles Times,* Nov 24, 1912, III1.

104. Untitled, n.p., Jan 1911, RLC, vol. 182, Reel 15, NYPL.

105. Untitled, n.p., Jan 1911, RLC, vol. 182, Reel 15, NYPL; "Eltinge Wanted in London," *Dramatic News,* Apr 1911, RLC, vol. 182, Reel 15, NYPL; "Julian Eltinge Intends to Play Masculine Roles," n.p., c. 1919, RLC, NYPL.

106. "Eltinge," *Dramatic News,* Aug 19, 1905, RLC, vol. 182, Reel 15, NYPL.

107. "World's Foremost Imitator of Women," n.p., n.d., RLC, vol. 182, Reel 15, NYPL.

108. Kasson, *Houdini, Tarzan, and the Perfect Man,* 4.

109. Ibid., 6.

110. Filene, *Him/Her/Self,* 77.

111. For an insightful analysis of Sandow, see Kasson, chap. 1, "Who Is The Perfect Man? Eugen Sandow and a New Standard for America," 21–75.

112. Eugen Sandow, *Body Building or Man in the Making: How to Become Healthy and Strong: Containing Sets of Exercises and Special Photos of Mr. Sandow and Family* (London: Gale and Polden, 1904); Eugen Sandow, *Strength and How to Obtain It: With Anatomical Chart Illustrating the Exercises for Physical Development* (London: Gale and Polden, 1897).

113. "Julian Eltinge," n.p., n.d., RLC, NYPL.

114. Moore, *Drag!* 106.

115. Ullman, *Sex Seen*, 9, 152, n42.

116. "World's Foremost Imitator of Women," n.p., n.d., RLC, vol. 182, Reel 15, NYPL.

117. "Would Let Woman Choose Own Way," *Boston Daily Globe*, May 13, 1912, 11.

118. "Mr. Eltinge Charmingly Feminine without Being Effeminate," n.p., Dec 31, 1909, RLC, vol. 182, Reel 15, NYPL. Emphasis mine.

119. For further examples see, "All These Are Pictures of the Same Person," n.p., 1904, RLC, vol. 182, Reel 15, NYPL.

120. See Bederman's introduction, "Remaking Manhood through Race and Civilization," *Manliness and Civilization*, 1–45.

122. The press repeated this claim several times. For example, see "The Prettiest Girl on the Stage is a Man," *The Julian Eltinge Magazine*, c. 1911, 22, TWC, NYPL; "Julian Eltinge." n.p., n.d., RLC, NYPL; "Julian Eltinge's Two Faces," *Pittsburgh Leader*, Oct 8. c. 1920, RLC, NYPL.

123. One reviewer approvingly commented on Eltinge's male role in his first musical comedy: "the wonder of Julian's impersonations will be intensified for the audience when they see him as a stalwart youngster with the biceps of a John L. Sullivan." "The Fascinating Widow," *New York Telegraph*, 1910, RLC, vol. 182, Reel 15, NYPL.

124. Untitled, n.p., Apr 1, 1910, RLC, vol. 182, Reel 15, 54, NYPL.

125. In later years, he also purchased a large undeveloped plot of land in California, on which he hoped to start a ranch for actors. "Julian Eltinge Back with A Most Widowish Plumpness," Jul 1, 1915, RLC, ser. 3, vol. 432, 99, NYPL.

126. "Julian Eltinge Tells of Life between Seasons on His Long Island Farm," *Julian Eltinge Magazine*, c. 1912, 21, TWC, NYPL.

127. Ibid., 21, 23. Emphasis mine.

128. Untitled, n.p., n.d., RLC, vol. 182, Reel 15, 52, NYPL.

129. "Julian Eltinge Advises Ladies to Learn Gentle Art of Boxing," *Julian Eltinge Magazine*, c. 1912, 17, 18, TWC, NYPL.

130. Bederman, *Manliness and Civilization*, 157.

131. Ibid., 3.

132. Lois Banner, *American Beauty* (New York, Alfred A. Knopf, 1983), 154.

133. "Julian Eltinge Advises Ladies to Learn Gentle Art of Boxing," *Julian Eltinge Magazine*, c. 1912, 17, 18, TWC, NYPL.

134. Banner, *American Beauty*, 157.

135. "Castle Square Will Present a Maggie Mitchell Success This Week," *Boston Sunday Journal*, Jul 19, 1903, 10.

136. Bederman, *Manliness and Civilization*, 8.
137. "Julian Eltinge's Ideal Husband and Wife," *Julian Eltinge Magazine*, 50, TWC, NYPL. Emphasis mine.
138. The lyrics to "The Modern Sandow Girl," also sung in Florenz Ziegfeld's "The Follies of 1907," described the notion of separate spheres as old-fashioned and celebrated the fashionable convergence of manliness and womanliness in both physical and cultural arenas. However, they also appeared to poke fun at such changes. Words by Harry B. Smith, Music by Gus Edwards, Gus Edwards Music Pub. Co, 1512, Broadway N.Y. HTC, HL, Harvard.
139. Marie Corelli, "The Palm of Beauty," *Julian Eltinge Magazine and Beauty Hints*, c. 1912, 5, TWC, NYPL. Emphasis mine.
140. Bederman, *Manliness and Civilization*, 25.
141. Untitled photographs, Chamberlain and Lyman Brown Theatrical Agency Collection, NYPL.
142. Eltinge affectionately referred to his corsets as "Old Ironsides" and publicly endorsed commercial brands such as "R and G Abdoband Corsets," which he claimed to wear "exclusively" to whittle his 38-inch waist down to 26 inches. *Julian Eltinge Magazine*, 65, TWC, NYPL.
143. Walter Anthony, "Eltinge's Show is Great Vaudeville," *Post-Intelligencer*, Jun 30, 1919, RLC, NYPL.
144. "English's-Cohan's Minstrels," *Indianapolis News*, Sep 30, 1908, RLC, vol. 182, Reel 15, NYPL. Emphasis mine.
145. Kellar, "Making a Woman of Himself."
146. Mizejewski, *Ziegfeld Girl*, 121.
147. "Julian Eltinge (Paramount Star)," 1918, RLC, NYPL.
148. Julian Eltinge, "How I Portray a Woman on the Stage," *Theatre Magazine*, Aug 1913, 58, RLC, NYPL.
149. Kellar, "Making a Woman of Himself."
150. Kathy Peiss, *Hope in a Jar* (New York: Henry Holt and Company, 1998), 39, 19.
151. Ibid., 40.
152. Ibid., 40, 21.
153. Ibid., 15, 41.
154. Ibid., 31.
155. Roediger, *Wages of Whiteness*, 12.
156. Ibid.
157. "Would Let Woman Choose Own Way," *Boston Daily Globe*, May 13, 1912, 11.
158. Roediger, *Wages of Whiteness*, 117.
159. Ibid.
160. "In Just a Minute," *Boston Daily Globe*, Feb 13, 1911, 3.
161. Guterl, *The Color of Race in America*, 5.
162. Ibid., 43.
163. Ibid.
164. In *The Wages of Whiteness*, Roediger's focus on the "interpenetration" of race and class leaves little room for exploring how gender and race shaped each other in meaningful ways, 11.

165. "Julian Eltinge Delights the Fair Ones," *The Julian Eltinge Magazine and Beauty Hints*, c. 1912, 57, TWC, NYPL.

166. Eltinge further enticed readers by offering six large photographs "showing him as Bride, Bathing Girl, Society Woman, Dressing for the Stage, Widow and Himself. Any of these beautiful pictures will be mailed free with every jar of cold cream." "Julian Eltinge Delights the Fair Ones," *The Julian Eltinge Magazine and Beauty Hints*, c. 1912, 57, TWC, NYPL.

167. "Be As Beautiful As Julian Eltinge," *The Julian Eltinge Magazine and Beauty Hints*, 60, TWC, NYPL.

168. "Julian's Own Recipe which He Uses for Making Up," *The Julian Eltinge Magazine and Beauty Hints*, c. 1912, 59, TWC, NYPL.

169. Untitled article, *The Julian Eltinge Magazine and Beauty Hints*, 40, TWC, NYPL.

170. *The Julian Eltinge Magazine and Beauty Hints*, c. 1912, 40, TWC, NYPL.

171. Peiss, *Hope in a Jar*, 44, 48.

172. For further discussion on the importance of whiteness in Anna Held's performances, see Pamela Brown Lavitt's article, "First of the Red Hot Mamas: 'Coon Shouting' and the Jewish Ziegfeld Girl," *American Jewish History* 87, no. 4 (Dec. 1999): 253–290, especially 267–270.

173. Ibid., 269.

174. Ibid., 268.

175. For instance, in 1914, Held published "My Own Beauty Secrets" in the *Atlanta Georgian*. Ibid., 270.

176. Moore, *Drag!* 101.

177. *Julian Eltinge Magazine*, 63, c. 1912, TWC, NYPL.

178. "Eltinge Packs a Wallop in his Delicate Mitt," *New York Telegraph*, Aug 16, 1917, RLC, NYPL.

179. Moore, *Drag!* 108.

180. Ibid., 107.

181. "Julian Eltinge Hurt When Auto Crashes into a Police Car," *Chicago Daily Tribune*, Jul 11, 1929, 7.

182. Chauncey, *Gay New York*, 9, 13, 23.

183. Moore, *Drag!* 108; Senelick, *The Changing Room*, 382.

184. Moore, *Drag!* 109.

185. "Critic Recalls the Career of Julian Eltinge," *Chicago Daily Tribune*, Mar 16, 1941, H8.

CHAPTER 3

1. Ralph Matthews, "Looking at the Stars," *The Baltimore Afro-American*, Jul 7, 1934, 9.

2. Robert Kya-Hill, Telephone communication with Kathleen Casey, Feb 10, 2010; Floyd G. Nelson, "Harlem Limited Broadway Bound," *Pittsburgh Courier*, Nov 1, 1930, B8.

3. Matthews, "Looking at the Stars," 9.

4. Floyd G. Snelson, "Harlem Limited Broadway Bound," B8. For a fascinating discussion of the primitive obsessions and interracial relationships of Nancy Cunard, see Ann Douglas, *Terrible Honesty*, chap. 7, "Black Man and White Ladyship," especially 272–282.

5. "Lillian [sic] Brown Wilson, 83, Dies; Vaudeville Star and an Actress," *New York Times,* Jun 11, 1969, 47.

6. Chad Heap, *Slumming: Sexual and Racial Encounters in American Nightlife, 1885-1940* (Chicago: University of Chicago, 2009), 10.

7. Harry J. Elam Jr. and David Krasner, Eds., *African American Performance and Theatre History: A Critical Reader* (New York: Oxford University Press, 2001), 139.

8. Karen Sotiropoulos argues that the first blues song, written by W.C. Handy, was not published until 1912. Sotiropoulos, *Staging Race,* 12.

9. Although not the first black woman to record the blues (Mamie Smith did so just seven months earlier on the OKeh label), Brown was the first black woman to record on the Emerson label. Among other works, Paul Oliver, *The Story of the Blues* and Samuel Charters, *Jazz* (Garden City, NY: Doubleday, 1962) credit Brown with this honor. The songs she recorded in this session are available on compact disc in *The Complete Recorded Works of Esther Bigeou, Lillyn Brown, Alberta Brown and the Remaining Titles of Ada Brown.*

10. For a discussion of how the earliest commercial recordings of "vaudeville blues" by singers such as Brown, Mamie Smith, Lucille Hegamin, and Lavinia Turner differed from "folk blues," see Steven C. Tracy, *Write Me a Few of Your Lines: A Blues Reader* (Amherst: University of Massachusetts Press, 1999), 4–5.

11. D. Antoinette Handy, *The International Sweethearts of Rhythm* (Metuchen, NJ: The Scarecrow Press, 1983), 62.

12. "'Dandies' Star an Atlanta Girl," *The Baltimore Afro-American,* Oct 10, 1924, 2.

13. Ibid.

14. For examples, see Hazel Carby, "'It Jus Be 'Dat Way Sometime:' The Sexual Politics of Women's Blues," *Radical America* 20, no. 4 (1987): 8–22; Daphne Duval Harrison, *Black Pearls: Blues Queens of the 1920s* (New Brunswick, N.J.: Rutgers University Press, 1988), and Angela Y. Davis, *Blues Legacies and Black Feminism: Gertrude "Ma" Rainey, Bessie Smith, and Billie Holiday* (New York: Pantheon Books, 1998).

15. Although no recordings exist of more celebrated sometime male impersonators such as Aida Overton Walker and Florence Mills, their histories have been explored more fully. On Florence Mills, see Bill Egan, *Florence Mills: Harlem Jazz Queen (Studies in Jazz)* (Oxford: Scarecrow Press, 2004). On Aida Overton Walker, see Richard Newman, "'The Brightest Star:' Aida Overton Walker in the Age of Ragtime and Cakewalk," *Prospects* no. 18 (1993), and David Krasner, *Resistance, Parody, and Double Consciousness in African American Theatre, 1895–1910.* Two recent works have analyzed black gender impersonators, though they have focused on nightclubs rather than vaudeville. See Heap, *Slumming* and Laura Grantmyre, "They lived their life and they didn't bother anybody": African American Female Impersonators and Pittsburgh's Hill District, 1920-1960," *American Quarterly* 63, no. 4 (Dec 2011): 983–1011. Though she does not examine vaudeville either, Anne Marie Bean has also helped fill the gap in this literature by focusing on race in gender impersonation in her essay "Black Minstrelsy and Double Inversion Circa 1890," *African American Performance and Theatre History,* 171–191.

16. Krasner, *A Beautiful Pageant*, 3.
17. For information on vaudeville's *de facto* seating policies and black patrons' attempts to challenge them, see Sotiropoulos, *Staging Race*, 63–74.
18. James Weldon Johnson, "The Dilemma of the Negro Author," *The Essential Writings of James Weldon Johnson* (Random House, 2008), 202. Originally published in *The American Mercury*, Dec 1938.
19. Mitchell, *Righteous Propagation*, 13.
20. Marshall Stearns's notes on "Brown, Lillyn 1952, Dec 20," IJS, Rutgers.
21. Ibid.
22. Leonard Kunstadt, "Lillyn Brown Discography," *Record Research* 2, no. 4, (Nov/Dec 1956): 12.
23. Heap, *Slumming*, 225.
24. Gershon Alexander Legman, "The Language of Homosexuality: An American Glossary," *Sex Variants: A Study of Homosexual Patterns*, George W. Henry, M.D. (New York: Paul B. Hoeber, 1941), 1170.
25. J.E. Lighter, Ed., *Random House Historical Dictionary of American Slang*, vol. 1 A-G (New York: Random House, 1997), 436.
26. Snelson, "Harlem Limited Broadway Bound," B8; Malcolm Poindexter, Jr. "Lillyan [*sic*] Brown Ends Stage Career With 'Kiss Me Kate,'" *Philadelphia Tribune*, Nov 24, 1951, 9; Marshall Stearns's notes on "Brown, Lillyn 1952, Dec 20," IJS, Rutgers.
27. Mura Dehn, Interview with Lillian [*sic*] Brown, Papers on Afro-American Dance, c. 1869–1987, JRDD, NYPL, 11.
28. Snelson, "Harlem Limited Broadway Bound," B8.
29. Ibid.
30. Dehn, Interview with Lillian [*sic*] Brown, 11.
31. Ibid., 12.
32. Ibid., 11.
33. Marshall Stearns's notes on "Brown, Lillyn 1952, Dec 20," IJS.
34. Kibler, *Rank Ladies*, 123.
35. Unlike Brown, Whitman was not characterized as a surprise act; in other words, her impersonations were not intended to trick anyone into believing she was a man.
36. In *Royalty of Negro Vaudeville* Nadine George-Graves provides an interesting study of the Whitman sisters, but does not focus on "Bert's" male impersonations. Nadine George-Graves, *The Royalty of Negro Vaudeville: The Whitman Sisters and the Negotiation of Race, Gender and Class in African American Theater, 1900-1940* (New York: St. Martin's Press, 2000).
37. Lulu Jones Garret, "Bert Whitman, Subbing for Man, Liked Role and Stuck," *The Baltimore Afro-American*, Dec 21, 1929, A10.
38. Brown is presumably referring to a song called "If I Was Only Pierpont Morgan." Dehn, Interview with Lillian [*sic*] Brown, 14.
39. Dehn, Interview with Lillian [*sic*] Brown, 13. Emphasis mine.
40. Sotiropoulos, *Staging Race*, 36–37; Bean, "Blackface Minstrelsy and Double Inversion," 180-181.
41. Dehn, Interview with Lillian [*sic*] Brown, 14. Emphasis mine.
42. Ibid.
43. "Gossip about People of the Stage," *Washington Post*, Apr 22, 1906, RA8.

44. English actresses dominated this first generation of male impersonators, of which Donner and Tilley were the most visible stars. Other male impersonators from the British music hall included Annie Hindle, Bessie Bonehill and later, Hetty King.

45. Judith Halberstam, "Mackdaddy, Superfly, Rapper: Gender, Race and Masculinity in the Drag King Scene," *Social Text* no. 52/53 (Autumn 1997): 113.

46. Gillian Rodger, "'He Isn't a Marrying Man:' Gender and Sexuality in the Repertoire of Male Impersonators, 1870–1930." In *Queer Episodes in Music and Modern Identity*, Eds. Sophie Fuller and Lloyd Whitesell (Urbana: University of Illinois Press, 2002), 105, 122. Rodger argues that "by the 1920s, if not earlier, the stigmatized social categories 'gay man' and 'lesbian,' had come to be associated with the central feature of this performance style: cross-dressing." 106. For more information on the two previous generations of male impersonators, see chap. 2 and 4, Gillian Rodger, "Male Impersonation on the North American Variety Stage, 1860–1930." PhD diss. University of Pittsburgh, 1998.

47. Ullman, "The 'Self-Made Man': Male Impersonation and the New Woman," in *Passing: Identity and Interpretation in Sexuality, Race and Religion*, Eds. Maria Carla Sanchez and Linda Schlossberg (New York: New York University Press, 2001), 197.

48. As a testament to her talents, black critics often cited white critics' comparisons of Brown to British male impersonator Kitty Donner. For example, "White critics in their praise have rated Miss Brown above the famous English impersonator, Miss Kitty Donner." "Film Operator Dies of Burns," *The Baltimore Afro-American*, May 16, 1931, 9. Like Eltinge, Donner was perceived as an artist. Though her act included several different male impersonations, *The Washington Post* described her as "just as much at home in feminine duds." "Keith's," Jan 17, 1927, 13.

49. Garber, *Vested Interests*, 63.

50. Ullman, "The 'Self-Made Man,'" 197.

51. Ibid.

52. Rodger, "He Isn't a Marrying Man," 123.

53. One exception was a contemporary group of white women cheekily called "The Beef Trust," who each weighed at least two hundred pounds.

54. In *The Changing Room*, Senelick includes a photograph of a large woman named Louise Rott, "a German serio-comic, billed as a '*weibliche Gesangskomiker*'" (female singing comedian), 333.

55. Ullman, "The 'Self-Made Man,'" 198.

56. Ibid.

57. Hailed as one of the most successful male impersonators, British performer Vesta Tilley was also considered one of the most realistic. Yet her impersonations, too, were characterized as "boys." Anthony Slide, *Selected Vaudeville Criticisms* (Lanham, Md.: Scarecrow Press, 1988), 184. Cited in Ullman, "The 'Self-Made Man,'" 197, n24.

58. Rodger, "He Isn't a Marrying Man," 123.

59. See *The Golden Years of Music Hall*, Compact Disc, Saydisc, 1995. In an interview, Tilley explained that she deliberately left "just enough of a woman in my impersonations to keep my work clean." Rodger, "He Isn't a Marrying Man," 123.

60. Rodger, "He Isn't a Marrying Man," 124.
61. Rodger, "He Isn't a Marrying Man," 125. Active between 1900 and 1930, Ella Shields is an interesting exception to this rule; she sang in the first person in at least one of her recordings.
62. Rodger, "He Isn't a Marrying Man," 124.
63. Ibid.
64. Ibid., 125.
65. Smith-Rosenberg, *Hidden From History*, 269. Emphasis mine. For Richard von Krafft-Ebing's work, see "Psychopathia Sexualis," 1886.
66. Smith-Rosenberg, *Hidden From History*, 279.
67. Ibid., 269.
68. "Article 4—No Title," *New York Amsterdam News*, Feb 15, 1940. 17; George D. Tyler, "Male Impersonator Must Quit Stage," *The Baltimore Afro-American*, Dec 12, 1931, 9.
69. Floyd G. Nelson, "Harlem Limited Broadway Bound," B8.
70. In contrast, white male impersonator Vesta Tilley declared her distaste for "mannish" women. Vesta Tilley, "The 'Mannish' Woman," *Pittsburgh Gazette Home Journal*, Apr 3, 1904, 5. Cited in Rodger, "He Isn't a Marrying Man," 132.
71. Smith-Rosenberg, *Hidden From History*, 267.
72. Lulu Jones Garret, "Bert Whitman, Subbing for Man, Liked Role and Stuck," *The Baltimore Afro-American*, Dec 21, 1929, A10.
73. Ibid.
74. Rodger, "He Isn't a Marrying Man," 130.
75. According to blues scholar Paul Oliver, most female blues singers started out singing in the South in poorly equipped tents lacking microphones. "The weaker voiced singers used a megaphone, but most of the featured women's blues singers scorned such aids to volume." Paul Oliver, *The Story of the Blues* (Philadelphia: Chilton Book Company, 1969), 60. Ann Douglas notes that the electric microphone was not invented until 1925. *Terrible Honesty*, 360.
76. "Serenaders Stand Out at Harlem Opera House," *New York Amsterdam News*, Dec 22, 1934, 10; Robert Kya Hill, Telephone Interview with Kathleen Casey, Feb 10, 2010.
77. Recorded one year after the Volstead amendment prohibited the sale, and manufacture of alcohol, the song announced the singer's disdain for the law as well as for the man who stole his lover. Information on the song's composer and its categorization as a "blues" number taken from Leonard Kunstadt's notes on Lillyn Brown, "Lillyn Brown with the Jazzbo Syncopators," Jul 29, 1952. IJS, Rutgers University.
78. Miles M. Jefferson, "The Negro on Broadway, 1949–1950," *Phylon* XI, no. 2 (Second Quarter, 1950): 105–113.
79. Reviews of British male impersonator Hetty King also noted the length of her long hair. Rodger, "He Isn't a Marrying Man," 132, n27.
80. Matthews, "Looking at the Stars," *The Baltimore Afro-American*, Jul 7, 1934, 9.
81. "At Harlem Theatres," *New York Amsterdam News*, Aug 7, 1929, 13.
82. Laurie, *Vaudeville*, 91.

83. Ibid., 90.
84. In a telephone interview with the author, Kya-Hill insisted Brown's impersonations "really had them fooled." Feb 10, 2010.
85. Bean suggests, "it is certainly possible, given the proliferation of black male impersonators in vaudeville, that these women were deftly performing one of many stock roles. . . . African American male impersonators inverted a theatrical playing out of dominance, turning over and around the assertion of power by the white male." Bean further claims, "The importance of their challenge is related to the performances of white male impersonators... who reconstituted women's bodies and marked them as almost male, as opposed to hyperfeminine." Bean, "Double Inversion," 186–7.
86. "Denies 'Father Divine' Song Reflects on Any Religion," *Los Angeles Sentinel,* Jan 8, 1948, 16.
87. Gladys Bentley, "I am a Woman Again," *Ebony* (Aug 1952), 93; Eric Garber, "Gladys Bentley: The Bulldagger who sang the Blues," 324; Dorothy Anderson, "Yawning After," *The Baltimore Afro-American,* Feb 16, 1935, 18.
88. In its profile of her, *The Baltimore Afro-American* detailed her "chauffeur, two homes, a country one for... and a summer town home with a domestic staff of four" and a prize-winning show dog valued at 1,000 dollars. Dorothy Anderson, "Yawning After," *The Baltimore Afro-American,* Feb 16, 1935, 18.
89. Anderson, "Yawning After," 18.
90. "Swingland's New Sensation," *Chicago Defender,* Apr 9, 1938, 18, col. 3.
91. Matthews, "Looking at the Stars," 9. Emphasis mine.
92. Ibid.
93. Heap, *Slumming,* 241.
94. See Chauncey, *Gay New York,* chap. 12, "The Exclusion of Homosexuality from the Public Sphere in the 1930s," especially 331–332, 337–349.
95. Mitchell, *Righteous Propagation,* 121.
96. Ullman, "The 'Self-Made Man,'" 203.
97. Ibid., 199.
98. *The Chicago Daily Tribune* called Eltinge "ambisextrous" on at least two occasions. Percy Hammond, "Music and Drama," Dec 6, 1910, 8; Untitled newspaper clipping, Mar 22, 1914, RLC, NYPL. This lengthy profile, "Bert Whitman, Subbing for Man, Liked Role and Stuck," featured subtitles highlighting Whitman's gender transgressions: "Takes Male Role," "Mannish Attire," and "Doesn't Like Long Dresses," Lulu Jones Garret, *The Baltimore Afro-American,* Dec 21, 1929, A10.
99. Heap, *Slumming,* 239.
100. "Many Actresses Have Worn Trousers," *The Baltimore Afro-American,* Mar 18, 1933, 8.
101. For additional primary sources on popular distaste for women wearing pants, see "Why an Actress Cannot Wear Trousers Like a Man," *New York Journal,* Feb 13, 1898; "Fascination of Masculine Garb for Ambitious Actresses," *New York Morning Telegraph,* Jul 5, 1903; "Stage Arts Adamless Eden," *New York Herald,* Jul 10, 1904; Perriton Maxwell, "Stage Beauty in Breeches," *Theatre Magazine,* Aug 24, 1916: 73, 75, 96. Cited by Rodger, "He Isn't a Marrying Man," 132, n24.
102. "Many Actresses Have Worn Trousers," *Afro-American,* Mar 18, 1933, 8.

103. Matthews, "Looking at the Stars," 9.
104. "Ellis Glenn Freed," *Washington Post*, Jun 4, 1905, 9.
105. "Male Impersonator Taken," *Atlanta Constitution*, Dec 11, 1901, 5.
106. *The Morning Oregonian*, Jun 4, 1912, 12.
107. Garber, "Spectacle of Color," 325.
108. Gerry, "Men Tenors, Women Wear Tuxedos at Costume Ball," *The Baltimore Afro-American*, Feb 22, 1930, A5.
109. Eric Garber, "Spectacle of Color," 328; Chauncey, *Gay New York*, 291–299.
110. Gerry, "Men Tenors," A5.
111. For examples, see "Brooklyn News and Social Briefs," *New York Amsterdam News*, Nov 7, 1928, 10; "Nursery and Dance," May 7, 1930, 6; "Impersonators' Ball at Modern," *Daily Defender*, Oct 17, 1957, 20, col. 4 and John Fuster, "About the Stage, Radio and Screen," *Cleveland Call and Post*, Feb 4, 1961, 7A.
112. In searching white-owned newspapers for impersonation ball advertisements, I located one advertisement for a contest sponsored by a City Parks Department. However, the contest did not solicit gender impersonators and specifically limited the contest to "characters of history, fiction, movies and stage." "Plays, Impersonations to Make Up Programs," *Atlanta Constitution*, Aug 1, 1937, 10B.
113. "Mask Dance at Masonic Hall," *Chicago Defender*, Feb 23, 1918, 5, col. 4.
114. For example, though she examined the significance psychologists and sexologists attributed to women's clothing, in her essay on the New Woman, historian Carroll Smith-Rosenberg argued: "Clothes are cultural artifacts, lightly donned or doffed, but words are rooted in our earliest and most profound experiences of social location and of the distribution of power." Smith-Rosenberg, *Hidden From History*, 264. In *Ladies of Labor, Girls of Adventure: Working Women, Popular Culture, and Labor Politics at the Turn of the Twentieth Century* (New York: Columbia University Press, 1999), Nan Enstad provides an insightful discussion of the ways in which working women's fashion was inherently political.
115. Smith-Rosenberg, *Hidden From History*, 269.
116. Kibler supports this contention in *Rank Ladies*, 93.
117. Laurie, *Vaudeville*, 93.
118. Kibler argues such actresses were motivated to take on these parts because they could seize the best roles. *Rank Ladies*, 89.
119. Rodger, "He Isn't a Marrying Man," 113.
120. Ibid., 115.
121. Judith Halberstam makes a similar criticism of scholarship on male impersonation in "Mack Daddy, Superfly, Rapper." She notes that "white and black male impersonation... have very different histories in the United States.... Histories of male impersonation tend to focus on white actresses and do not allow for very different productions of drag in communities of color." 112.
122. Mitchell, *Righteous Propagation*, 81.
123. Lynn Abbott and Doug Seroff, *Out of Sight: The Rise of African American Popular Music, 1889-1895 (American Made Music)* (Jackson: University Press of Mississippi, 2002), 156.
124. Sotiropoulos, *Staging Race*, 9–10.

125. Though both were urban figures, the Zip Coon differed in its specific dero-
gation of free blacks. Unlike the suave black dandy, the antebellum Zip
Coon was "an urban buffoon who derided free blacks and insinuated that
African Americans were unfit for freedom and urban life." Sotiropoulos,
Staging Race, 21.

126. Bederman, *Manliness and Civilization*, 25.

127. Monica L. Miller, *Slaves to Fashion: Black Dandyism and the Styling of
Black Diasporic Identity* (Durham: Duke University Press, 2009), 178.

128. Ibid., 202.

129. Ibid., 82.

130. Ibid., 92.

131. Ibid., 92–93.

132. Sotiropoulos, *Staging Race*, 50.

133. Miller, 202.

134. Laurie, *Vaudeville*, 95; Kibler, *Rank Ladies*, 111–142. Interestingly, very
few white actresses wore blackface while impersonating men (dandies or
otherwise). In chapter 5, "The Corking Girls," of *Rank Ladies*, Kibler provides rare insight on these women.

135. *The Chicago Defender* praised the equally fair-skinned dandy impersonator Alberta Whitman, "who works under cork," adding that "comediennes who work in blackface are so few that Miss Whitman is a distinct
novelty." "New Monogram," *Chicago Defender*, Mar 4, 1916, 5. For more
information on black women's beauty products, see chap. 2 of Davarian
Baldwin, *Chicago's New Negroes* and Peiss, *Hope In a Jar*.

136. "Lillian [*sic*] Brown Wilson," *Variety*, Jun 18, 1969, Lillyn Brown clippings
file, Theatre Division, NYPL.

137. Snelson, "Harlem Limited Broadway Bound," B8.

138. About "Dixie to Broadway," a revue in which Brown performed with
Florence Mills, theatre historian Krasner argues, "White critics struggled to
locate the show's 'blackness.'" The same might be said about Brown herself.
Krasner, *A Beautiful Pageant*, 282; "Lillian [*sic*] Brown Wilson, 83, Dies;
Vaudeville Star and an Actress," Jun 11, 1969, *New York Times*, Lillyn Brown
clippings file, BRTD, NYPL; Heywood Broun, "The New Play," *New York
World*, Oct 30, 1924, Florence Mills clipping file, Dance Collection, NYPL.

139. For more information on the history of black blues "queens," the connections between their art and personal experiences, and an in-depth treatment of Sippie Wallace, Victoria Spivey, Edith Wilson, and Alberta Hunter,
see Daphne Duval Harrison, *Black Pearls*.

140. In addition to Florence Hines, Brown and DeMont likely took inspiration
from George Walker and Bert Williams, whose act featured the two men
singing and dancing in formal suits. Malcolm Poindexter Jr., "Lillyan [*sic*]
Brown Ends Stage Career With 'Kiss Me Kate,'" *Philadelphia Tribune*,
Nov 24, 1951, 9.

141. For example, in May 1919, while performing on the vaudeville circuit
with DeMont, a Buffalo newspaper called the two "blackface comedians,"
noting that, as the only 'black act,' the two added "a touch of color" to the
bill. "At The Lyric," *Illustrated Buffalo Express*, May 11, 1919, 3.

142. Sotiropoulos makes such an argument about black performers generally in *Staging Race*. When parodying Jewish blackface singer/comedian

Al Jolson, Brown questioned Jolson's claim to whiteness and his right to mock blackness. Her imitation of Jolson imitating black Americans paralleled the forces at work when black performers did the cakewalk, which originated from slaves' imitations of their white slave owners. Adding yet another layer of inversion, at the turn of the century, well-heeled whites hired African American performers like Aida Overton Walker to teach them this "black" dance.

143. Sotiropoulos, *Staging Race*, 3, 64, 89.
144. "Gaiety Will Offer Stars of Southland," *Utica Daily Press*, Dec 17, 1927, 13.
145. "'Dandies' Star an Atlanta Girl," *The Baltimore Afro-American*, Oct 10, 1924, 2.
146. Under the headline "Good Clean Comedy," in 1918, *Utica Herald Dispatch* described the two as "meritorious entertainers" that provide a "study in black and tan." *Utica Herald Dispatch*, Dec 10, 1918.
147. Sotiropoulos, *Staging Race*, 48, 90–94.
148. Untitled, *Chicago Defender*, Jun 25, 1921, 8, col. 2.
149. Charters, *Jazz*, 98.
150. In introducing her new moniker, newspapers did not reveal her real name, though they acknowledged "Elbrown" was a male impersonator, thereby implying she was a woman.
151. Leon Abbey, "Paris Gossip," *Philadelphia Tribune*, Sep 4, 1930. 7; "Singers to Tour Switzerland," *The Baltimore Afro-American*, Sep 6, 1930, A9.
152. Snelson, "Harlem Limited Broadway Bound," B8.
153. Ibid.
154. Ibid.
155. "Here and There with Bob Hayes," *Chicago Defender (National edition)* Apr 12, 1930, 7.
156. Sotiropoulos makes a similar point in *Staging Race*, 7.
157. Birdie Brass, Untitled letter to the editor, *Chicago Defender*, Jul 29, 1916, 4, col. 5.
158. Douglas, *Terrible Honesty*, 98–107.
159. On Johnson and DuBois as black dandies, see chap. 3, "W.E.B. DuBois's 'Different' Race Man" and chap. 4, "'Passing Fancies:' Dandyism, Harlem Modernism, and the Politics of Visuality," in Miller, *Slaves to Fashion*.
160. Dehn, Interview with Lillian [sic] Brown, 14.
161. Garber, "Gladys Bentley," 60.
162. Gladys Bentley, "I am a Woman Again." *Ebony* (Aug 1952), 92–98; "Baby Dies as Mother Sees Show," *The Baltimore Afro-American*, Jul 26, 1952, 20; Florence Cadrez, "Mostly 'Bout Musicians," *Los Angeles Sentinel*, Oct 27, 1955, A11.
163. Bentley, "I am a Woman Again," 92.
164. Ibid.
165. Garber, "Gladys Bentley," 61.
166. "Services Set for Mrs. Wilson," *New York Amsterdam News*, Jun 14, 1969, 16.
167. "March King Pianist Dies," *New York Amsterdam News*, Feb 7, 1959, 22.
168. On Bentley's death see Garber, "Gladys Bentley," 60-61. On Brown's last recording, see Victoria Spivey, "Blues are My Business," *Record Research*

68 (May 1965), 6. My search for "I'm Blue and Rockin'" yielded no results. Dan Morgenstern, Director of the Institute for Jazz Studies at Rutgers, confirms that, despite Spivey's promise to release Brown's record by the end of the year, Spivey Records never did so. Dan Morgenstern, email correspondence with Kathleen Casey, Feb 22, 2010.

169. For more information on the connections between fashion and visual deviance from the 1930s to the 1960s, see Elizabeth Lapovsky Kennedy and Madeline D. Davis, *Boots of Leather, Slippers of Gold: The History of a Lesbian Community* (New York: Routledge, 1993).

170. W.E.B. DuBois. *The Souls of Black Folk* (Chicago: A.C. McClurg and Co, 1972), vii.

CHAPTER 4

1. Michael Awkward uses the term transraciality "to describe the adoption of physical traits of difference for the purpose of impersonating a racial other." Michael Awkward, *Negotiating Difference: Race, Gender, and the Politics of Positionality (Black Literature and Culture)* (Chicago: University of Chicago Press, 1995), 19. As quoted by Susan Gubar, *Racechanges: White Skin, Black Face in American Culture (Race and American Culture)* (New York: Oxford University Press, 1997), 248.

2. By June Sochen, see "From Sophie Tucker to Barbra Streisand: Jewish Women Entertainers as Reformers," in Joyce Antler, Ed., *Talking Back: Images of Jewish Women in American Popular Culture (Brandeis Series in American Jewish, History, Culture, and Life)* (Hanover: Brandeis University Press, 1998), 68–84; "Fanny Brice and Sophie Tucker: Blending the Particular with the Universal," Sarah Blacher Cohen, Ed., *From Hester Street to Hollywood: The Jewish-American Stage and Screen* (Bloomington: Indiana University Press, 1983), 44–57.

3. For a more nuanced recent treatment of Tucker, see, Harrison-Kahan, *The White Negress.*

4. Harrison-Kahan, *The White Negress,* 13.

5. Archeophone records released twenty-four of Tucker's earliest recordings on the compact disc "Origins of the Red Hot Mama, 1910-1922" in May 2009. Archeophone Records. In this chapter I also rely heavily on archives located at the Robinson Locke and Sophie Tucker Collections at the New York Public Library.

6. According to Tucker's biographer, Tucker was born in January 1886. Armond Fields, *Sophie Tucker: First Lady of Show Business,* 251, chap. 1, n4.

7. Robert Snyder, *The Voice of the City,* 48, 62–6, 117–20.

8. Goldstein, *The Price of Whiteness,* 3.

9. Ibid., 35.

10. Ibid., 3.

11. Fields, *Sophie Tucker,* 14.

12. Fields, *Sophie Tucker,* 15; Tucker, *Some of These Days,* 15.

13. Tucker, *Some of These Days,* 60.

14. "Sophie Tucker: She's Indebted to a Maid who was Worth a Fortune," *The Baltimore Afro-American,* Jan 31, 1948, M3.

15. "Shout, Coon, Shout!" *The Musical Quarterly* 16, no. 4 (Oct 1930): 517.

16. "Sophie Tucker 'Mary Garden of Ragtime' at Orpheum; Educated Canine a Feature," *Duluth News-Tribune* (published as *Sunday News Tribune*), Oct 10, 1916, 6. In reality, May Irwin had already honed a similar style using dialect in the 1890s, though she did not appear in blackface.

17. "Queen of All Ragtime Airs: Sophie Tucker—Singer of Joy Songs: Sophie Tucker Explains Change in Her Songs," *Los Angeles Times*, Dec 16, 1917, III, 22.

18. "The Vaudeville Bill Has Caught On and Audiences are Delighted," n.p., c. 1908, STC, BRTD, NYPL.

19. "Music with a Kick Was Always Popular," *Boston Daily Globe*, Nov 16, 1919, 64.

20. Michael Seiler, "Eubie Blake, Treasure of Musical Past, Dies at 100," *Los Angeles Times*, Feb 13, 1983, 30.

21. Leone Cass Baer, "Coon Shouter Shouts Brother an Education," *Oregonian* (Published as *Morning Oregonian*), Aug 10, 1912, 7.

22. Baer, "Coon Shouter Shouts Brother an Education," 7.

23. Ibid.

24. Johnson, "Sophie Tucker; Barney Bernard," H5.

25. Fields, *Sophie Tucker*, 25.

26. "Music with a Kick was Always Popular," *Boston Daily Globe*, Nov 16, 1919, 64.

27. "Bill Robinson Taps his Toes at Palace," *New York Times*, Feb 15, 1932, 13.

28. Julian Johnson, "Sophie Tucker; Barney Bernard," *Los Angeles Times*, Jul 23, 1912, H5.

29. Tucker, *Some of These Days*, 33.

30. Ibid., 34.

31. Ibid., 33.

32. Ibid., 35.

33. Ibid.

34. Ibid., 40.

35. "The Vaudeville Bill Has Caught On and Audiences are Delighted," n.p., c. 1908, STC, BRTD, NYPL.

36. Ibid.

37. "New Orpheum," n.p., c.1908, STC, BRTC, NYPL.

38. Waters, *His Eye is on the Sparrow*, 139.

39. Tucker, *Some of These Days*, 52. In *Rank Ladies*, Kibler examines a fascinating dancing group of cross-dressing women called the "The Minstrel Misses." The group applied blackface on stage during their act and headlined on the Keith circuit in 1903. She also discusses the blackface performances of Josephine Gassman, and Lulu and Mabel Nichols. See chap. 5, "The Corking Girls."

40. Tucker, *Some of These Days*, 60.

41. Though she felt it denied her femininity, Tucker later acknowledged, "blackface molded my performance style, enhancing the physicality of my performance and introducing me to the modern syncopated style of music that would facilitate my later embrace of jazz." Lois Tulin-Young, *Sophie and Me: Some of These Days* (San Jose: iUniverse, 2001), 132.

42. Untitled newspaper clipping, *South Bend Tribune*, Mar 18, 1913, Envelope 1614, RLC, NYPL, as cited by Kibler, 123, 241, n55.

43. These songs were probably intended to be sung by a man, as "Don't Put a Tax on the Beautiful Girls" was also famously sung by Eddie Cantor, "You're A Dog-gone Dangerous Girl" by Al Jolson and "High Brown Blues" by Irish-American singer Billy Murray. Other male-centered songs in Tucker's repertoire included "I've Found My Sweetheart Sally," "Oh, You Beautiful Doll," and "You'll never Know the Good Fellow I've Been." Inventory of the Sophie Tucker Collection. New York Public Library for the Performing Arts. Music Division. JPB 81–7. <http://www.nypl.org/research/manuscripts/music/mustucker.xml>. Jan 3, 2010.

44. Bederman, *Manliness and Civilization*, 25.

45. At the same session she recorded "Bad Land Blues," Brown also recorded "Ever Lovin' Blues," in which a female narrator bemoans her loneliness in the same voice.

46. Kibler, *Rank Ladies*, 132.

47. Ibid.

48. This changed briefly in 1929, when twenty-four year old Albert entered the public eye with a brief foray as a vaudeville dancer. Tucker was apparently less than pleased by Albert's attempt to follow in her professional footsteps; according to her biographer, she once cancelled an engagement to avoid being billed alongside her son. Fields, *Sophie Tucker*, 117.

49. "Queen of All Ragtime Airs," III22. Emphasis mine.

50. "Sophie Tucker Takes Role of Pacifier; Gets Black Eye," *Chicago Daily Tribune*, Sep 6, 1934, 1.

51. "Sophie Tucker Saves Child in Path of Auto," *Los Angeles Times*, Jun 15, 1934, 1. See also, "Sophie Tucker Saves Child from Auto and Is Bruised," *New York Times*, Jun 15, 1934, 46.

52. See chap. 1, "Some Could Suckle Over Their Shoulder," Morgan, *Laboring Women*; Briggs, "The Race of Hysteria," 262.

53. Roosevelt, "The Duties of a Great Nation," *Campaigns and Controversies* (1898), 291; Cited in Hoganson, *Fighting for American Manhood*, 144, 244 n18.

54. Beard, *American Nervousness*, 127.

55. Ibid., 120.

56. Grace Kingsley, "Jest and Melody," II3; "Sophie Tucker in Keith's Vaudeville: Her Jazz Jingles Feature of a Bill That Includes Many Good Numbers," *Boston Daily Globe*, Mar 26, 1918, 4; "Sophie Tucker at William Penn," *Philadelphia Inquirer*, Feb 1, 1916, 5.

57. Baer, "Coon Shouter Shouts Brother an Education," 7.

58. Kibler, *Rank Ladies*, 113, 119.

59. Pamela Lavitt has convincingly argued that Held was Jewish, though she went to great lengths to deny this to the public. "The First of the Red Hot Mamas," 288. Mizejewski makes a similar claim in chap. 1 of *Ziegfeld Girl*.

60. Glenn, *Female Spectacle*, 171.

61. Pierre Van Paassen, "Lights of London," *Atlanta Constitution*, Aug 16, 1926, 4.

62. Moore, *Drag!*, 107.

63. Tucker's first biographer seemed to agree she was decidedly unattractive. Although one contemporary critic suggested that, as a young woman, Tucker "possessed... good looks," Freedland countered, "perhaps [he] did need a new pair of glasses—or maybe he was sitting too far back in the theatre." Michael Freedland, *Sophie: Sophie Tucker Story* (London: Woburn Press, 1978), 25.

64. Tucker, *Some of These Days*, 90.

65. John A. Garraty and Mark C. Carnes, Eds., "Tucker, Sophie," *American National Biography*, vol. 21 (New York: Oxford University Press, 1999), 906. In other accounts, Abe Lackerman is called Al Lackerman.

66. Freedland, *Sophie*, 24.

67. Ibid., 19.

68. "Sophie Tucker Keith Headliner," *Boston Journal*, Jun 5, 1917, 9.

69. Mordaunt Hall, "The Screen," *New York Times*, Jun 5, 1929, 26.

70. Tucker, *Some of These Days*, 94.

71. Ibid.

72. Peter Antelyes, "Red Hot Mamas: Bessie Smith, Sophie Tucker, and the Ethnic Maternal Voice in American Popular Song," Leslie C. Dunn and Nancy A. Jones, Eds., *Embodied Voices: Representing Female Vocality in Western Culture (New Perspectives in Music History and Criticism)*, (New York: Cambridge University Press, 1996), 215.

73. Fields, *Sophie Tucker*, 30.

74. "Ministers are Shocked. Sophie Tucker Sings at University Club Stag Affair," *Morning Oregonian*, Nov 20, 1910, 47.

75. Tucker, *Some of These Days*, 95.

76. Ibid., 96.

77. Review by "Dash." "Sophie Taylor. Songs. 12 Minutes; One. Pastor's," *Variety*. c. 1908, STC, BRTD, NYPL.

78. "Sophie Tucker Will Bring New Act to Orpheum," *Los Angeles Times*, May 10, 1925, 20.

79. Van Paassen, "Lights of London," 4.

80. *The Jazz Singer*, Directed by Alan Crosland (Los Angeles: Warner Bros. Pictures, 1927).

81. Mae Noell described a performance in 1949 when she realized the ramifications of her blackface performance: "a lot of things had been happening worldwide, and we didn't realize that we were doing anything that was going to hurt anyone's feelings. We were doing the act and the audience was laughing." Noell added that she laughed "then looked back at the audience, and with a most horrible, sinking feeling, we watched every black patron walk off the lot. Then her husband said, 'I'll never put the cork on again.'" Browder, *Slippery Characters*, 204.

82. Tucker later claimed that her manager only said her trunk failed to arrive to give her the chance she wanted. Yet newspapers confirm the likelihood that Tucker's first performance without blackface was accidental: "Brought over from New York at the eleventh hour to replace the Richards, [Tucker] was obliged to appear in street dress but that fact did not detract from her ability to please her hearers." "Variety at the American," c. 1909, STC, BRTD, NYPL.

83. Tucker, *Some of These Days*, 63.

84. Ibid.
85. "American Music Hall Offers Many Diversions," Newark, c.1909, STC, BRTD, NYPL. According to Kibler, Tucker's experience was not unique because "racial masquerade was one route to success and celebrity in vaudeville for women who were not conventionally attractive (particularly women who were fat)." 113.
86. Fields, *Sophie Tucker*, 30.
87. Untitled newspaper clipping, n.p., c.1909, STC, BRTD, NYPL.
88. "American Music Hall," New Orleans, Dec 5, 1909, STC, BRTD, NYPL.
89. "Queen of All Ragtime Airs: Sophie Tucker—Singer of Joy Songs: Sophie Tucker Explains Change in Her Songs," *Los Angeles Times*, Dec 16, 1917, III22.
90. Fields, *Sophie Tucker*, 27. In 1913, Tucker also played a black-faced nanny named "Jennie Wimp" in the successful revue *Louisiana Lou*. This show ran in Chicago for over a year and featured "Now Am de Time!," a solo Tucker performed in dialect.
91. *San Francisco Chronicle*, Nov 19, 1917. Cited in Fields, *Sophie Tucker*, 252, chap. 6, n3.
92. "Music with a Kick was Always Popular," *Boston Daily Globe*, Nov 16, 1919, 64.
93. For a review of this performance, see *New York Clipper*, Mar 12, 1919. Cited in Fields, *Sophie Tucker*, 82, 252, chap. 6, n9.
94. In 1923, *The Baltimore Afro-American* announced that, after performing for a season with Tucker, black female dancer Ida Forsyne went on vacation. It is possible that Forsyne was the dancer to whom Fields refers. J.A. Jackson, "National Amusement News," *The Baltimore Afro-American*, Mar 30, 1923, 15.
95. "Going Backstage with the Scribe," *Chicago Defender*, Apr 25, 1931, 5. In 1924, the *Pittsburgh Courier* also reported that Tucker performed with Leroy Smith and Sam Wooding's black orchestras. Floyd G. Snelson, "Theatrical Comment," Nov 15, 1924, 9.
96. Larry Starr and Christopher Waterman, *American Popular Music* (New York: Oxford University Press, 2003), 87. It is unclear whether Smith was called to fill in because Tucker declined the offer or because the company chose Smith over Tucker. In any event, the fact that OKeh executives saw Smith as an appropriate alternative to Tucker suggests that Tucker was not without peers. This became abundantly clear when Smith's records had enormous commercial success.
97. Laurie Stras, "White Face, Black Voice: Race, Gender and Region in the Music of the Boswell Sisters," *Journal of the Society for American Music*, 1 (2007), 216.
98. For more info, see Fields, *Sophie Tucker*, 252, chap. 8, n27, *Variety*, Oct 8, 1924.
99. Fields, *Sophie Tucker*, 119.
100. Robert Dawidoff, *Making History Matter*, (Philadelphia: Temple University Press, 2000), 131.
101. Ibid., 142.
102. In *Racechanges*, Susan Gubar explains that contemporary white poets and writers such as Vachel Lindsay, Nancy Cunard, and Carl Van Vechten also

engaged in racialized "linguistic experimentation." See chap. 4, "De Modern Do Mr. Bones (And All That Ventriloquist Jazz)," 134–168.

103. Stras, "White Face, Black Voice," 212.
104. Harrison-Kahan, *The White Negress*, 50.
105. Douglas, *Terrible Honesty*, 376.
106. "Sophie Tucker and Her Kings Please," *Duluth-News Tribune*, Oct 2, 1916, 2; "Tucker Joy Syncopated at Orpheum," *Duluth-News Tribune*, Feb 25, 1918, 6.
107. Goldstein, *The Price of Whiteness*, 62.
108. Ibid., 109.
109. Ibid.
110. Ibid., 36.
111. Stras, "White Face, Black Voice," 210.
112. Ibid., 209–11.
113. Ibid., 216.
114. Ibid., 229.
115. Ibid.
116. Guterl, *The Color of Race*, 43. See also Jacobson, *Whiteness of a Different Color*, and Roediger, *Wages of Whiteness*.
117. Display Ad 36—No Title, *Pittsburgh Courier*, Jan 22, 1927, A3. According to *Shuffle Along* creator and composer Eubie Blake, record companies would "segregate the records... They'd call them 'race records.' They weren't supposed to be sold to the white people. Colored people, maids for white people, would play the records and the white people would hear them and tell their maids to get them that record."
118. Tucker, *Some of These Days*, 275.
119. "Julien [*sic*] Eltinge," n.p., n.d., RLC, NYPL.
120. "'I Thought You Were a Negro,' Luise Rainer to Sophie Tucker," *Chicago Defender*, Apr 17, 1937, 21.
121. Interestingly, just four months after this incident, the *Los Angeles Times* reported that Luise Rainer had become a "pupil" of Tucker's, taking lessons to learn her "Red Hot Mamma" style. The same year the fair-skinned Rainer began her tutelage under Tucker, Rainer portrayed characters as racially diverse as the lily-white Anna Held in *The Great Ziegfeld* (1937), "O-Lan, the slave girl" in *The Good Earth* (1937), and a slave-owning white Southern woman in *The Toy Wife* (1938), opposite several contemporary black actors and actresses. "Viennese Star Studies with Sophie Tucker," *Los Angeles Times*, Sep 24, 1937, 15; "Scenes in 'Toy Wife' Criticized," *New Journal and Guide*, Aug 6, 1938, 16.
122. "Razaf Stock Rising," *The Baltimore Afro-American*, Aug 10, 1929, 8. *Pittsburgh Courier* also noted that Andrea Razafkeriefo, known as Andy Razaf, was the "nephew of an African queen" and had previously written music for Mamie Smith, Sophie Tucker, and Ethel Waters. "Nephew of African Queen," *Pittsburgh Courier*, Apr 2, 1927, A1.
123. "Miss Sophie Tucker Lauds Songsmiths," *Duluth-News Tribune*, Oct 7, 1916, 7.
124. "Defender Forum," *Chicago Defender*, Sep 1, 1934, 14.
125. Further examples of black newspapers promoting Tucker's work abound. *The Chicago Defender* profiled black composers such as Luckeyth Roberts,

Mule Bradford, Perry Bradford, Tyus and Tyus, and Chris Smith, advertising that they all wrote hits performed by Tucker. Other articles and advertisements mentioned music sung by Tucker that was being published and sold by black presses, such as Triangle Music Publishers of New York City.

126. Mark Slobin, *Tenement Songs* (Urbana: University of Illinois Press, 1982), 202. Cited in Antelyes, "Red Hot Mamas," in *Embodied Voices*, 223.

127. Mel Tapley, "Alberta Hunter: Blues Queen," *New Amsterdam News*, Jan 21, 1978, D8. Emphasis mine.

128. Maurice Dancer, "Tan Manhattan," *Chicago Defender*, Oct 18, 1941, 20.

129. Ethel Waters with Charles Samuels, *His Eye is on the Sparrow* (Garden City: Double Day and Company, 1951), 135. Though Tucker did not die until fifteen years after Waters published her autobiography, she does not appear to have responded publicly to Waters's claim.

130. Harrison-Kahan, *The White Negress*, 36–40.

131. "Sophie Tucker: She's Indebted to a Maid Who Was Worth a Fortune," M3.

132. Ibid.

133. Ibid.

134. Ibid.

135. In "Negro Woman's Advice Helped Her to Fame—Sophie Tucker," Tucker recalled that Mollie "was also a mother to my son and daughter... and a daughter to my parents during my long trips abroad." *Los Angeles Sentinel*, Oct 28, 1948, 19.

136. In her analysis of the relationship between Alberta Hunter and Sophie Tucker, Daphne Duval Harrison bypasses the role of Elkins, concluding that both Tucker and Hunter influenced each other's careers. Although Tucker never publicly acknowledged Hunter as an influence, she probably borrowed from Hunter more than the other way around. Harrison, *Black Pearls*, 210.

137. This article was first printed by London's *Daily Express* and shortly thereafter republished in *New York Amsterdam News*. "Nora Scores in London Town," Sep 25, 1929, 9.

138. Goldstein, *The Price of Whiteness*, 130.

139. Ibid., 44.

140. Rogin, *Blackface, White Noise*, 99.

141. "How to Act in Vaudeville," Mar 1, 1900, RLC, vol. 264 (Anna Held, vol. 1), BRTD, NYPL. As cited by Lavitt, "The First of the Red Hot Mamas," 277, n102.

142. "Music with a Kick was Always Popular," *Boston Daily Globe*, Nov 16, 1919, 64.

143. "Tastes in Night Clubs Variable as Fashions," *Washington Post*, May 19, 1926, 14.

144. Lavitt, "The First of the Red Hot Mamas," 280.

145. Ibid., 254.

146. See chap. 6, "Racial Masquerade and Ethnic Assimilation" in Rogin, *Blackface, White Noise*.

147. Rogin, *Blackface, White Noise*, 70. Browder similarly argues that blackface and dialect provided distinct ways for ethnic impersonators to "free themselves from the historical trap of an unwanted identity by passing into a new one." *Slippery Characters*, 10.

148. See chap. 5, "Race and the 'Jewish Problem' in Interwar America," Goldstein, *The Price of Whiteness.*
149. Goldstein, *The Price of Whiteness,* 122.
150. "Sophie Tucker: She's Indebted to a Maid who was Worth a Fortune," M3.
151. Lee, *The Black and White of American Popular Music,* 110.

EPILOGUE

1. Professional, Business Contracts 1911–1928, Box 1, ETP, BFRC, THF.
2. Rodger, "Male Impersonation on the North American Variety Stage, 1860–1930," 9.
3. Chauncey, *Gay New York,* 9, 13, 23.
4. Ullman, *Sex Seen,* 140.
5. Correspondence with Henry Ford, 1934, Personal, Correspondence and Writings, 1919 and undated, Box 1, ETP, BFRC, THF.
6. Tucker, *Some of These Days,* 81. Cited by Westerfield, "An Investigation," 7.
7. Karl Schriftgiesser, "Rebirth of Vaudeville," *New York Times Magazine,* Apr 19, 1942, 18.
8. The nine-minute music video "Telephone" opens in jail as two masculine women escort Gaga to a prison cell. Once in the cell, they strip Gaga; as the guards walk away, one mutters "I told ya she didn't have a dick." The other guard responds, "Too bad." "Telephone," Written by Lady Gaga and Jonas Akerlund, Directed by Jonas Akerlund (Serial Pictures, Streamline Records, 2010).
9. Buzz Bissinger, "Call Me Caitlyn," *Vanity Fair,* Jul 2015.
10. For example, see Richard Pérez-Peña, "Black or White? Woman's Story Stirs Up Furor," *New York Times,* Jun 12, 2015.
11. Jonathan Capehart, "Caitlyn Jenner and Rachel Dolezal: Clash of Identity and Authenticity," *Washington Post,* Jun 15, 2015; Vanessa Vitiello Urquhart, "It Isn't Crazy to Compare Rachel Dolezal with Caitlyn Jenner," *Slate,* Jun 15, 2015.
12. See Dumenil, *The Modern Temper.* Dumenil's title plays on Joseph Wood Krutch's contemporary collection of essays, *The Modern Temper: A Study and A Confession* (New York: Harcourt Brace,1929).

BIBLIOGRAPHY

PRIMARY SOURCES

Archival and Manuscript Collections

Brown, Lillian, Clippings File. Billy Rose Theatre Division. New York Public Library for the Performing Arts. Lincoln Center, New York City.

Brown, Lillyn, Collection. Negro Actors Guild of America Collection. Photographs and Prints Division. Schomburg Center for Black Studies, New York City.

Brown, Lillian, Interview 1960. Mura Dehn Papers on Afro-American Social Dance, c. 1869–1987. Folder 24. Jerome Robbins Dance Division. New York Public Library for the Performing Arts. Lincoln Center, New York City.

Brown, Lillyn, Marshall Stearns' Notes. "Brown, Lillyn 1952, Dec 20." Institute of Jazz Studies. Dana Library, Rutgers University. Newark, New Jersey.

Eltinge, Julian, Clippings File. Harvard Theatre Collection. Houghton Library, Harvard University.

Eltinge, Julian, Clippings File. Robinson Locke Collection of Theatrical Scrapbooks. Series 1, Reel 15. New York Public Library for the Performing Arts. Lincoln Center, New York City.

Historic Sheet Music Collection. Music Services. University of Oregon Libraries.

The Julian Eltinge Magazine, Townshend Walsh Collection. New York Public Library for the Performing Arts. Lincoln Center, New York City.

Sheet Music for Popular Songs, 1875–1986. Harvard Theatre Collection. Houghton Library. Harvard University.

Tanguay, Eva, Clippings 14. Harvard Theatre Collection. Houghton Library, Harvard University.

Tanguay, Eva, Clippings File. Robinson Locke Collection of Theatrical Scrapbooks. Series 1, Reel 39. New York Public Library for Performing Arts. Lincoln Center, New York City.

Tanguay, Eva, Papers. Benson Ford Research Center. The Henry Ford Museum. Dearborn, Michigan.

Tucker, Sophie, Collection. Billy Rose Theatre Division. New York Public Library for the Performing Arts. Lincoln Center, New York City.

Oral History

Kya-Hill, Robert. Telephone communication with Kathleen Casey. Feb 10, 2010.

Newspapers and Magazines

The Atlanta Constitution
Atlanta Daily World

The Baltimore Afro-American
The Bellingham Herald
The Boston Daily Globe
The Boston Journal
The Chicago Daily News
The Chicago Daily Tribune
The Chicago Defender
The Cincinnati Enquirer
Cleveland Call and Post
The Cleveland Plain-Dealer
The Daily Defender
The Detroit Journal
The Detroit News
Dramatic Mirror
Dramatic News
The Duluth News-Tribune
Ebony
Grand Forks Daily Herald
Green Book Album
Green Book Magazine
The Illustrated Buffalo Express
The Indianapolis News
The Julian Eltinge Magazine and Beauty Hints
The Kansas City Star
The Los Angeles Examiner
Los Angeles Sentinel
The Los Angeles Times
The Morning Oregonian
New Journal and Guide
The New York American Journal
New York Amsterdam News
The New York Clipper
New York Dramatic News
The New York Herald Tribune
The New York Mirror
The New York Telegraph
The New York Times
Niagara Falls New York Gazette
The Philadelphia Inquirer
The Philadelphia Tribune
Pittsburgh Courier
Record Research
The San Jose Mercury News
The South Bend Tribune
The State
St. Louis Republic
Talking Machine World
Theatre Magazine
The Toledo Times
The Utica Daily Press
Utica Herald Dispatch

Vanity Fair
Variety
The Washington Post

Articles

Davis, Michael Marks. "Exploitation of Pleasure: A Study of Commercial Regions in New York City." New York: Department of Child Hygiene of the Russell Sage Foundation, 1911.
Niles, John T. "Shout, Coon, Shout!" *The Musical Quarterly* 16, no. 4 (Oct 1930): 516–30.

Books

Beard, George M. *American Nervousness: Its Causes and Consequences, A Supplement to Nervous Exhaustion (Neurasthenia)*. New York: G.P. Putnam and Sons, 1881.
Beard, George M. *Sexual Neurasthenia (Nervous Exhaustion): Its Hygiene, Causes, Symptoms and Treatment*. New York: E. B. Treat and Company, 1898.
Bernhardt, Sarah. *My Double Life: Memoirs of Sarah Bernhardt*. London: William Heinemann, 1907.
Caffin, Caroline. *Vaudeville: The Book*. New York: Mitchell Kennerley, 1914.
DuBois, W. E. B. *The Souls of Black Folk*. Chicago: A. C. McClurg and Co., 1972.
Laurie, Joe, Jr. *Vaudeville: From the Honky Tonks to the Palace*. New York: Henry Holt and Company, 1953.
Legman, Gershon Alexander. "The Language of Homosexuality: An American Glossary." *Sex Variants: A Study of Homosexual Patterns*, George W. Henry, MD. New York: Paul B. Hoeber, 1941.
Potter, LaForest. *Strange Loves: A Study in Sexual Abnormality*. New York: Robert Dodlsey Co., 1933.
Tucker, Sophie. *Some of These Days: The Autobiography of Sophie Tucker*. New York, 1945.
von Krafft-Ebing, Richard. *Psychopathia Sexualis*. 1886.
Waters, Ethel with Charles Samuels. *His Eye is on the Sparrow: An Autobiography*. Garden City: Double Day and Company, 1951.

Recordings

Brown, Lillyn. "The Complete Recorded Works of Esther Bigeou, Lillyn Brown, Alberta Brown and the Remaining Titles of Ada Brown, in chronological order, 1921–1928." Compact Disc. Document Records, 1996.
Lennox, Jean and Harry O. Sutton. "I Don't Care." Published by Jerome H. Remick and Company, 1905. Recorded by Eva Tanguay, n.p., 1922.
Tilley, Vesta. "Jolly Good Luck to the Girl Who Loves a Soldier." *The Golden Years of Music Hall*. Compact Disc. Saydisc, 1995.
Tucker, Sophie. "Sophie Tucker: Origins of the Red Hot Mama, 1910–1922." Compact Disc. Arch 5010. Archeophone Records, 2009.

SECONDARY SOURCES

Articles and Book Chapters

Antelyes, Peter. "Red Hot Mamas: Bessie Smith, Sophie Tucker, and the Ethnic Maternal Voice in American Popular Song." In *Embodied Voices: Representing Female Vocality in Western Culture*, Eds. Leslie C. Dunn and Nancy A. Jones, 212–229. New York: Cambridge University Press, 1996.

Bean, Annemarie. "Black Minstrelsy and Double Inversion Circa 1890." In *African-American Performance and Theatre History: A Critical Reader*, Eds. Harry J. Elam and David Krasner, 171–91. New York: Oxford University Press, 2001.

———. "Presenting the Prima Donna: Black Femininity and Performance in Nineteenth-Century American Blackface Minstrelsy." *Performance Research* 1, no. 3 (1996): 32–42.

———. "Transgressing the Gender Divide: The Female Impersonator in Nineteenth-Century Blackface Minstrelsy." In *Inside the Minstrel Mask: Readings in Nineteenth-Century Blackface Minstrelsy*, Eds. Annemarie Bean, James Hatch, and Brooks McNamara, 145–56. Hanover, Pa.: Wesleyan University Press, 1996.

Berger, Iris, Elsa Barkley Brown and Nancy A. Hewitt. "Intersections and Collision Courses: Women, Blacks, and Workers Confront Gender, Race and Class." *Feminist Studies* 18, no. 2 (Summer 1992): 283–94.

Briggs, Laura. "The Race of Hysteria: 'Overcivilization' and the 'Savage' Woman in Late Nineteenth-Century Obstetrics and Gynecology." *American Quarterly* 52, no. 2 (June 2000): 246–73.

Carby, Hazel. "It Jus Be Dat Way Sometime:' The Sexual Politics of Women's Blues." *Radical America* 20, no. 4 (1987): 8–22.

———. "Policing the Black Woman's Body in an Urban Context." *Critical Inquiry* 18 (Summer 1992): 738–55.

Crenshaw, Kimberly. "Mapping the Margins: Intersectionality, Identity Politics, and Violence Against Women of Color." *Stanford Law Review* 43, no. 6 (1991): 1241–99.

Garber, Eric. "Gladys Bentley: The Bulldagger who sang the Blues." *Out/look* (Spring 1988): 52–61.

Halberstam, Judith. "Mackdaddy, Superfly, Rapper: Gender, Race and Masculinity in the Drag King Scene." *Social Text* no. 52/53 (Autumn 1997): 104–31.

Higginbotham, Evelyn Brooks. "African-American Women's History and the Metalanguage of Race." *Signs* 17, no. 2 (Winter 1992): 251–74.

Jefferson, Miles M. "The Negro on Broadway, 1949–1950." *Phylon* 11, no. 2 (Second Qtr, 1950): 105–13.

Lavitt, Pamela B. "The First of the Red Hot Mamas: 'Coon Shouting' and the Jewish Ziegfeld Girl." *American Jewish History* 87, no. 4 (Dec. 1999): 253–90.

Price, Charles Gower. "Sources of American Styles in the Music of the Beatles." *American Music* 15, no. 2 (Summer 1997): 208–32.

Rodger, Gillian. "'He Isn't a Marrying Man:' Gender and Sexuality in the Repertoire of Male Impersonators, 1870–1930." In *Queer Episodes in Music and Modern Identity*, Eds. Sophie Fuller and Lloyd Whitesell, 105–33. Urbana: University of Illinois Press, 2002.

Rubin, Gayle. "The Traffic in Women: Notes on the Political Economy of Sex." *Toward an Anthropology of Women*. Edited by Rayna Reiter. New York: Monthly Review Press, 1975.

Senelick, Laurence. "The Evolution of the Male Impersonator of the Nineteenth-Century Popular Stage." In *Homosexuality and Homosexuals in the Arts*. New York: Garland Publishing, 1992. 261–74.

Siegrist, Sarah Elizabeth. "He's a Great Lookin' Dame: A Feminist Account of Gender Performance at the Turn of the Twentieth Century." *International Journal of the Arts in Society* 2, no. 2 (2006): 119–26.

Sochen, June. "Fanny Brice and Sophie Tucker: Blending the Particular with the Universal." In *From Hester Street to Hollywood: The Jewish American Stage and Screen*. Edited by Sarah Blacher Cohen, 44–57. Bloomington: Indiana University Press, 1983.

———. "From Sophie Tucker to Barbra Streisand: Jewish Women Entertainers as Reformers." In *Talking Back: Images of Jewish Women in American Popular Culture*. Edited by Joyce Antler, 68–84. Hanover: Brandeis University Press, 1998.

Stras, Laurie. "White Face, Black Voice: Race, Gender and Region in the Music of the Boswell Sisters." *Journal of the Society for American Music* 1 (2007): 207–55.

Ullman, Sharon R. "The 'Self-Made Man:' Male Impersonation and the New Woman." In *Passing: Identity and Interpretation in Sexuality, Race and Religion*, Eds. Maria Carla Sanchez and Linda Schlossberg, 187–207. New York: New York University Press, 2001.

Verter, Bradford. "Interracial Festivity and Power in Antebellum New York: The Case of Pinkster." *The Journal of Urban History* 28, no. 4 (May 2002): 398–428.

Weinbrenner, Melissa. "Movies, Model-T's and Morality: The Impact of Technology on Standards of Behavior in the Early Twentieth Century." *Journal of American Culture* 44, no. 3 (Jun 2011): 647–59.

Books

Abbott, Lynn and Doug Seroff. *Out of Sight: The Rise of African-American Popular Music, 1889–1895*. Jackson: University Press of Mississippi, 2002.

Allen, Robert C. *Horrible Prettiness: Burlesque and American Culture*. Chapel Hill: University of North Carolina Press, 1991.

Antler, Joyce. *The Journey Home: Jewish Women and the American Century*. New York: The Free Press, 1997.

Antler, Joyce, ed. *Talking Back: Images of Jewish Women in American Popular Culture*. Hanover: Brandeis University, 1998.

Baldwin, Davarian L. *Chicago's New Negroes: Modernity, The Great Migration, and Black Urban Life*. Chapel Hill: University of North Carolina Press, 2007.

Banner, Lois W. *American Beauty*. New York, Alfred A. Knopf, 1983.

Bederman, Gail. *Manliness and Civilization: A Cultural History of Gender and Race in the United States, 1880–1917*. Chicago: University of Chicago Press, 1996.

Browder, Laura. *Slippery Characters: Ethnic Impersonators and American Identities*. Chapel Hill: University of North Carolina Press, 2000.

Butler, Judith. *Gender Trouble: Feminism and the Subversion of Identity,* Third Edition. New York: Routledge, 2006.

Carter, Julian B. *The Heart of Whiteness: Normal Sexuality and Race in America, 1880–1940.* Durham: Duke University Press, 2007.

Charters, Samuel and Leonard Kunstadt. *Jazz: A History of the New York Scene.* Garden City, NY: Doubleday, 1962.

Chauncey, George. *Gay New York: Gender, Urban Culture, and the Making of the Gay Male World, 1890–1940.* New York: Basic Books, 1994.

Cockrell, Dale. *Demons of Disorder: Early Blackface Minstrels and their World.* New York: Cambridge University Press, 1997.

Cott, Nancy F. *The Bonds of Womanhood: "Woman's Sphere" in New England, 1780– 1835.* New Haven: Yale University Press, 1977.

———. *The Grounding of Modern Feminism.* New Haven: Yale University Press, 1987.

———. *Public Vows: A History of Marriage and the Nation.* Cambridge, Mass.: Harvard University Press, 2000.

Davis, Angela Y. *Blues Legacies and Black Feminism: Gertrude "Ma" Rainey, Bessie Smith and Billie Holiday.* New York: Pantheon Books, 1998.

Dawidoff, Robert. *Making History Matter.* Philadelphia: Temple University Press, 2000.

Douglas, Ann. *Terrible Honesty: Mongrel Manhattan in the 1920s.* New York: Farrar, Straus and Giroux, 1995.

Duberman, Martin, George Chauncey, and Carroll Smith-Rosenberg, Eds. *Hidden From History: Reclaiming the Gay and Lesbian Past.* New York: Penguin, 1990.

Dudden, Faye E. *Women in the American Theatre.* New Haven: Yale University Press, 1994.

Dumenil, Lynn. *The Modern Temper: American Culture and Society in the 1920s.* New York: Hill and Wang, 1995.

Edwards, Laura. *Gendered Strife and Confusion: The Political Culture of Reconstruction.* Chicago: University of Illinois Press, 1997.

Elam, Harry J., Jr. and David Krasner, Eds. *African-American Performance and Theatre History: A Critical Reader.* New York: Oxford University Press, 2001.

Enstad, Nan. *Ladies of Labor, Girls of Pleasure: Working Women, Popular Culture, and Labor Politics at the Turn of the Twentieth Century.* New York: Columbia University Press, 1999.

Erdman, Andrew. *Blue Vaudeville: Sex, Morals, and the Mass Marketing of Amusement, 1895–1915.* Jefferson, NC: McFarland and Company, 2004.

———. *Queen of Vaudeville: The Story of Eva Tanguay.* Ithaca: Cornell University Press, 2012.

Erenberg, Lewis. *Steppin' Out: New York Nightlife and the Transformation of American Culture, 1890–1930.* Chicago: University of Chicago Press, 1981.

Faderman, Lillian. *Odd Girls and Twilight Lovers: A History of Lesbian Life in Twentieth-Century America.* New York: Columbia University Press, 1991.

Ferris, Lesley, ed. *Crossing the Stage: Controversies on Cross-dressing.* New York: Routledge, 1993.

Fields, Armond. *Sophie Tucker: First Lady of Show Business.* Jefferson, NC: McFarland and Company, 2003.

Filene, Peter G. *Him/Her/Self: Gender Identities in Modern America*, Third Edition. Baltimore: The Johns Hopkins University Press, 1998.

Freedland, Michael. *Sophie: The Sophie Tucker Story*. London: Woburn Press, 1978.

Frost, Linda. *Never One Nation: Freaks, Savages, and Whiteness in U.S. Popular Culture, 1850–1877*. Minneapolis: University of Minnesota Press, 2005.

Garber, Marjorie. *Vested Interests: Cross-dressing and Cultural Anxiety*. New York: Routledge, Chapman and Hall, Inc., 1992.

George-Graves, Nadine. *The Royalty of Negro Vaudeville: The Whitman Sisters and the Negotiation of Race, Gender and Class in African American Theatre 1900–1940*. New York: St. Martin's Press, 2000.

Gilbert, Douglas. *American Vaudeville: Its Life and Times*. New York: Dover Publications Inc., 1963.

Glenn, Susan. *Female Spectacle: The Theatrical Roots of Modern Feminism*. Cambridge, Mass.: Harvard University Press, 2000.

Goldstein, Eric. *The Price of Whiteness: Jews, Race and American Identity*. Princeton: Princeton University Press, 2008.

Gordon, Lynn. *Gender and Higher Education in the Progressive Era*. New Haven: Yale University Press, 1990.

Grossman, Barbara. *Funny Woman: The Life and Times of Fanny Brice*. Indianapolis: Indiana University Press, 1992.

Gubar, Susan. *Racechanges: White Skin, Black Face in American Culture*. New York: Oxford University Press, 1997.

Guglielmo, Thomas. *White on Arrival: Italians, Race, Color and Power in Chicago, 1890–1945*. Cambridge: Oxford University Press, 2004.

Guterl, Matthew Pratt. *The Color of Race in America, 1900–1940*. Cambridge, Mass.: Harvard University Press, 2001.

Halberstam, Judith. *Female Masculinity*. Durham: Duke University Press, 1998.

Handy, D. Antoinette. *The International Sweethearts of Rhythm*. Metuchen, NJ: The Scarecrow Press, 1983.

Harrison, Daphne Duval. *Black Pearls: Blues Queens of the 1920s*. Newark: Rutgers University Press, 1990.

Harrison-Kahan, Lori. *The White Negress: Literature, Minstrelsy, and the Black Jewish Imaginary*. New Brunswick: Rutgers, 2011.

Hartog, Hendrik. *Man and Wife in America: A History*. Cambridge, Mass.: Harvard University Press, 2000.

Heap, Chad. *Slumming: Sexual and Racial Encounters in American Nightlife, 1885–1940*. Chicago: University of Chicago Press, 2009.

Hoganson, Kristin L. *Fighting for American Manhood: How Gender Politics Provoked the Spanish-American and Philippine-American Wars*. New Haven: Yale University Press, 1998.

Hull, Gloria and Patricia Bell Scott, Barbara Smith, Eds. *All the Women are White, All the Blacks Are Men, But Some of Us Are Brave*. Old Westbury, New York: The Feminist Press, 1982.

Hurewitz, Daniel. *Bohemian Los Angeles and the Making of Modern Politics*. Berkeley: University of California Press, 2007.

Ignatiev, Noel. *How The Irish Became White*. New York: Routledge, 1995.

Jacobson, Matthew Frye. *Whiteness of a Different Color: European Immigrants and the Alchemy of Race*. Cambridge, Mass.: Harvard University Press, 1998.

Johnson, E. Patrick and Mae G. Henderson, Eds., *Black Queer Studies: A Critical Anthology*. Durham: Duke University Press, 2005.

Kasson, John F. *Houdini, Tarzan, and the Perfect Man: The White Male Body and the Challenge of Modernity in America*. New York: Hill and Wang, 2001.

Kenney, William Howland. *Recorded Music in American Life: The Phonograph and Popular Memory, 1890–1945*. New York: Oxford University Press, 1999.

Kibler, M. Alison. *Rank Ladies: Gender and Cultural Hierarchy in American Vaudeville*. Chapel Hill: University of North Carolina Press, 1999.

Krasner, David. *A Beautiful Pageant: African-American Theatre, Drama, and Performance in the Harlem Renaissance, 1910–1927*. New York: Palgrave Macmillan, 2002.

———. *Resistance, Parody, and Double Consciousness in African American Theatre, 1895–1910*. New York: St. Martin's Press, 1997.

Lee, Vera. *The Black and White of American Popular Music from Slavery to World War II*. Rochester, Vt.: Schenkman Books, Inc., 2007.

Lewis, Robert M., ed., *From Traveling Show to Vaudeville: Theatrical Spectacle in America, 1830–1910*. Baltimore: Johns Hopkins Press, 2003.

Lhamon, W. T. *Raising Cain: Blackface Performance from Jim Crow to Hip Hop*. Cambridge, Mass.: Harvard University Press, 1998.

Lieb, Sandra. *Mother of the Blues: A Study of Ma Rainey*. Amherst: University of Massachusetts Press, 1981.

Lott, Eric. *Love and Theft: Blackface Minstrelsy and the American Working Class*. New York: Oxford University Press, 1993.

McAllister, Marvin. *Whiting Up: Whiteface Minstrels and Stage Europeans in African American Performance*. Chapel Hill: University of North Carolina Press, 2011.

McLean, Albert F., Jr. *American Vaudeville as Ritual*. Lexington, Ky.: University of Kentucky Press, 1965.

Melnick, Jeffrey. *A Right to Sing the Blues: African Americans, Jews and American Popular Song*. Cambridge, Mass.: Harvard College, 1999.

Miller, Monica. *Slaves to Fashion: Black Dandyism and the Styling of Black Diasporic Identity*. Durham: Duke University Press, 2009.

Mitchell, Michele. *Righteous Propagation: African Americans and the Politics of Racial Destiny after Reconstruction*. Chapel Hill: University of North Carolina Press, 2004.

Moore, F. Michael. *Drag! Male and Female Impersonators on Stage, Screen and Television*. Jefferson, N.C.: McFarland and Co. Inc., 1994.

Morgan, Jennifer. *Laboring Women: Reproduction and Gender in New World Slavery*. Philadelphia: University of Pennsylvania Press, 2004.

Oliver, Paul. *The Story of the Blues*. Philadelphia: Chilton Book, Company, 1969.

Patterson, Martha. *Beyond the Gibson Girl: Reimagining the American New Women, 1895–1915*. Urbana: University of Illinois Press, 2005.

Peiss, Kathy. *Cheap Amusements: Working Women and Leisure in Turn-of-the-Century New York*. Philadelphia: Temple University Press, 1985.

———. *Hope in a Jar: The Making of America's Beauty Culture*. New York: Henry Holt and Company, 1998.

Peiss, Kathy and Christina Simmons, eds. *Passion and Power: Sexuality in History*. Philadelphia, Temple University Press, 1989.

Roediger, David R. *The Wages of Whiteness: Race and the Making of the American Working Class*, Third Edition. London: Verso, 1991.

Rogin, Michael. *Blackface, White Noise: Jewish Immigrants in the Hollywood Melting Pot*. Berkeley: University of California Press, 1996.

Samuels, Charles and Louise. *Once Upon a Stage: The Merry World of Vaudeville*. New York: Dodd, Mead and Company, 1974.

Senelick, Laurence. *The Changing Room: Sex, Drag and Theatre*. New York: Routledge, 2000.

Smith-Rosenberg, Carroll. *Disorderly Conduct: Visions of Gender in Victorian America*. New York: Alfred A. Knopf, 1985.

Snyder, Robert. *The Voice of the City: Vaudeville and Popular Culture in New York*. New York: Oxford University Press, 1989.

Somerville, Siobhan. *Queering the Color Line: Race and the Invention of Homosexuality in American Culture*. Durham: Duke University Press, 2000.

Sotiropoulos, Karen. *Staging Race: Black Performers in Turn of the Century America*. Cambridge, Mass.: Harvard University Press, 2006.

Starr, Larry and Christopher Waterman. *American Popular Music: From Minstrelsy to MTV*. New York: Oxford University Press, 2003.

Stein, Charles, Ed. *American Vaudeville as Seen by Its Contemporaries*. New York: Alfred A. Knopf, 1984.

Stulman, Andrea Dennett. *Weird and Wonderful: The Dime Museum in America*. New York: New York University Press, 1997.

Toll, Robert C. *Blacking Up: The Minstrel Show in Nineteenth Century America*. New York: Oxford University Press, 1974.

———. *On With The Show: The First Century of Show Business in America*. New York: Oxford University Press, 1976.

Torgovnick, Marianna. *Gone Primitive: Savage Intellects, Modern Lives*. Chicago: University of Chicago Press, 1990.

Tracy, Steven Carl. *Write Me a Few of Your Lines: A Blues Reader*. Amherst: University of Massachusetts Press, 1999.

Ullman, Sharon R. *Sex Seen: The Emergence of Modern Sexuality in America*. Berkeley: University of California Press, 1997.

Ulrich, Laurel Thatcher. *Well-Behaved Women Seldom Make History*. New York: Alfred A. Knopf, 2007.

White, Deborah Gray. *Ar'n't I a Woman? Female Slaves in the Plantation South*, Revised Edition. New York: W.W. Norton & Company, 1999.

Williams, Katherine, Zachary Ross, Kathleen Spies, Amanda Glesmann and Claire Perry. *Women on the Verge: The Culture of Neurasthenia in Nineteenth-Century America*. The Iris and B. Gerald Cantor Center for Visual Arts at Stanford University, 2004.

Williams, Martin. *Jazz in Its Time*. New York: Oxford University Press, 1989.

———. *Jazz Master's of New Orleans*. New York: MacMillan Co, 1967.

Wolcott, Victoria. *Race, Riots, and Rollercoasters: The Struggle Over Segregated Recreation in America*. Philadelphia: University of Pennsylvania, 2012.

Young-Tulin, Lois. *Sophie and Me: Some of These Days*. San Jose: iUniverse, 2001.

Dissertations and Theses

Foreman, Ronald. "Jazz and Race Records 1920–1932: Their Origins and Their Significance for the Record Industry and Society." PhD diss, University of Illinois, 1968.

Kainer, Eden Elizabeth. "Vocal Racial Crossover in the Song Performance of Three Iconic American Vocalists." PhD diss, University of Wisconsin, Madison, 2008.

Pittenger, Peach. "Women in Popular Entertainment: Creating a Niche in the Vaudevillian Era, 1890s to 1930s." PhD diss, Ohio State University, 2005.

Rodger, Gillian. "Male Impersonation on the North American Variety and Vaudeville Stage, 1868–1930." PhD diss, University of Pittsburgh, 1998.

Vale, Joan M. "Tin-Type Ambitions: Three Vaudevillians in Search of Hollywood Fame." MA thesis, University of San Diego, 1985.

Westerfield, Jane. "Investigation of the Lifestyles and Performances of Three Singer- Comediennes of American Vaudeville: Eva Tanguay, Nora Bayes and Sophie Tucker." PhD diss, Ball State University, 1987.

Films

Before Stonewall: The Making of a Gay and Lesbian Community. Directed by Greta Schiller. New York: First Run Features, 1999.

Birth of a Nation. Directed by D.W. Griffith. Epoch Producing Co, 1915.

The I Don't Care Girl. Directed by Lloyd Bacon. Twentieth Century Fox Film Corporation, 1953.

The Jazz Singer. Directed by Alan Crosland. Los Angeles: Warner Bros. Pictures, 1927.

The Ladies Sing the Blues. VHS. Produced by Tom Jentz. New York: View Video, 1988.

Stormé: The Lady of the Jewel Box. VHS. Directed by Michelle Parkerson. New York: Women Make Movies, 1987.

Unforgivable Blackness: The Rise and Fall of Jack Johnson. Directed by Ken Burns. Hollywood, California: PBS Home Video, 2004.

The Wild Girl. Directed by Howard Estabrook. Eva Tanguay Film Corporation, 1917.

Wild Women Don't Have the Blues. VHS. Directed by Christine Dall. Calliope Film Resources, Inc. San Francisco, California: California Newsreel, 1989.

Without Fear or Shame 1920–1937. VHS. Directed by Sam Pollard. Alexandria, Virginia: PBS video, 1999.

References and Bibliographies

Cullen, Frank, Florence Hackman, and Donald McNeilly. *Vaudeville Old and New: An Encyclopedia of Variety Performers in America.* Vols. 1 and 2. New York: Routledge, 2007.

Garraty, John A. and Mark C. Carnes, Eds. *American National Biography.* New York: Oxford University Press, 1999.

Harris, Sheldon. *Blues Who's Who: A Biographical Dictionary of Blues Singers.* New Rochelle, New York: Arlington House Publishers, 1979.

Kellner, Bruce, Ed. *The Harlem Renaissance: A Historical Dictionary for the Era.* Westport, Connecticut: Greenwood Press, 1984.

Laird, Ross. *Moanin' Low: A Discography of Female Popular Recordings, 1920–1933.* Westport, Ct.: Greenwood Press, 1996.

Lighter, J. E., Ed. *Random House Historical Dictionary of American Slang.* Vols. 1 and 2. New York: Random House, 1994.

Major, Clarence, Ed. *Juba to Jive: A Dictionary of African-American Slang.*
    London: Penguin Books, 1970.
Peterson, Bernard L. *A Century of Musicals in Black and White: An Encyclo-
    pedia of Musical Stage Works By, About, or Involving African Americans.*
    London: Greenwood Press, 1993.
Sampson, Henry T. *Blacks in Blackface: A Sourcebook on Early Black Musical
    Shows.* Metuchen, NJ: Scarecrow Press, 1980.
Sampson, Henry T. *The Ghost Walks: A Chronological History of Blacks in
    Show Business, 1865–1910.* Metuchen, NJ: The Scarecrow Press, Inc.,
    1988.
Slide, Anthony. *The Vaudevillians: A Dictionary of Vaudeville Performers.*
    Westport, Ct.: Arlington House, 1981.

INDEX